For all those appearing for NATA/ JEE (B. ARCH)

National Aptitude Test in Architecture/ Joint Entrance Examinations

B. ARCHITECTURE

About Architecture:

Architecture deals with planning, designing and constructing form, space and ambience to reflect functional, technical, social, environmental and aesthetic considerations. It requires the creative manipulation and coordination of materials and technology, and of light and shadow.

The Bachelor of Architecture, Bachelor of Architecture (Interior Design) is a five-year full time professional degree programme accredited by the Council of Architecture, New Delhi- a statutory body of Government of India that regulates architectural education in India.

About N.A.T.A 2017:

NATA measures the aptitude of the applicant for specific field of study, i.e. Architecture. The test makes an assessment of drawing and observation skills, sense of proportion, aesthetic sensitivity, Mathematics and critical thinking ability that have been acquired over a long period of time and are related to the specific field of study.

There will be three sections, DRAWING, APTITUDE & MATHEMATICS.

DRAWING - Candidate has to attempt two questions within 90 minutes. The drawing aptitude is judged on the following aspects -

- Ability to sketch a given object proportionately and rendering the same in visually appealing manner; Visualizing and drawing the effects of light on the object and shadows cast on surroundings;
- Sense of perspective drawing;
- Combining and composing given three dimensional elements to form a building or structural form;
- Creating interesting two dimensional composition using given shapes and forms; Creating visual harmony using colors in given composition; Understanding of scale and proportions;
- Drawing from memory through pencil sketch on themes from day to day experiences.

GENERAL APTITUDE- Objects, texture related to architecture and built environment. Interpretation of pictorial compositions, Visualizing three-dimensional objects from two-dimensional drawing. Visualizing different sides of 3D objects. Analytical reasoning, mental ability (visual, numerical and verbal), General awareness of national/ international architects and famous architectural creations.

Mathematical reasoning: Statements, logical operations like and, or, if and only if, implies, implied by. Understanding of tautology, converse, contradiction and contrapositive.

Sets and Relations: Idea of sets, subsets, power set, complement, union, intersection and difference of sets, Venn diagram, De Morgan's Laws, Relation and its properties. Equivalence relation — definition and elementary examples

MATHEMATICS- Mathematics will include the following topics-

- **Algebra**
- **Logarithms**
- **Matrices**
- **Trigonometry**
- **Coordinate geometry**
- **3-Dimensional Co-ordinate geometry**
- **Theory of Calculus**
- **Application of Calculus**
- **Permutation and combination**
- **Statistics and Probability**

Subject and Marks of Examination

Subject and Marks of Examination		
Part-A (FIRST 90 minutes)		**TOTAL 120 Marks**
Mathematics (MCQ)	**20X2 = 40 Marks (OMR BASED)**	
General Aptitude (MCQ)	**40X2 = 80 Marks (OMR BASED)**	
Part-B (LAST 90 minutes)		**TOTAL 80 Marks**
Drawings (TWO SETS) in A4 Size paper 2X 40 = 80 Marks		

N.A.T.A CLASSES

PHONE NO: - 965-443-2033(NEW DELHI), 09215800625 (ALL INDIA),

WEBSITE:- WWW.NATACALSSES.IN

REGISTRATION FORM FOR REGULAR STUDENTS

I came to know about NATA CLASSES from

Name of the Newspaper……………………………

Name of the website………………………

Name of the Friend……………………………………

Other Source…………………………………………….

Particulars of the Candidate:

1. Name (Capital Letter) Master/Miss………………………………………………………………………

2. Date of Birth…………………………………………………………………………(Attach proof)

3. Name of the School last attended……………………………………………………………………

(a) Class Passed………… (b) Percentage………….. (c) Year Of Passing……………………

4. Father's Name…………………………………………………(i)Academic Qualification…………………

(ii) Profession…………………………………………….Office Phone No…………………………………

5. Mother's Name…………………………………………… (i)Academic Qualification……………………

(ii) Profession……………………………………………..Office Phone No…………………………………

6. Email ID..……………………………………………………………………………………………...

7. Residential Address………………………………………………………………………………………….

………………………………………………………………Phone No……………………………………..

8. Crash Course Type……………………………………………………………………………………….

9. Fees Status………………………………………………………..Receipt No…………………………….

10. Course Period From (DD/MM/YY)………………………………………..Till(DD/MM/YY)…………………………………….

Note:- Issue of registration form does mean that admission is ensured. Fee is not Refundable.

Date………………………………….

Place………………………………… **Signature**

FEES STRUCTURE OF N.A.T.A CLASSES

Course	Fees (Installment)	Fees (One Time)
FOR 12TH PASSOUTS (MON-FRI)		
• 3 Weeks	-	15500/-
• 6 Weeks	-	22500/-
FOR 12TH STANDARD (WEEKEND BATCH)		
• 6 Months	13000 X 2	24000/-
• 1 Year (Free 6 weeks crash course)	19000 X 2	36000/-
FOR 12TH STANDARD (REGULAR BATCH)		
• 6 Months	19000 X 2	36000/-
• 1 Year (Free 6 weeks crash course)	25000 X 2	48000/-
FOR 11TH STANDARD (WEEKEND BATCH)		
• 2 Year (Free 6 weeks crash course)	25000 X 2	48000/-
FOR 11TH STANDARD (REGULAR BATCH)		
• 2 Year (Free 6 weeks crash course)	32000 X 2	60000/-

INCLUDES

- Drawing Study Material & Question Papers of Previous Years

Student's Reference Drawing Book Including Best Drawings of the Students Based on previous Year Papers.

- Aptitude Study Material & Aptitude Mock Tests

E-book Contain Images of Buildings, Monuments, Temples, Textures & Materials, Famous Architects, Aptitude Picture Gallery etc.

Registration Fee is Rs. 2000, which will be later deducted from the Total Fee.

PAYMENT OPTIONS

1. CASH DEPOSITE

(Candidate can deposit cash Fee Payment or NEFT transfer in any branch of PUNJAB NATIONAL BANK throughout the country in Account of N.A.T.A CLASSES

A/C NO. 3267 0021 0000 4573

IFSC CODE - PUNB0326700 (FOR NEFT TRANSFER ONLY)

2. CHEQUE

Candidate can deposit Cheque in their nearest branch of Punjab National Bank, Cheque should be in favor of "N.A.T.A CLASSES"

A/C NO. 3267 0021 0000 4573

After fee payment please send us scanned Bank deposit slip copy or Transaction Number at delhinataclasses@gmail.com along with your Complete Form and scanned photo of the candidate

APTITUDE & DRAWING BOOK FOR NATIONAL APTITUDE TEST IN ARCHITECTURE (N.A.T.A)

TABLE OF CONTENTS

PART–01

DRAWING

Q.1) Imagine you are a child in a crib & your mother is giving you a toy. Draw what you see from your point.

Q.2) Imagine your height is reduced to 6" & you are standing on the kitchen counter & your mother is cooking food. Draw what you see from your point.

Q.3) Imagine you are sitting in a lawyer's office in front of his table and you see a wall behind his chair full of racks holding neatly arranged similar looking books. His desk also has a few books removed from that rack lying on it along with a telephone, a notepad, pen stand. Draw what you see from your point.

Q.4) Imagine you are standing in the queue to buy a movie ticket. You can view others standing in a queue till the booking window, people standing around (not in a queue) looking at hoardings /banners. Draw what you see from your point.

Q.5) Imagine you are standing in a metro .Draw what you see from your point.

Q.6) Imagine you are sitting in a open to sky food court. It has fast food counters and few People are sitting around you. Draw what you see from your point.

Q.7) Imagine you are sitting in the last row of an auditorium to see the live dance performance. Lights on the stage are on and rest of auditorium is dark. Draw what you see from your point

Q.8) Imagine you are sitting in your grandfather's study, draw what you see from your point.

Q.9) Imagine you are standing in front of a mall & there are lot of people . Draw what you see from your point in 2 point perspective.

Q.10) Imagine you are a bird flying over a historical monument. Draw what you see From your point.

Q.11) Imagine you are a bird sitting in your nest & your nest has eggs in it. A boy is climbing the tree in front of your nest. Draw what you see from your point.

Q.12) Draw a street view through a 2-point perspective.

Q.13) Imagine you are standing in a park & there is a sculpture made of 8 cubes at the centre and you are standing at the corner of cube . Draw what you see from your point.

Q.14 There is a match going on in your university ground and imagine you are a wicket keeper in the match. Draw what you see from your point.

Q.15) Imagine you are a bird and you are flying over a ruined fort. Draw what you see from your point.

Q.16) Children from your neighborhood are fl ying kites. Imagine you are reduced to small size to ride a kite & you are riding one of the kites. Draw the view of city from your point of view.

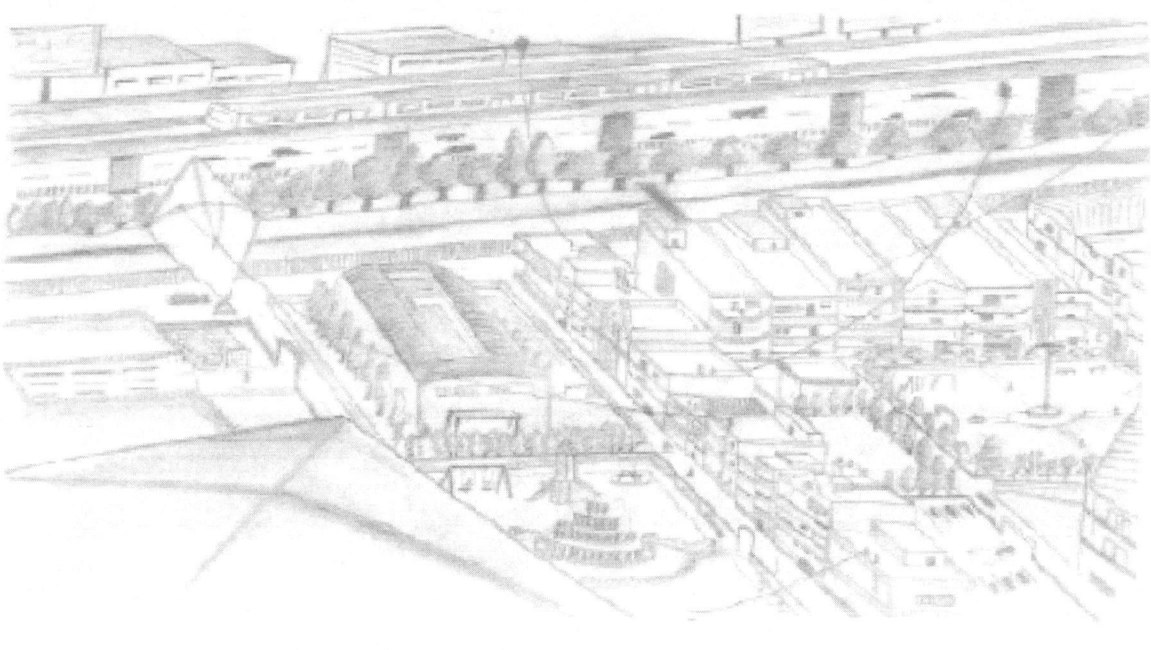

Q.17) Imagine you are sitting behind the seat of driver, but facing opposite side towards students in your college bus, Draw what you see from your point.

Q.18) Imagine you are a bird & you are flying around India gate .Draw what you see from your point

Q.19) Imagine you are a hockey player penalty corner specialist & you are playing in a world cup, you are about to execute a penalty corner & all the players are on their position & your team mate is about to push in the ball. Draw what you see from your point.

Q.20) Imagine you are standing on a railway platform & a train is standing on the track and there are people around you. Draw what you see from your point.

Q.21) Imagine you are standing on a bus stop & a bus is coming and there are people around you. Draw what you see from your point.

Q.22) Imagine you are standing on a round about. Draw what you see from your point.

Q.23) Imagine you are a bird flying above a house. Draw the aerial view of the house from your point.

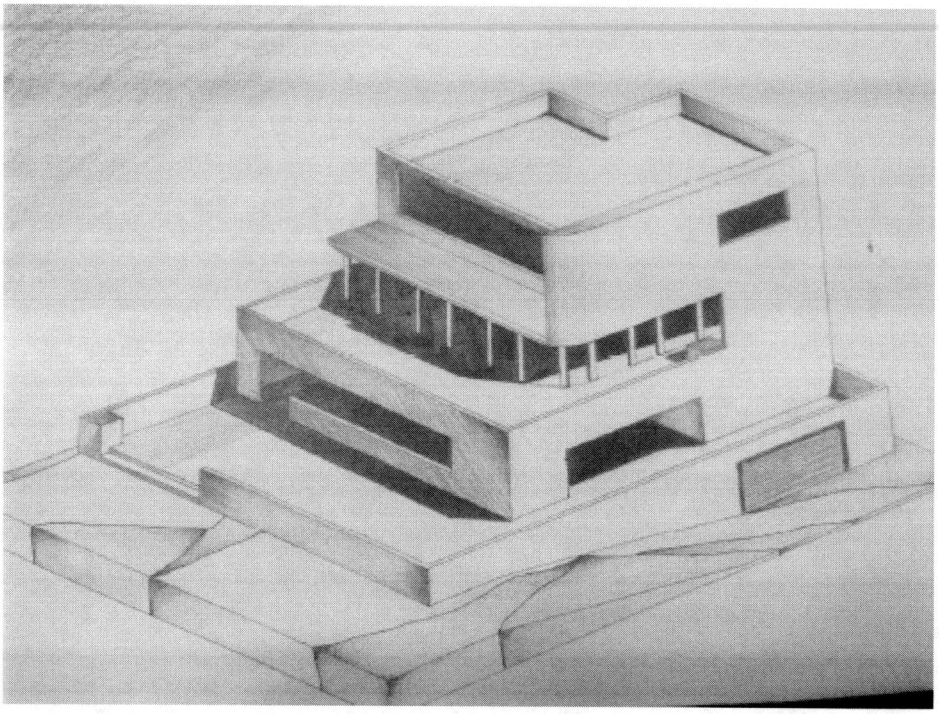

Q.24) Imagine you are standing in your balcony & there is a park in front of your house & children are playing cricket in the park. Draw what you see from your point.

Q.25) Imagine you are a bird sitting on the nest on the top of a building. There is another bird sitting in your nest.Draw what you see from your point.

26) Imagine you are playing basketball with your college team in your college ground. Draw what you see from your point.

Q.27) Imagine you are a fish in an aquarium with your friends. A family of four is watching you from outside and young girl from the family is pointing at you. Draw what you see from your point.

Q.28) Imagine you are standing in front of a road side dhaba. Draw what you see from your point.

Q.29) Imagine you are standing with your schoolmates in the assembly ground with your teachers on flag hosting day. Draw what you see from your point.

Q.30) Imagine that your size has been reduced to 6cms and you are sitting along with a mouse & a frog in a paperboat in a big bucket inside your bathroom.. Draw what you see from your point sitting with your companions.

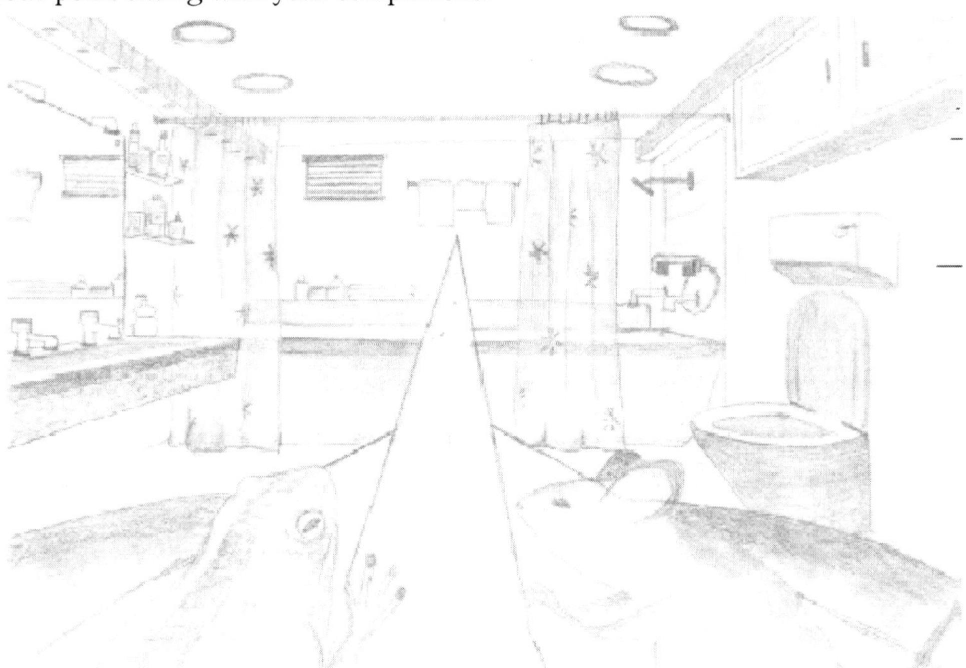

Q.31) Imagine your height is reduced to 6" & you are inside a fridge. Draw what you see from Your point.

Q.32) Imagine you are a salesman inside a cloth shop & there are people around buying clothes. Draw what you see from your point.

Q.33) Imagine you are inside a library & there are students around. Draw what you see from your point.

Q.34) Imagine you are inside a waiting lobby of a hospital. Draw what you see from your point.

Q.35) Imagine your height is reduced to 6" & you are standing on the table of a world renowned explorer. There is a map spread out on the table and there is also 1 fountain pen and 1 pencil. You can also see side window panel which is partially curtained and you also have to draw 3 thick books .

Q.36) Imagine you are inside your bedroom & your sister is searching something in the cupboard. Draw what you see from your point.

Q.37) Imagine you are inside a local market & there are people around you buying vegetables & clothes. Draw what you see from your point.

Q.38) Imagine you are inside the study room & your grandfather is sitting on a chair. Draw what you see from your point.

Q.39) Imagine you are inside an old building. Draw what you see from your point.

Q.40) Imagine you are standing in your balcony and you are looking at the bus stop on other side of the road. Draw what you see from your point.

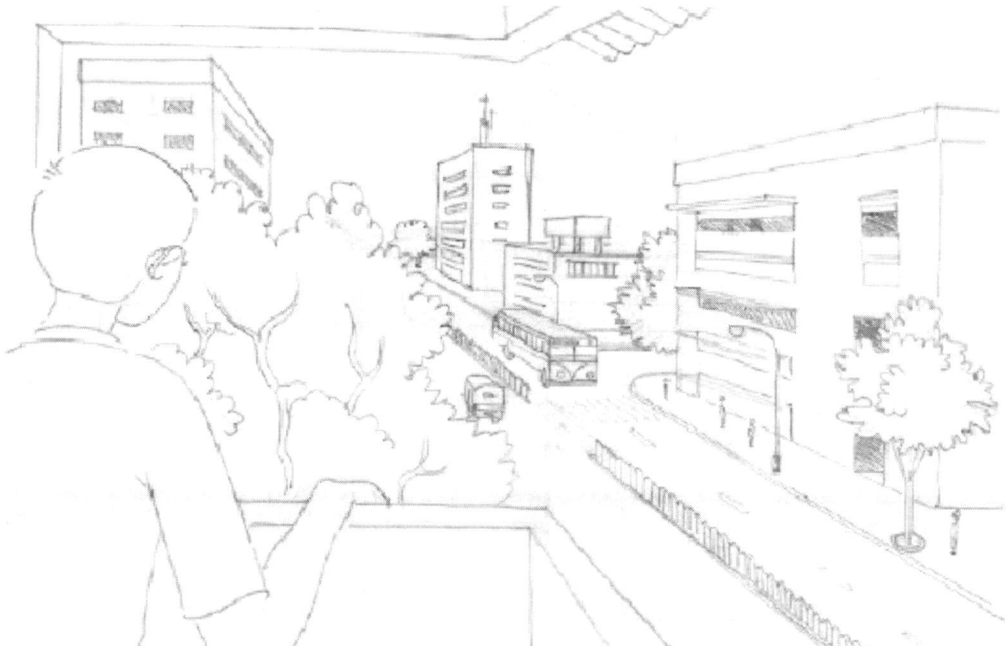

3-D DRAWINGS

Q.1) Draw a 3- d composition using 7 cylinders. Also show the effects of shade & shadow.

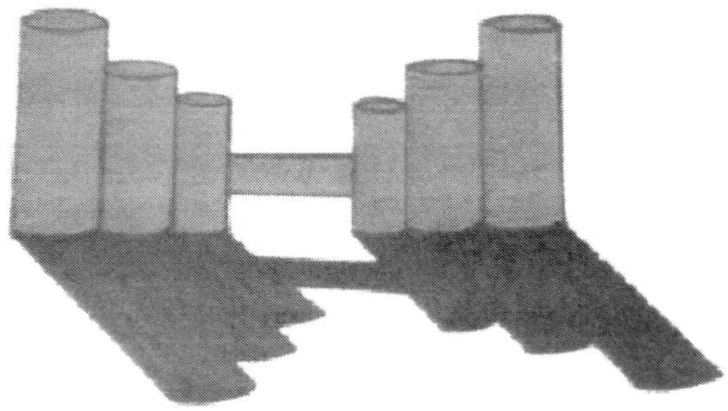

Q.2) Draw a 3- d composition using 1 bucket, 1 pot, 1 tumbler & 1 piece of cloth. Also show the effects of shade & shadow.

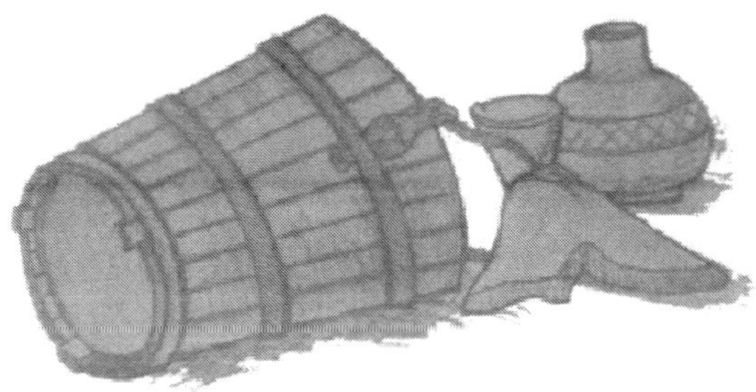

Q.3) Draw a 3- d composition using 3 bricks & 2 stones. Also show the effects of shade & shadow.

Q.4) Draw a 3- d composition using 3 cubes & 2 cuboids. Also show the effects of shade & shadow.

Q.5) Draw a 3- d composition using 3 books, 1magnifying glass, 1 clock, 1glass & 1spectacles. Also show the effects of shade & shadow.

Q.6) Draw a 3- d composition using 2 cubes, 1 cuboid & 1 glass pyramid. Also show the effects of shade & shadow.

Q.7) Draw a 3- d composition using 6 automobile tyres. Also show the effects of shade & shadow.

Q8.) Draw an interesting 3- D composition by using three books, one magnifying glass, one spectacles & table clock. Show the effect of shade and shadow.

Q.9) Draw a 3- d composition using 5 wooden logs & 4 cubes. Also show the effects of shade & shadow.

Q.10) Draw a 3- d composition using 5 earthen pots. Also show the effects of light & shadow.

Q.11) Draw a 3- d composition using 6 wooden logs, 4 cubes & 1 piece of cloth. Also show the effects of shade & shadow.

Q.12) Draw a 3- d composition using 4 cyclinders, , 1 sphere& 1cuboid ,1 hemisphere . Also show the effects of shade & shadow.

Q.13) Draw a 3- d composition using 1 apple , 1 banana& 1 earthen pot,1 book. Also show the effects of shade & shadow.

Q.14) There are 12 apples kept in a plate .Make an interesting 3D composition using them and also show the effects of shade and shadow .

Q.15) Draw a 3- d composition using some eggs in a plate, a packet of bread opened and a cup of tea and show the effects of shade & shadow.

Q.16) Draw a 3- d composition using 5 earthen pots and show the effects of shade & shadow.

Q.17) Draw a 3- d composition using 3 cubes, 2 pyramids and 4 cylinders show the effects of shade & shadow.

Q18)Draw an interesting 3- D composition by using 1 cubical box and 1 sphere and show the effect of shade and shadow.

Q19)Draw an interesting 2- D composition by using 1 bat, 1 cap, 2 wickets & 3 balls Also show the effect of shade and shadow.

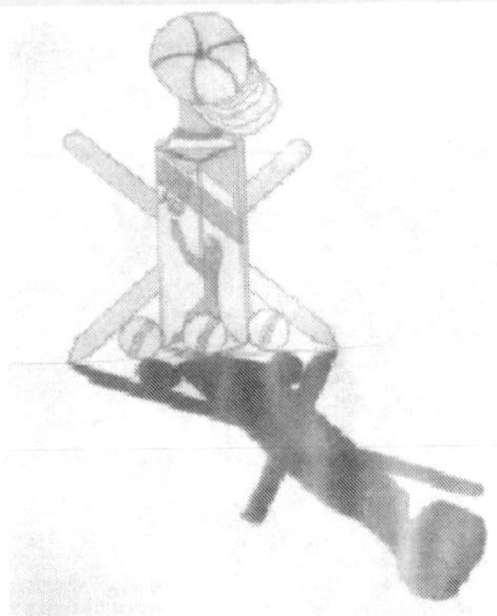

Q20)Draw an interesting 2- D composition by using 1 bat, 1 cap, 2 wickets & 3 balls Also show the effect of shade and shadow.

Q21)Draw an interesting 3- D composition by using 2 cuboids, 3 cylinders, 1 hemisphere and 1 sphere. Show the effect of shade and shadow.

Q22) Draw an interesting 3- D composition by using three types of biscuits. Show the effect of shade and shadow.

Q.23) In the given space make an interesting 3- dimensional stable composition using 1 cricket bat, 1 cap, 2 wickets & 3 cricket balls. Also show the effects of light & shadow on the composition.

Q.24) Draw a 3-D composition using one bowl, two earthen pots & show the shade & shadow of the same.

2-D DRAWINGS

Design a logo for global warming & color it by using 4 colors.

Draw a 2-d composition using profile of pet animals.

Design a logo for a car company using primary shapes like circle, triangle & square and Color it using 3 colors

Design a logo for the bag of an architecture student & color it using 2 colors.

Design a logo for Google.

Design a logo for your favorite IPL team.

Design a logo for a pre primary school & color it using primary colors.

Design a logo for a t-shirt on save planet and colour it by using fi ve colors of your choice.

Design a logo for a t-shirt to save water and color it by using any 4 colors of your choice.

Draw a 2-d composition using 5 playing cards with playing faces up.

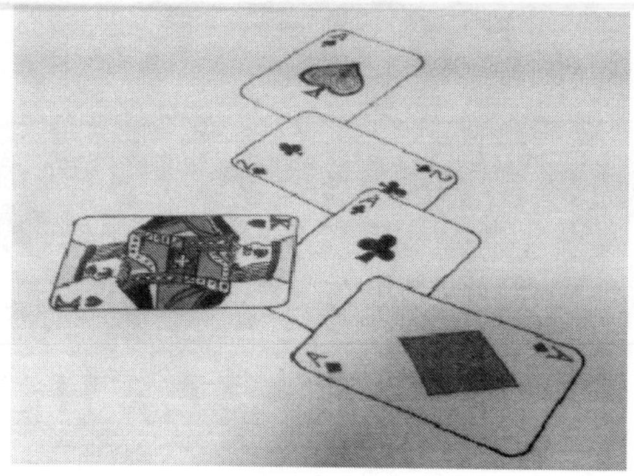

Design a logo on Indian politics.

Design a logo for Indian cricket team & color it using four colors

Design a logo for a t-shirt to save trees & color it by using four colors.

Design a logo for water polo game & color it by using different colors.

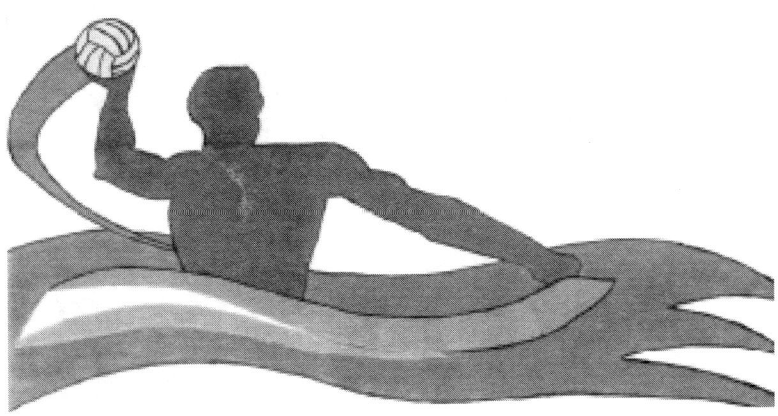

Design a logo for a laptop bags on music.

Design a 2D composition for games and color the same by using any color of your choice.

Draw a 2-d composition using primary shapes like circle, triangle & square & color its voids using any one primary color.

Design a logo for the bag of architecture student and colour it by using different colors

By using different parts of bicycle draw a 2- D composition by using suitable colors

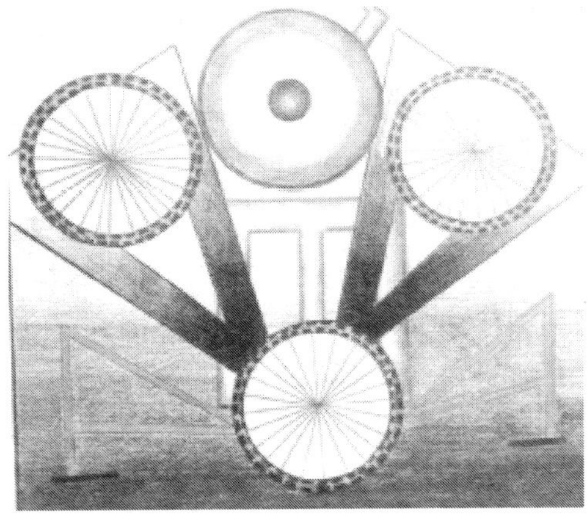

Design a bed sheet & color it by using different colors

Design a logo for a TV show

Using three color.

Design a logo for a restaurant & color it

ARCHITECTURE STYLES

(FOR ANALYSING)

- ARCHITECTURE IN PRE HISTORIC TIME
- ANCIENT EGYPT (3050 BC to 900 BC)
- CLASSICAL ARCHITECTURE (850 BC TO 476 AD)
- EARLY CHRISTIAN & MEDIEVAL (373 TO 500 AD)
- BASILICA
- ROMANESQUE ARCHITECTURE (500 TO 1200 AD)
- BYZANTINE ARCHITECTURE
- GOTHIC (1100 TO 1450 AD)
- RENAISSANCE (1400 TO 1600 AD)
- BAROQUE (1600 TO 1830 AD)
- ROCOCO (1650 TO 1790 AD)
- AMERICAN COLONIAL (1600 TO 1780 AD)
- GEORGIAN ARCHITECTURE (1720 TO 1800 AD)
- NEOCLASSICAL/ FEDERALIST (1730 TO 1925 AD)
- GREEK REVIVAL
- VICTORIAN ARCHITECTURE
- ART/CRAFT MOVEMENT IN ARCHITECTURE
- ART NOUVEAU ARCHITECTURE
- NEO- GOTHIC
- ART- DECO

• ARCHITECTURE IN PRE HISTORIC TIMES

Before recorded history, humans constructed stone circles, megaliths & other structures.

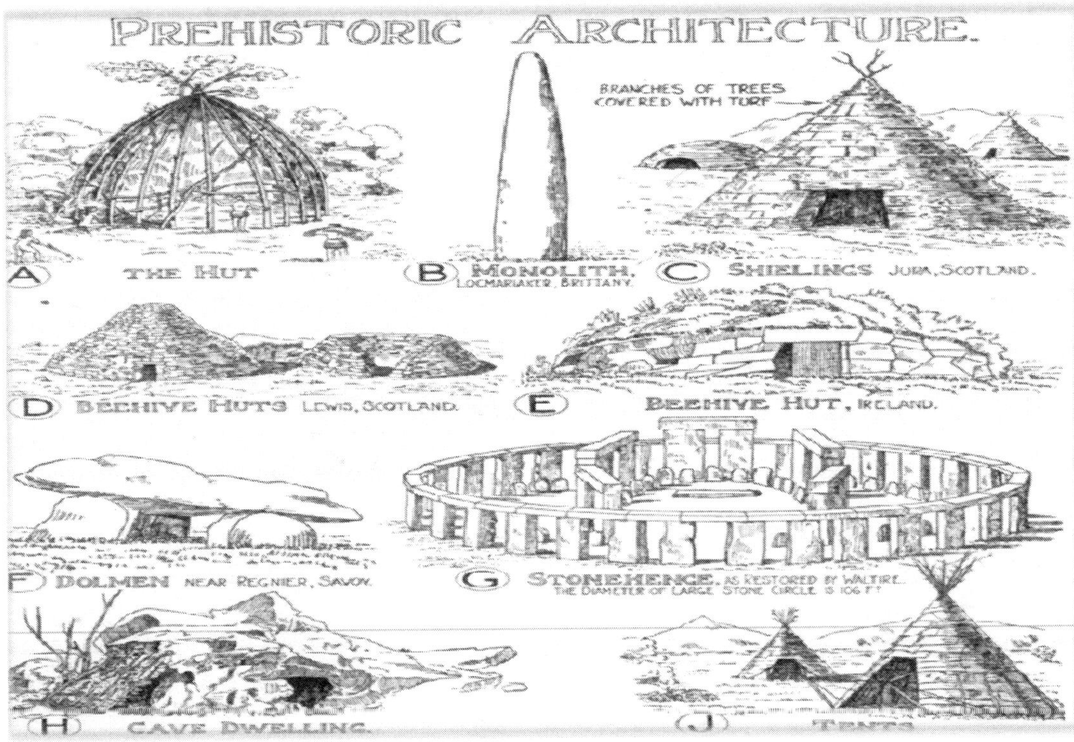

EXAMPLES:

STONE HENGE

ROMAN BRIDGE

- **ANCIENT EGYPT(3050 BC to 900 BC)**

- Egyptian architecture is based mainly on religious monuments, massive structures characterized by **thick, sloping walls** with **few openings**, possibly echoing a method of construction used to obtain stability in **mud walls**.

FEATURE :

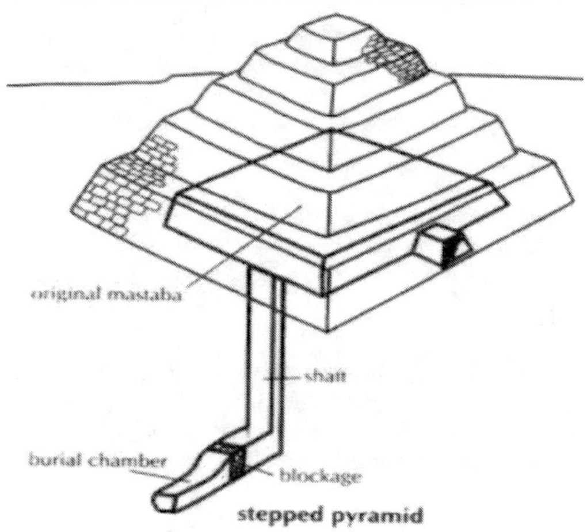

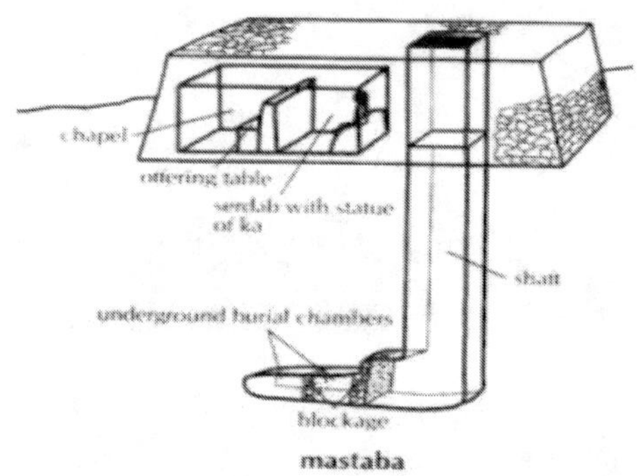

A typical Old Kingdom simple mastaba tomb

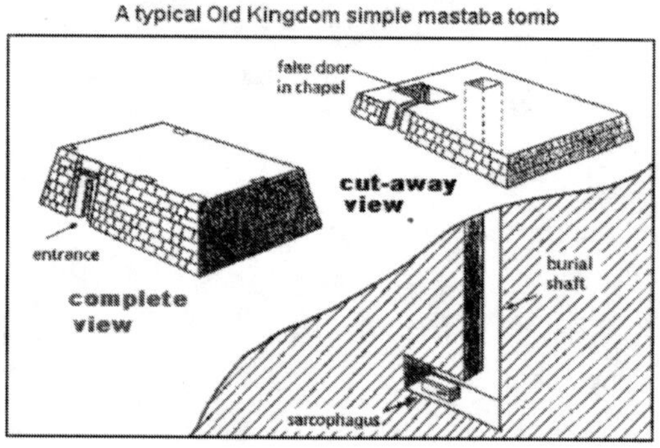

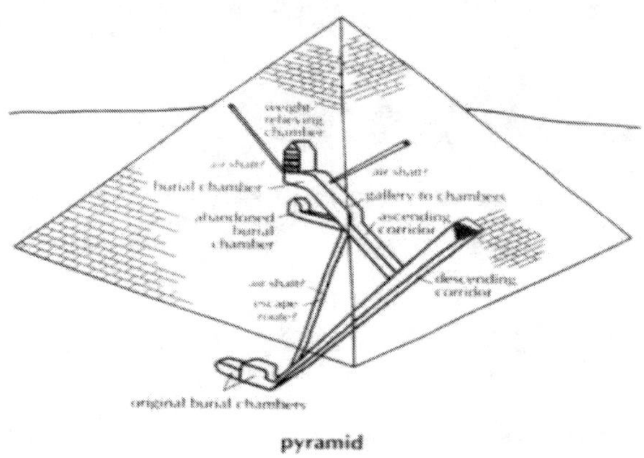

EXAMPLES:

• CLASSICAL ARCHITECTURE (850 BC TO 476 AD)

FEATURE:

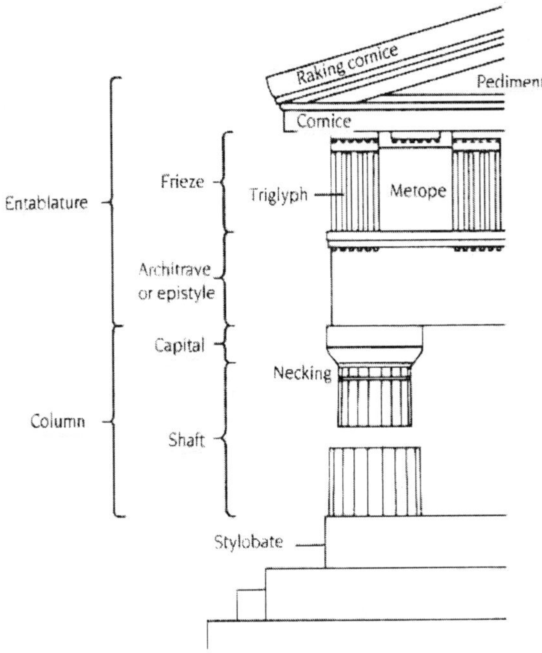

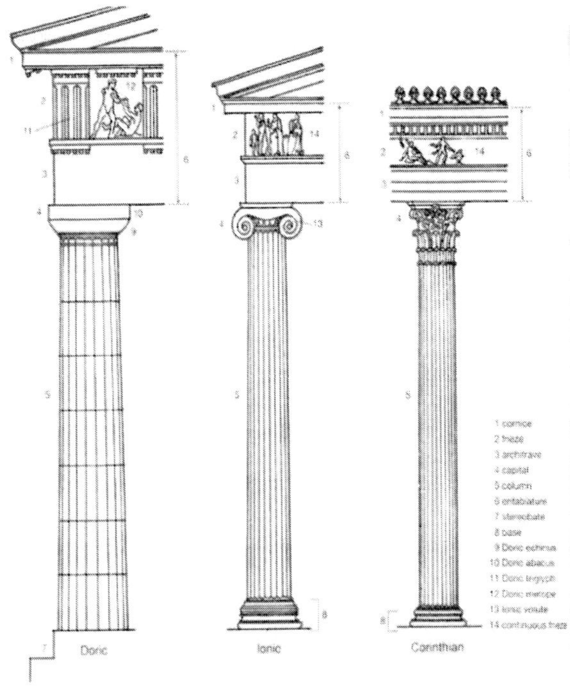

GLYPTOTHEK

IN MUNICH

- **EARLY CHRISTIAN & MEDIEVAL (373 TO 500 AD)**

European architecture moved from the rectangular basilica forms tothe classically inspired byzantine style.

Basilica

Romanesque

Byzantine

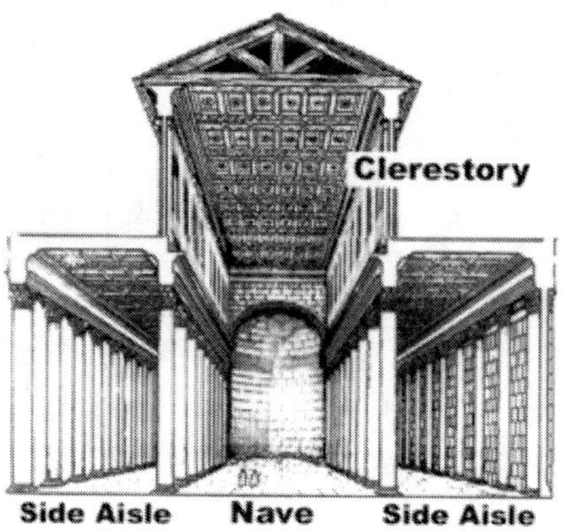

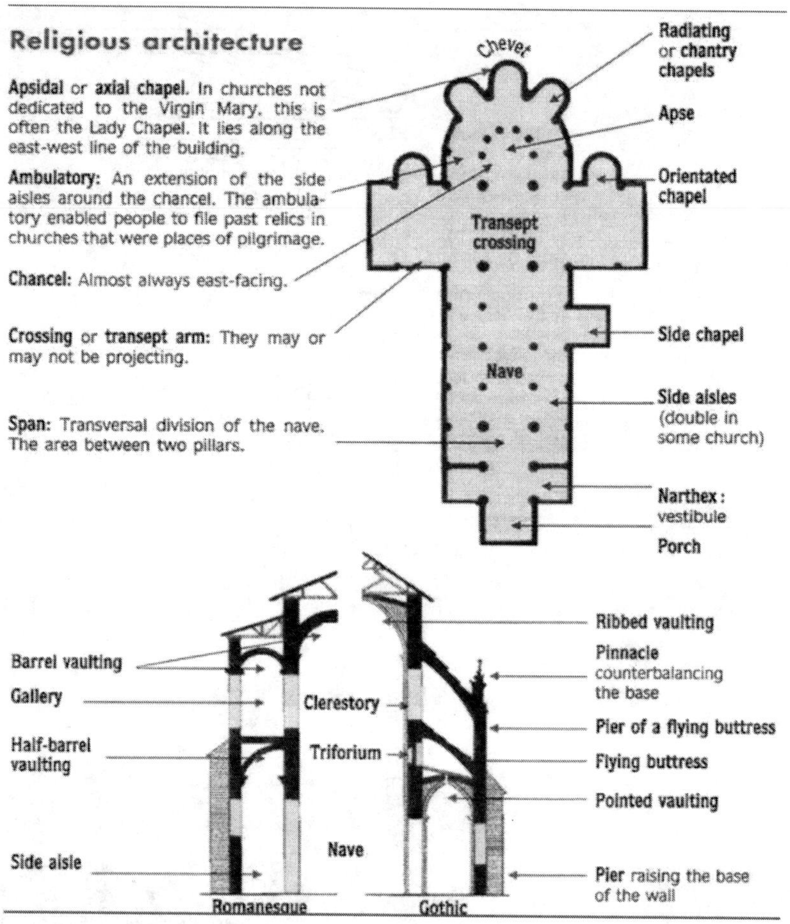

EXAMPLES:

- **BASILICA**

"In architecture, the term basilica signifies a kingly, and secondarily a beautiful, hall."

FEATURES:

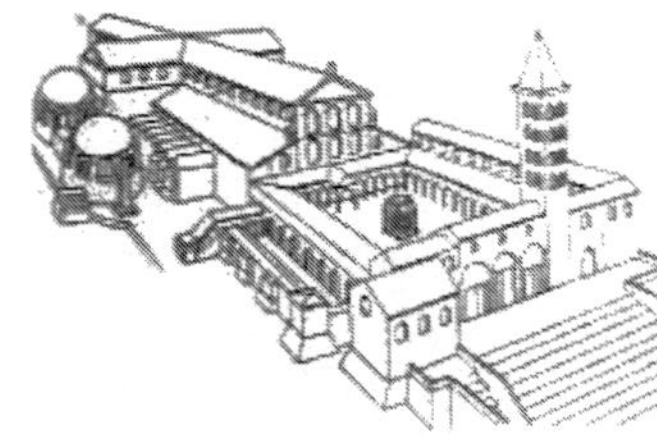

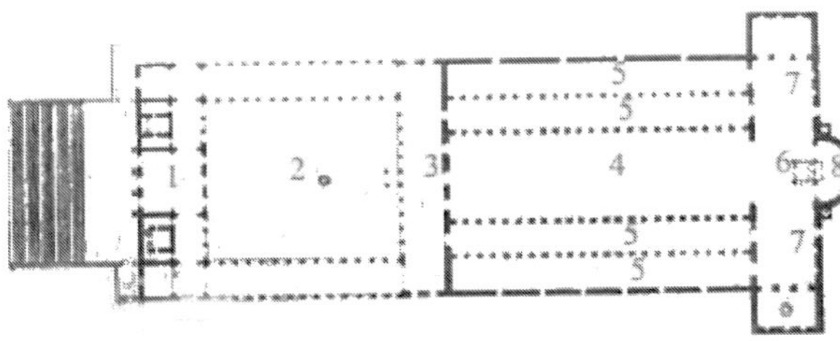

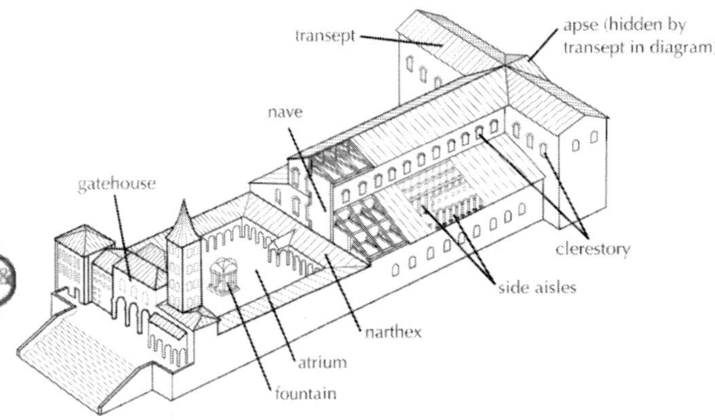

1) **Propylaeum**- the entrance building of a sacred precinct, whether church or imperial palace.

2) **Atrium**- in early Christian, Byzantine, and medieval architecture, the forecourt of a church; as a rule enveloped by four colonnaded porticoes.

3) **Narthex**- the entrance hall or porch proceding the nave of a church.

4) **Nave**- the great central space in a church. In longitudinal churches, it extends from the entrance to the apse (or only to the crossing if the church has one) and is usually flanked by side aisles.

5) **Side Aisle**- one of the corridors running parallel to the nave of a church and separated from it by an arcade or colonnade.

6) **Crossing**- the area in a church where the transept and the nave intersect.

7) **Transept**- in a cruciform church, the whole arm set at right angles to the nave.

EXAMPLES:

Old St. Peter's | ChurchSta_ Sabina | Church in Italy

- **ROMANESQUE ARCHITECTURE (500 TO 1200 AD)**

As Rome spread across Europe, **heavier, stocky** Romanesque architecture with **rounded arches** emerged.

FEATURE :

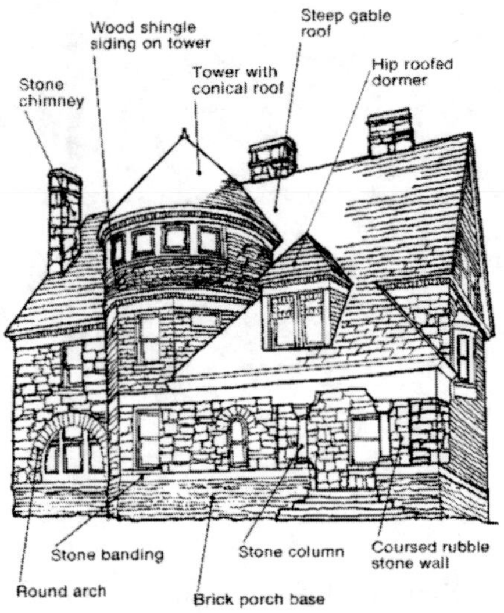

EXAMPLE: Lessay Abbey, Normandy, France

CHURCH PORTAL:

Tympanum: the surface enclosed by the arch and lintel of an arched doorway, frequently carved with relief sculptures.

Archivolt: the molding fram an arch. In Romanesque and Gothic architecture, each one of a series of arches framing the tympanum of a portal.

Lintel: a horizontal beam spanning an openings, as over a window or door, or between two posts.

Trumeau: doorpost supporting lintel.

Jamb: the side of a doorway or window frame. The jambs of the portals of Romanesque and Gothic churches are frequently decorated with figure sculpture.

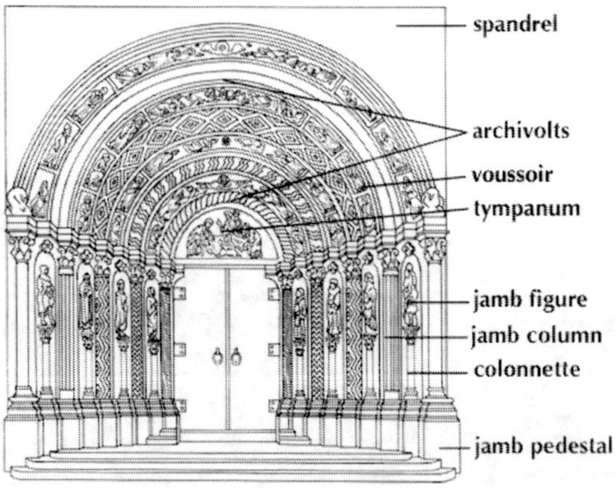

Romanesque church portal

- **BYZANTINE ARCHITECTURE:**

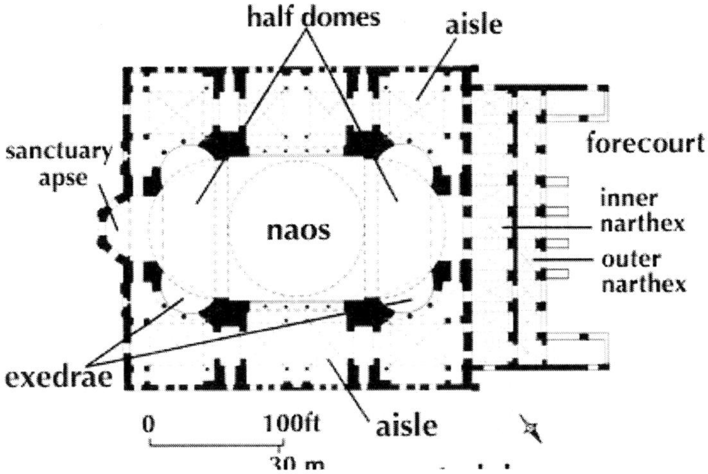

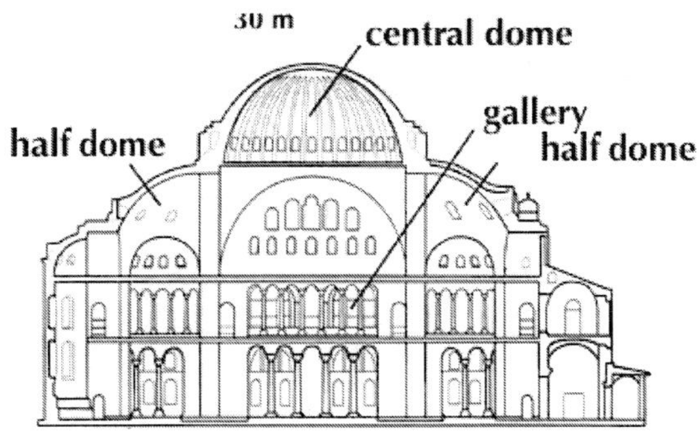

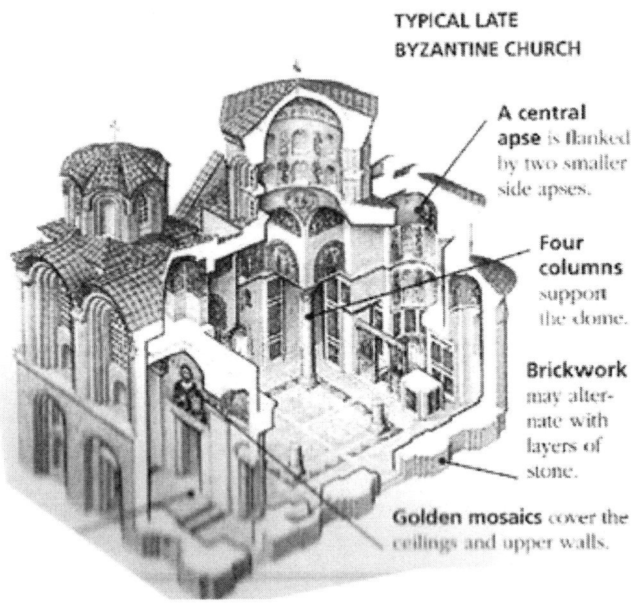

EXAMPLE :Aya Sofa

EXAMPLE : Hagia Sophia

- **GOTHIC (1100 TO 1450 AD)**

Innovative builders created the great cathedrals of europe. Gothic architecture was about flamboyancy, elegance, details, and asymmetry.

FEATURE

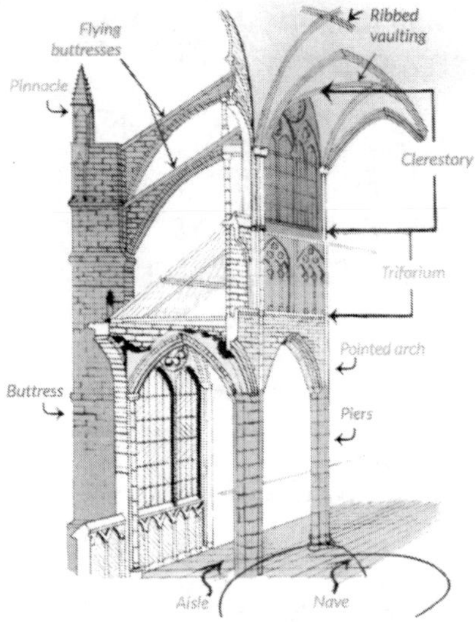

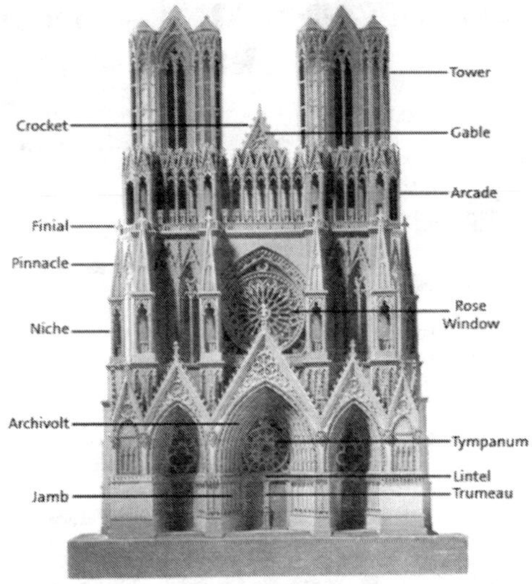

EXAMPLE : Westminster Abbey

EXAMPLE : Charles Cathedral

EXAMPLE : Basilica Of St. Denis

EXAMPLE : Cologne Cathedral

• RENAISSANCE (1400 TO 1600 AD)

Renaissance meant the revival, rebirth, or new age. It adapted some architectural features from the romanesque and gothic architecture such as, pediments, triangular shaped architectural feature found at the top most of the front facade. Arches, the curved open space that are sometimes used as entrances in some buildings and also windows. Renaissance architecture basically, was a combination of romanesque and gothic architecture that focused mostly on symmetry, proportion, balance, equilibrium. Renaissance for short, is obsessive compulsive to proportion and equality.

Renaissance tower and spire

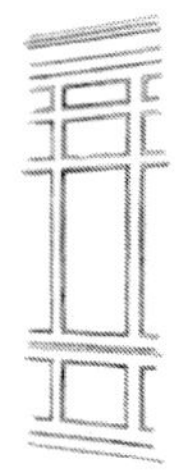
Panelling

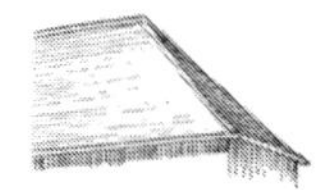
Hipped Roof

Dormer window

A Wren-style house

- Symmetrical arrangement of windows and doors
- Extensive use of Classical columns and pilasters
- Triangular pediments
- Square lintels
- Arches and Domes
- Niches with sculptures

EXAMPLE :

El Escorial (Madrid, Spain)
St. Peter (Rome - Vatican, Italy)
Chateau de Chambord (Chambord, France)
Queen Anne Summer palace (Prague, Czech Republic)
The Queen's House (Greenwich, England)
Antwerp - City Hall (Antwerp, Belgium)

• BAROQUE (1600 TO 1830 AD)

FEATURE:

In churches, broader naves and sometimes given oval forms.

Fragmentary or deliberately incomplete architectural elements

Dramatic use of light; either strong light-and-shade contrasts

Opulent use of colour and ornaments , plaster or stucco, marble or faux finishing

Large-scale ceiling frescoes

An external façade often characterized by a dramatic central projection

The interior is a shell for painting, sculpture and stucco (especially in the late Baroque)

Illusory effects like trompe l'oeil (an art technique involving extremely realistic imagery in order to create the optical illusion that the depicted objects appear in three dimensions.) and the blending of painting and architecture

Pear-shaped domes

São Roque Church in Lisbon

Copenhagen Amalienborg

• ROCOCO (1650 TO 1790 AD)

FEATURE:

Natural motives

Elaborate carved forms

Asymmetry

S and c scrolls

Rocaille

Acanthus leaf

Igreja de São Francisco de Assis

Marek & Ewa Wojciechowscy

• AMERICAN COLONIAL (1600 TO 1780 AD)

FEATURE:

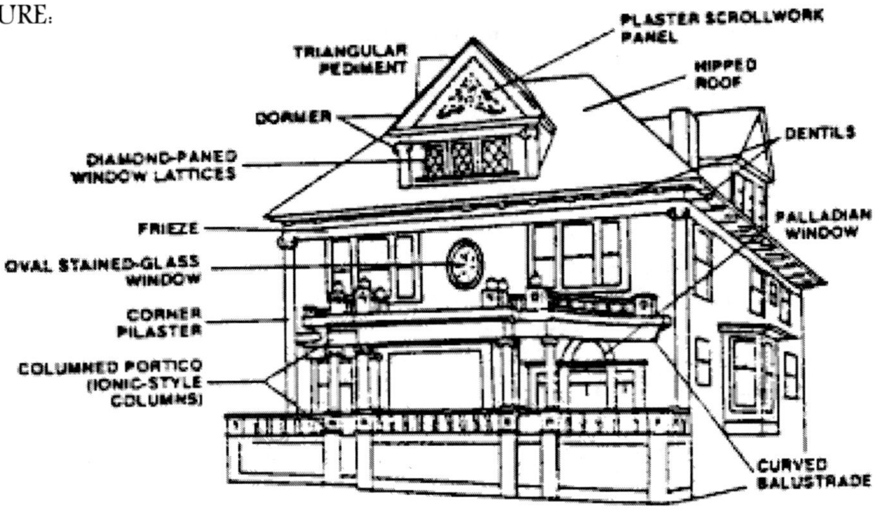

EARLY COLONIAL REVIVAL DETAILS

A cornucopia of Georgian/Federal classical elements often embellish a basically late-Victorian house.

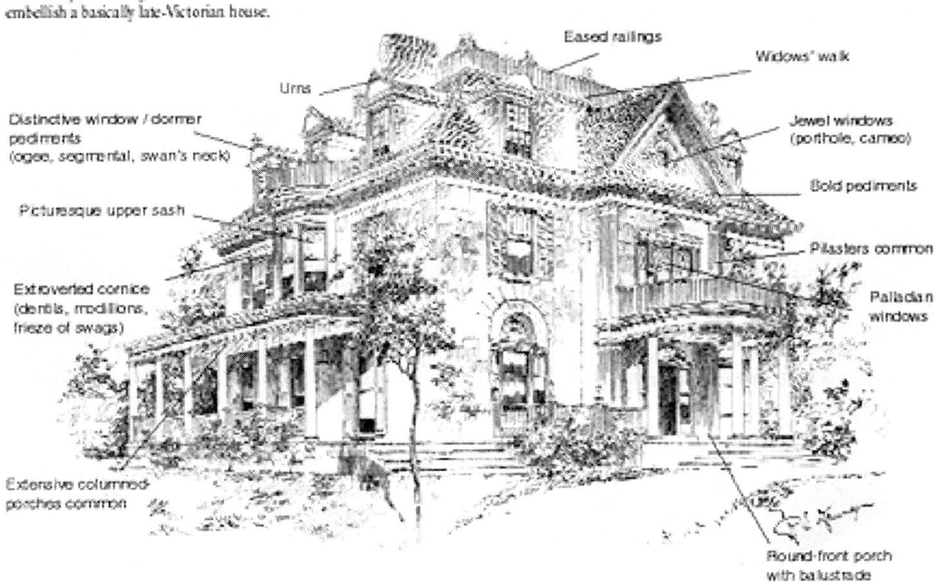

EXAMPLE:

- **GEORGIAN ARCHITECTURE (1720 TO 1800 AD)**

Georgian was a stately, symmetrical style that dominating in great Britain and Ireland and influenced building style in the American colonies.

FEATURE:

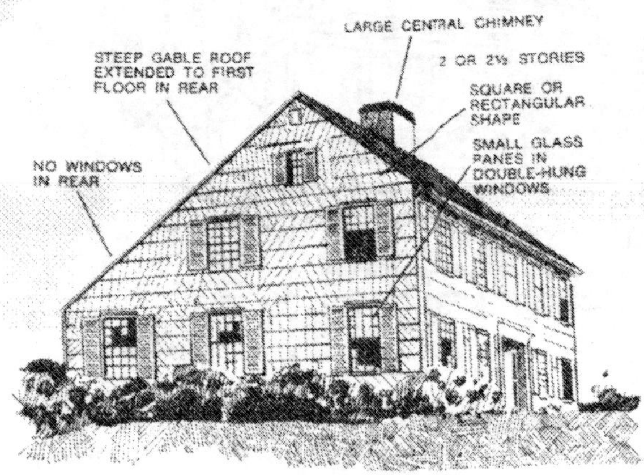

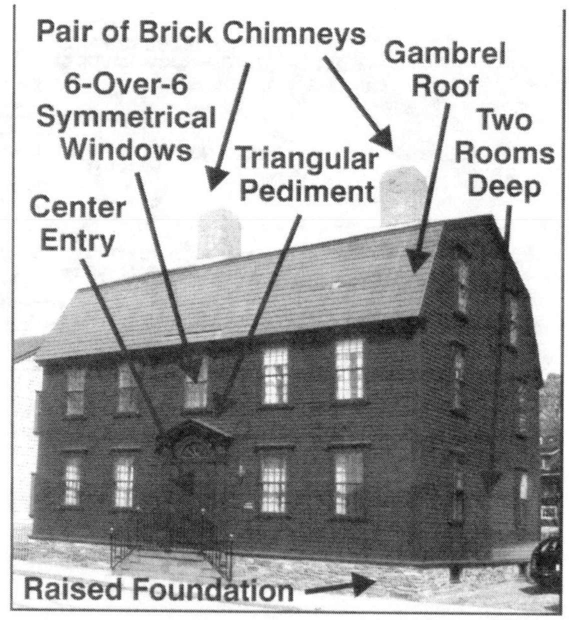

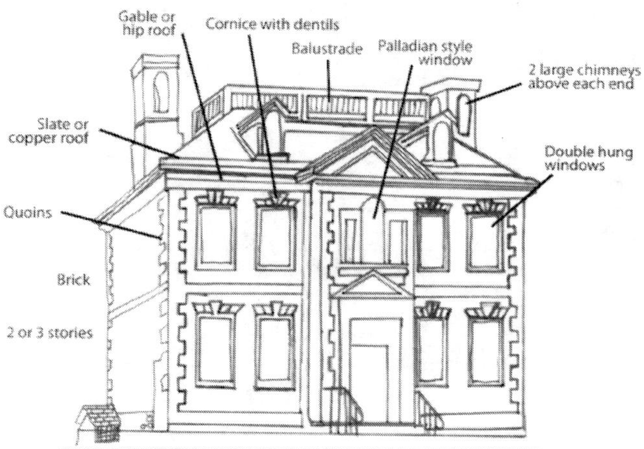

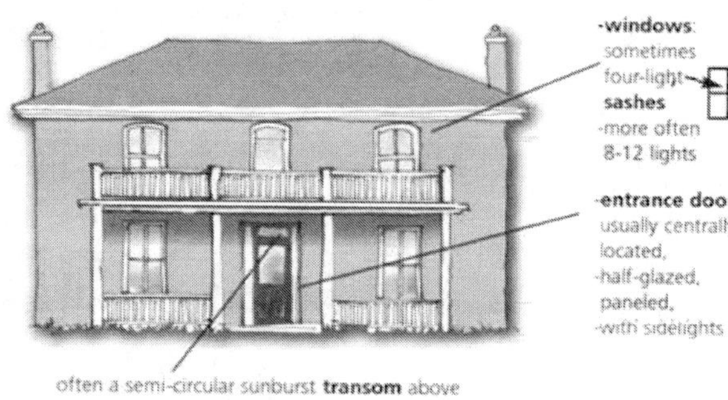

EXAMPLE:

• NEOCLASSICAL/ FEDERALIST (1730 TO 1925 AD)

NEOCLASSICAL

FEATURE:

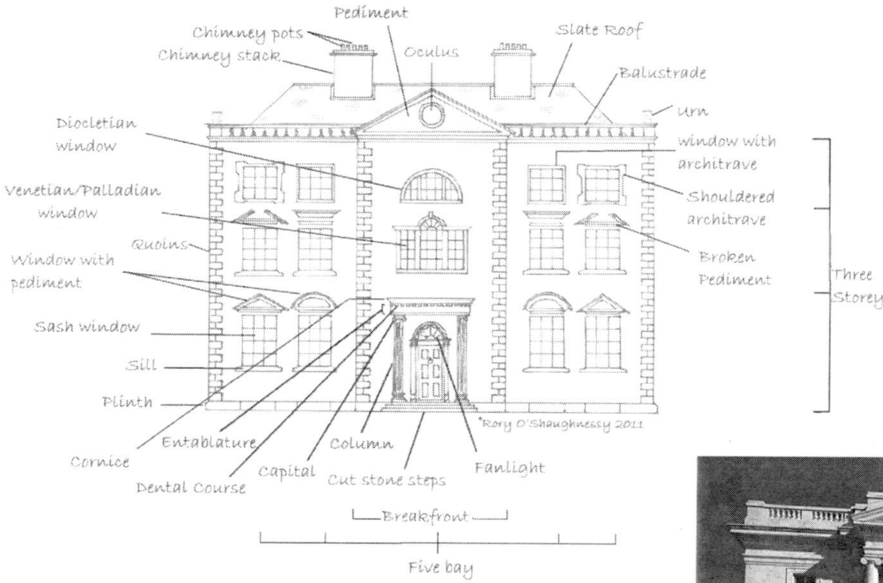

EXAMPLE:

FEDERALIST

FEATURE:

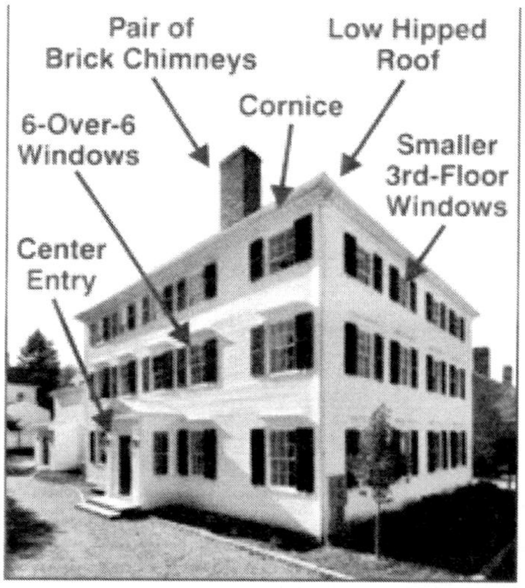

EXAMPLE:

- **GREEK REVIVAL ARCHITECTURE (1790 TO 1850 AD)**

These classical building and homes often feature columns, pediments and other details inspired by GREEK forms.

FEATURE:

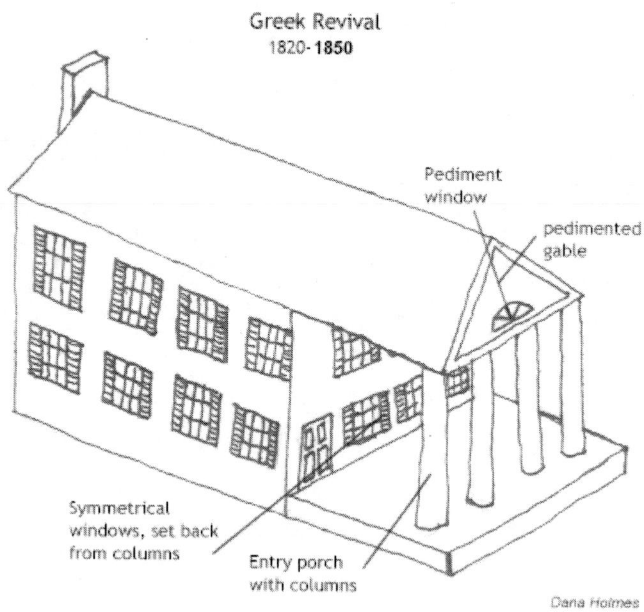

EXAMPLE:

• VICTORIAN ARCHITECTURE (1840 TO 1900 AD)

Industrialization brought many innovation in architecture .Victorian style include gothic revival, Italianate .sticks, Eastlake, Queen Anne, Romanesque and second empire.

FEATURE:

EXAMPLE:

• ART AND CRAFTS MOVEMENT IN ARCHITECTURE (1860 TO 1900 AD)

Art and craft was a late 19 Th– century backlash against the force of industrialization. The arts and crafts movement revived an interest in handicraft and sought a spiritualconnection with the surrounding environment, both natural and manmade.

William Morris's Red House in London

- **ART NOUVEAU ARCHITECTURE (1890 TO 1914 AD)**

FEATURE:

Asymmetrical shapes,

Extensive use of arches and curved forms

Flowering lines and buildings

CASA MILACASA MILA (AERIAL VIEW)

CASA BATLLO

CASA BATLLO (INTERIOR)

RAGA LITWA

PARK GUELL

• NEO-GOTHIC ARCHITECTURE (1905 TO 1930 AD)

In the early 20th century, medieval gothic ideas were applied to modern skyscrapers.

FEATURE:

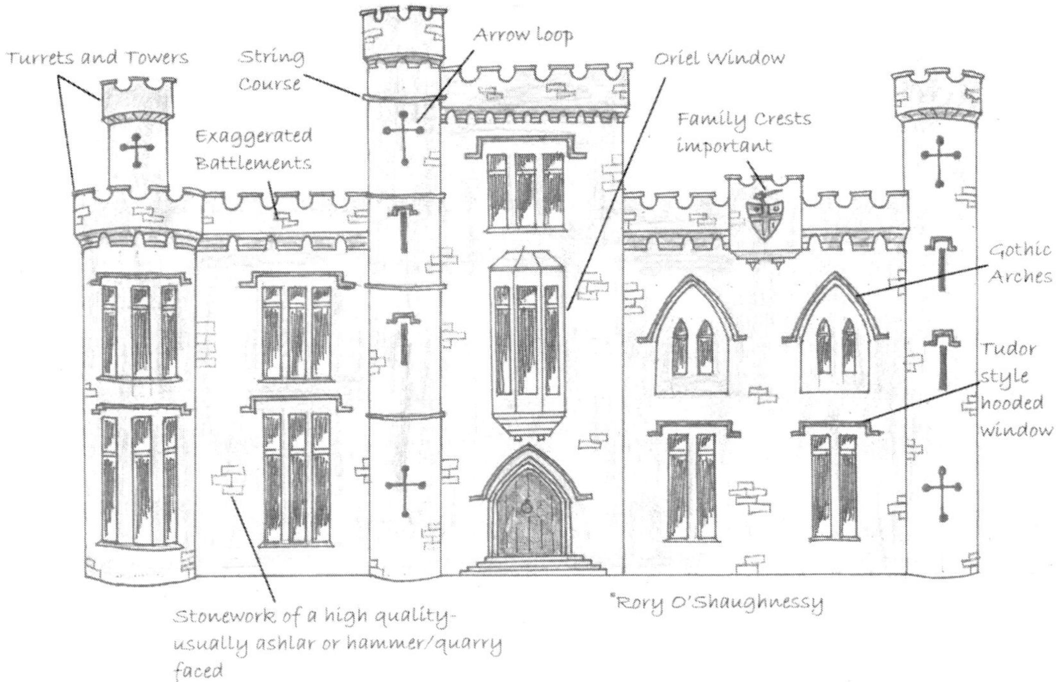

WASHINGTON NATIONAL CATHEDRAL

• ART – DECO ARCHITECTURE (1925 to 1937 AD)

FEATURE:

Zigzag patterns and vertical lines

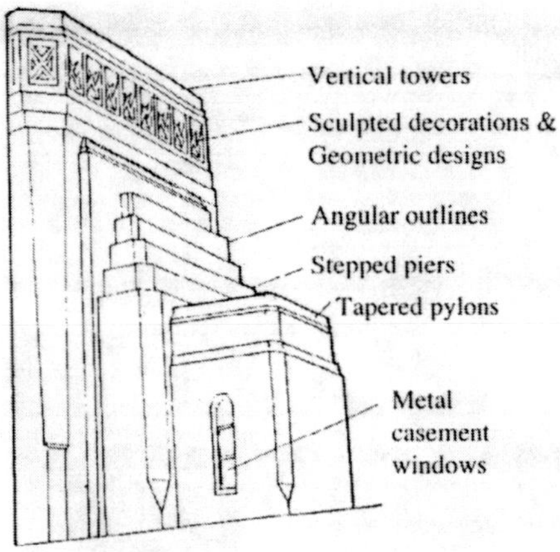

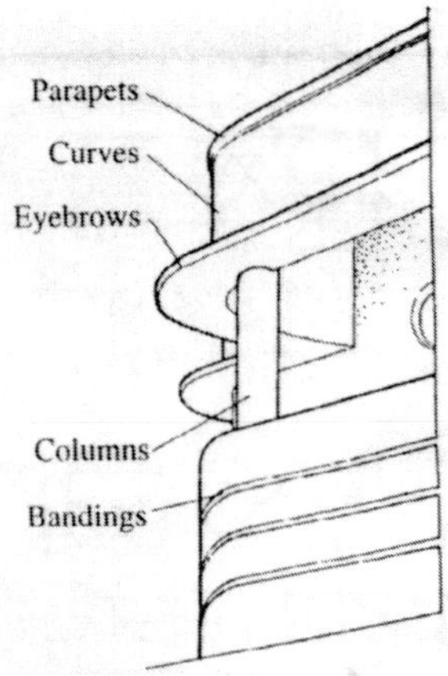

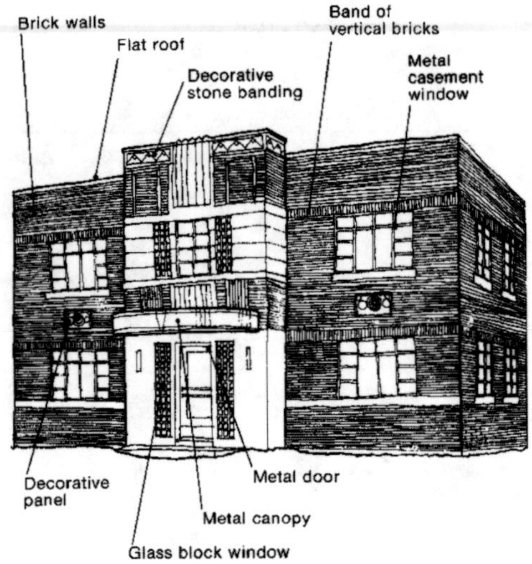

EXAMPLE:

THE CHRYSLER BUILDING

DAILY EXPRESS BUILDING

MICHAEL ROUX-SPITZ

ALDRED BUILDING

COLLEGE PARK,TORONTO

333 North Michigan

INDIAN BUILDINGS

(FOR VISUAL RECOGNITION)

 GOL GUMBAZ BIJAPUR	 MYSORE PALACE	 ST. MARY BASILICA,KARNATAKA
 WORLD TRADE CENTRE BANGALORE (NORTH STAR)	 UB CITY BANGALORE COMMERCIAL C OMPLEX	 PUBLIC UTILITY BUILDING (SUBHASH CHANDAR BOSE TOWER) BANGALORE
 BANGALORE TOWN HALL	 VIDHAN SABHA BENGLURU	 VEMBANAND LAKE KERALA
 HIGH COURT KERELA	 MANTRI PINNACLE	 KERALA GOVT. SECRETERIAT
 **St. Francis CSI** Church, KOCHI	 HAWA MEHAL, JAIPUR	 AMBER FORT NEAR JAIPUR

JAL MEHAL JAIPUR

CITY PALACE, JAIPUR

JAIGARH FORT, NEAR AMBER IN JAIPUR

JANTAR MANTAR, JAIPUR

ALBERT HALL MUSEUM, JAIPUR

DARGAH SHARIF OR AJMER SHARIF

JUNAGARH FORT

LAXMI NIWAS PALACE, JAIPUR

JAWAHAR KALA KENDRA, JAIPUR

DILWARA JAIN TEMPLES, RAJASTHAN

CHITTORGARH FORT, RAJASTHAN

VIJAY STHAMB (TOWER OF VICTORY)

JAG MANDIR , UDAIPUR (LAKE GARDEN PALACE)

CITY PALACE UDAIPUR

LAKE PALACE UDAIPUR (JAG NIWAS PALACE)

 INDIA GATE, DELHI	 SANSAD BHAWAN, DELHI(PARLIAMENT HOUSE)	 RASHTRAPATI BHAWAN DELHI
 PURANA QUILA DELHI	 RED FORT, DELHI	 QUTUB MINAR, DELHI
 HUMAYUN'S TOMB	 AKSHARDHAM TEMPLE, DELHI	 LAXMI NARAYAN TEMPLE, DELHI (BIRLA MANDIR)
 **ISKON TEMPLE, DELHI**	 **JAMA MASJID, DELHI**	 **LOTUS TEMPLE, DELHI**
 JANTAR MANTAR, DELHI	 PRAGATI MAIDAN, DELHI	 TEEN MURTI BHAWAN, DELHI

RAJIV GANDHI BHAWAN, DELHI

SUPREME COURT, DELHI

IIT DELHI

LIC BUILDING CONNAUGHT PLACE DELHI

ASIAN GAMES VILLAGE, DELHI

TRIVENI KALA SANGAM, DELHI

GOLDEN TEMPLE, PUNJAB

SHEESH MEHAL, PATIALA

PALACE OF ASSEMBLY, CHANDIGARH

SECRETERIAT CHANDIGARH

HIGH COURT, CHANDIGARH

SANCHI STUPA, M.P

KENDRIYA MAHADEVA TEMPLE, M.P

MATANGESHWAR TEMPLE, M.P

PARSAVNATH TEMPLE, M.P

JAHAGIR MEHAL, M.P

BHARAT BHAWAN, BHOPAL

CHASHME SHAHI, KASHMIR

INDIAN INST. OF ADVANCE STUDIES, KASHMIR

NATIONAL INST. OF TECHNOLOGY HAMIRPUR, H.P

STONE ERECTIONS, MANIPUR

FIROZ SHAH PALACE COMPLEX,HISAR,HARYANA

KINGDOM OF DREAMS, GURGAON, HARYANA

GODAVARI ARCH BRIDGE, A.P

CHAR MINAR, HYDERABAD

GOLCONDA FORT

RANCHI, SCIENCE CENTRE

INDIRA GANDHI, PLANETERIUM, PATNA

TOMB OF SHER SHAH SURI, BIHAR

BUDDHIST STUPA (NALANDA)

JAL MANDIR

MILL OWNERS ASSOCIATION BUILDING, AHEMDABAD

LAXMI VILAS PALACE, GUJRAT

SOMNATH TEMPLE, GUJRAT

SUN TEMPLE, MODHERA, GUJRAT

CEPT UNIV. AHEMDABAD

IIM AHEMDABAD

AGHA KHAN, PALACE

ELEPHANTA CAVES, MMBAI

ANTILA (MUKESH AMBANI'S HOUSE)

IMPERIAL, MUMBAI

GATEWAY OF MUMBAI

CHATARPATI SHIVAJI INTERNATIONAL AIRPORT, MUMBAI

INDIA TOWER, MUMBAI

JEEJEEBHOY TOWER, MUMBAI

NATIONAL GALERY OF MODERN ART, MUMBAI

FOREST RESEARCH INST., DEHRADUN

TOWN HALL KOLKATA

WRITER'S BUILDING, KOLKATA

BIRLA PLANETERIUM, KOLKATA

NATIONAL LIBRARY OF INDIA, KOLKATA

FOREIGN BUILDINGS

(FOR VISUAL RECOGNITION)

EMPIRE STATE BUILDING, USA

GOLDEN GATE BRIDGE, USA

FALLING WATER HOUSE, USA

THE WHITE HOUSE, WASHINGTON

FRANSWORTH HOUSE, USA

GATEWAY ARCH, USA

BROOKLYN BRIDGE, USA

STATUE OF LIBERTY, NEW YORK

SEAGRAM BUILDING, NEW YORK

GUGGENHEIM MUSEUM, N.Y.

TWA TERMINAL, N.Y

PENTAGON, NEW YORK

PARLIAMENT HILL, CANADA

EL ANGEL, MAXICO

ST.STEPHEN'S CATHEDRAL,AUSTRIA

BIG BEN, ENGLAND

BUKINGHAM PALACE, ENGLAND

ST.PAUL'S CATHEDRAL, ENGLAND

LONDON EYE

TOWER OF LONDON

TOWER BRIDGE (LONDON BRIDGE)

STONEHENGE, LONDON

NOTRE DAM DE PARIS

ARC DE TRIOMPHE, PARIS

EIFFEL TOWER, PARIS

PALACE OF VERSAILLES, PARIS

PANTHEON, PARIS

LOUVRE MUSEUM, PARIS

BMW MUSEUM, GERMANY

NEW TOWN HALL, GERMANY

REICHSTAG DOME, GERMANY

BERLIN CATHEDRAL, GERMANY

ACROPOLIS, GREECE

 PARTHENON, GREECE	 ACROPOLIS MUSEUM, GREECE	 TEMPLE OF ZEUS, GREECE
 LEANING TOWER OF PISA, ITALY	 COLOSEUM, ITALY	 BAPISTERY, ITALY
 ST.PETER'SBASALICA,VATICAN CITY	 ST.PETER'S SQUARE, VATICAN CITY	 PANTHEON, ROME (ITALY)
 PALAZZO PITTI, ITALY	 CESA MILA, SPAIN	 GUGGENHEIM MUSEUM, SPAIN
 INT. RED CROSS AND RED CRECESENT MUSEUM, GENEVA	 SULTAN AHMED MOSQUE, ISTANBUL	 SYDNEY OPERA HOUSE
 SYDNEY HARBOUR BRIDGE	 SYDNEY TOWER	 RIALTO TOWER, SYDNEY

WORLD TOWER, SYDNEY	BEEHIVE, NEWZELAND	BURJ KHALIFA, DUBAI
 GREAT PYRAMID OF GIZA, EGYPT	 STEP PYRAMID OF DIJOSER, DUBAI	 ABU SIMBEL, EGYPT
 FORBIDDEN CITY, CHINA	 BANK OF CHINA, TOWER	 GREAT WALL OF, CHINA
 TOKYO TOWER, JAPAN	 PETRONAS TWIN TOWER, MALASIYA	 MOHAN JO DARO

INDIAN ARCHITECTS

(TO LEARN ABOUT THE MASTER ARCHITECTS, THEIR ARCHITECTURAL STYLES AND BUILDINGS)

- ANANT RAJE
- CHARLES MARK CORREA
- B.V. DOSHI
- LAURENCE WILFRED BAKER
- RAJ REWAL
- ACHYUT KANVINDE
- HAFEEZ CONTRACTOR
- CHRISTOPHER CHARLES BENNINGER

ANANT RAJE

Anant Raje is a well known Indian architect born in Mumbai in 1929. He studied at the SirJ. J. School of Architecture and later worked with Louis Kahn in Philadelphia, where he also taught at the University of Pennsylvania.

M.A.F.C.O. Wholesale Market (1975) ,

MumbaiGalbabhai Training Institute (1983) - Palanpur

Institute of Forest Management (1984) – Bhopal

The Indian Statistical Institute in New Delhi

CHARLES MARK CORREA

Charles Correa is an Indian architect, planner, activist, and theoretician who studied architecture at the Massachusetts Institute of Technology (MIT) and the University of Michigan. He is known for the wide range of his architectural work in India on urbanization and low-cost shelter. His architectural designs have been internationally acclaimed and he has received many awards including the Royal Institute of British Architects Gold Medal in 1984, the Indian Institute of Architects Gold Medal in 1987, the International Union of Architects Gold Medal in 1990, and the Premium Imperial for Architecture from the Japan Art Association in 1994.

Astronomy and Astrophysics Centre,

Bharat Bhawan, Bhopal

KanchanjungaApparments

Jawaharlal Nehru Kala Kendra

B.V. DOSHI

B. V. Doshi was born in Pune, India. He studied at the J. J. School of Architecture, Mumbai. B.V. Doshi worked in London then for four years with Le Corbusier. He returned to Ahmedabad to supervise Le Corbusier's work. His studio, Vastu-Shilpa(environmental design), was established in 1955. Doshi is a Fellow of the Royal Institute of British Architects, and has been on the selection committee for the Pritzker Prize, the Indira Gandhi National Centre for Arts, and the Agha Khan Award. He is also a Fellow of the Indian Institute of Architects.

Ahemdavad Ni Gufa, Ahmedabad

IIM Bangalore

4. LAURENCE WILFRED BAKER (LAURIE BAKER)

Laurence W.Baker, well known as Laurie Baker, was born in Birmingham, England on 2nd March 1917. He joined the Birmingham School of Architecture. In 1945, he came to India, to convert old refugee centers into actual treatment hospitals, with knowledge of leprosy and its treatment, apart from his planning and building experience. The Bakers remained in Pithoragarh for the next sixteen years. Living there, in a hilly terrain in the most adverse climatic conditions, amidst the poor, he understood the importance of Himalayan domestic architecture, which to him was a perfect example of vernacular architecture. Baker became well known for designing and building low cost, high quality, beautiful homes, with a great portion of his work suited to or built for lower-middle to lower class clients. While the jaalis, the traditional roofs, the stepped arches, the overhanging eaves and the skylights etc., are some of the well-known elements that characterize Baker's style, it is his high regard for nature that makes him unique. The local materials like brick, tile, lime, palm thatch, stone, granite and laterite thus replace the conventional steel and glass of modern architecture. Laurie Baker died at 7:30 am on April 1, 2007, aged 90.

WORKS:

Centre for Development Studies

The Hamlet – Laurie Bakers Own residence

Indian Coffee House

Chapel, CMC Vellore

RAJ REWAL

Raj Rewal is an Indian architect and urban design consultant who studied architecture in New Delhi and London. Rewal worked in Michel Ecochards's office in Paris before starting his practice in New Delhi

WORKS:

Asian Games Village

Hall Of Nation, PragatiMaidan

Parliament Library, New Delhi

Civic Centre

Indian National Science Academy

STC Building

ACHYUT KANVINDE

Padma ShriAchyut P. Kanvinde is considered as one of forefathers of modern Indian architecture. Along with his partner S. Rai, he opened a firm Kanvinde and Rai in New Delhi (which is currently run by Mr. Sanjay Kanvinde, Mrs. B.K. Tanuja and Mr. Murad Chaudhury).

Kanvinde was born in 1916 in a small village on the Konkan coast. He entered the Architecture Department at Sir J.J. School of Art in 1935, the first of the three existing architecture programs in the country then. Achyut Kanvinde attended Harvard Graduate school of Design in 1945 becoming the first Indian architect to have studied in America .Later he would be often termed as one of the doyens of modern Indian Architecture.

WORKS:

IIT, Kanpur

Milk Processing Plant

National Science Centre, New Delhi

Iskon Temple, New Delhi

HAFEEZ CONTRACTOR

He started his firm, Architect Hafeez Contractor, in 1983 with two people. One of his first success stories was the Vastu building at Worli Sea face. His work is controversial from the perspective of social impact and originality. His design approach is often thought of as uninspiring by architecture academics. Despite being one of India's most successful commercial architects, he publicly stated that Western standards for "green" buildings are a joke arguing that the problems present in India require unique solutions. His own unique solutions for India are however blatant replicas of Western landmarks, such as I. M. Pei's glass pyramid at the Louvre or the St. Peter's Basilica in Vatican City. His works are often condemned by the end users and inhabitants as being glitzy and dysfunctional for the unique conditions of the Indian sub-continent.

Works:

Vastu Building, Worli,Mumbai

The Imperial Towers

Lokhandwala Minerva

NICMAR , Pune

Mumbai Airport redesign

CHRISTOPHER CHARLES BENNINGER

Great Master Architect of India **Christopher Charles Benninger** is an American-Indian architect and planner born in the United States in 1942. He studied urban planning at the Massachusetts Institute of Technology and architecture at Harvard's Graduate School of Design, where he later taught (1969–72). The YMCA International Camp, Nilshi, India won the Arches Award for the best Institutional Building 2006 and the Indian Institute of Architects Award for the Best Public Building 2006.

WORK:

SuzlonOn Earth

Tshechu Ground or the National Ceremonial Plaza

India House

YMCA International Camp, Nilshi, India

FOREIGN ARCHITECTS

(TO LEARN ABOUT THE MASTER ARCHITECTS , THEIR ARCHITECTURAL STYLES AND BUILDINGS)

- FRANK O GEHRY
- F.L. WRIGHT
- LE CORBUSIER
- MIES VAN DEROHE
- NORMAN FOSTER
- LOUIS I KAHN
- I M PEI
- EERO SAARINEN
- JORN UTZON
- JOSEPH ALLEN STEIN
- ZAHA HADID

FRANK O GEHRY

Frank Gehry was born in Toronto, Ontario, Canada in 1929. He studied at the Universities of Southern California and Harvard, before he established his first practice,

Frank O. Gehry and Associates in 1963. In 1979 this practice was succeeded by the firm Gehry & Krueger Inc. Gehry's architecture has undergone the plywood and corrugated-metal vernacular of his early works to the distorted but pristine concrete of his later works.

WORKS:.

American Center, at Paris,France, 1988.

Gehry House, at Santa Monica, California, 1979 and 1987.

Goldwyn Branch Library, at Hollywood, CA, 1982

Guggenheim Museum Bilbao, at Bilbao, Spain, 1997

FRANK LLOYD WRIGHT

Frank Lloyd Wright was born in Richland Center, Wisconsin in1867. He and his family settled in Madison, Wisconsin in 1877.Wright departed for Chicago where he spent several months in J. L. Silsbee's office before seeking employment with Adler and Sullivan.

Wright evolved a new concept of interior space in architecture. Rejecting the existing view of rooms as single-function boxes, Wright created overlapping and interpenetrating rooms with shared spaces. He integrated simple materials such as brick, wood, and plaster into the designs. During the last part of his life, Wright produced a wide range of work. Particularly important was Taliesin West, a winter retreat and studio he built in Phoenix, Arizona. Hedied at Taliesin West in 1959.

WORKS:

Guggenheim Museum, at New York, New York, 1956 to 1959.

Imperial Hotel, at Tokyo, Japan, 1916 to 1922.

Falling Waters, USA

LE CORBUSIER

Charles-Edouard Jeanneret-Gris was born in La Chaux de Fonds, Switzerland, 1887. Trained as an artist, he travelled extensively through Germany and the East. In Paris he studied under Auguste Perret and absorbed the cultural and artistic life of the city. During this period he developed a keen interest in the synthesis of the various arts. Jeanneret-Gris adopted the name Le Corbusier in the early 1920s. Le Corbusier's post-war buildings rejected his earlier industrial forms and utilized vernacular materials, brute concrete and articulated structure. Near the end of his career he worked on several projects in India, which utilized brutal materials and sculptural forms. In these buildings he readopted the recessed structural column, the expressive staircase, and the flat undecorated plane of his celebrated five points of architecture.

WORKS:

Museum at Ahmedabad, India, 1953 to 1957

Notre-Dame-du-Haut, at Ronchamp, France,

United Nations Headquarters, New York

Assembly Hall, Chandigarh

LUDWIG MIES VAN DER ROHE

Ludwig Mies Van der Rohe was born in Aachen, Germany in 1886. He worked in the family stone-carving business before he joined the office of Bruno Paul in Berlin. He entered the studio of Peter Behrens in 1908 and remained until 1912. Famous for his dictum **'Less is More'**, Mies attempted to create contemplative, neutral spaces through an architecture based on material honesty and structural integrity. Mies died in Chicago, Illinois in 1969.

WORKS:

Barcelona Pavilion

Fransworth House

Seagram Building

Crown Hall

National Gallery at Berlin

NORMAN FOSTER

Norman Foster was born in Manchester, England in 1935. He received his architectural training at Manchester University School of Architecture and Yale University. The "High Tech" vocabulary of Foster Associates shows an uncompromising exploration of technological innovations and forms. The firm's work also shows a dedication to architectural detailing and craftsmanship. Their designs emphasize the repetition of industrialized "modular" units in which prefabricated off-site-manufactured e l e m e n t s are frequently employed. The firm often designs specialist components for individual projects. Foster was awarded the RIBA Royal Gold Medal in 1983, and in 1990 the RIBA Trustees Medal was made for the Willis Faber Dumas building. He was knighted in 1990, and received the Gold Medal of the AIA in 1994. On June 7, 1999, Sir Norman will receive the Pritzer Architecture Prize.

WORKS:

Hong Kong and Shanghai Bank, at Hong Kong

IBM Pilot Head Office, at Cosham, England

London City Hall, at London, England, 2003

London Millennium Bridge, at London, England

LOUIS I. KAHN

Louis Kahn was born in Saaremaa (Saaremaa), Estonia in 1901. His family emigrated to the U.S. in 1905. He graduated from the University of Pennsylvania with a thorough grounding the the Beaux Art school of architecture. During the 1920s and 1930s he worked as a Draughtsman and, later, as a head designer for several Philadelphia based firms. Kahn's architecture is notable for its simple, platonic forms and Compositions. Through the use of brick and poured-in place concrete asonry, he developed a contemporary and monumental architecture that maintained a sympathy for the site. While rooted in the International Style, Kahn's architecture was an amalgam of his Beaux Arts education and a personal aesthetic impulse to develop his own architectural forms. Considered one of the foremost architects of the late twentieth century, Kahn received the AIA Gold Medal in 1971 and the RIBA Gold Medal in 1972. He was elected a member of the American Academy of Arts and Letters in 1971.

WORKS:

IIM Ahmedabad

National Assembly Building

Salk Institute

Yale University Art Gallery

I. M. P EI

Ieoh Ming Pei was born in Canton, China in 1917. He left China when he was eighteen to study architecture at MIT and Harvard. Between 1942 and 1945, He worked as a concrete designer for Stone and Webster, and in 1946 he began work in the office of Hugh Asher Stubbins, in M Boston. Pei generally designs 297 sophisticated glass clad buildings loosely related to the high-tech Movement. However, many of his designs result from original design concepts.

WORKS:

Bank of China, at Hong Kong

National Centre for Atmospheric Research

East Wing, National Gallery, at Washington

Christian Science Center, at Boston,Massachusetts

Pyramiddu Louvre, at Paris, France, 1989.

EERO SAARINEN

Eero Saarinen was born in Kirkkonummi, Finland in 1910. He studied in Paris and at Yale University, after which he joined his father's practice. Eero initially pursued sculpture as his art of choice. After a year in art school, he decided to become an architect instead. Much of his work shows a relation to sculpture. Saarinen developed a remarkable range which depended on color, form and materials. Saarinen showed a marked dependence on innovative structures and sculptural forms, but not at the cost of pragmatic considerations. He easily moved back and forth between the International Style and Expressionism, utilizing a vocabulary of curves and cantilevered forms. Eero Saarinen died in Ann Arbor, Michigan in 1961.

Gateway Arch, at St. Louis, Missouri,

IBM Research Building, at Yorktown

TWA at New York, at New York

Dulles Airport

IBM Research at Yorktown, New York

JORN UTZON

Jørn Utzon was born in Copenhagen in 1918. He studied at the Academy of Arts in Copenhagen, under Kay Fisker and Steen Eiler Rasmussen. He established his own practice in Copenhagen in 1950 when he returned from his travels. Utzon has created a style marked by monumental civic buildings and unobtrusive housing projects. He incorporates the balanced discipline of Asplund, the sculptural quality of Alvar Aalto, and the organic 300structures of Frank Lloyd Wright into his designs. Influenced by architectural tradition, he attempts to create architecture for living that adheres to a strict structural and constructive process. Utzon always considers site conditions and program requirements before he designs each building. He transcends architecture as art and develops his forms into poetic inventions that Possess thoughtful programming, structural integrity and sculptural harmony.

WORKS:

Church at Bagsvaerd

Houses in Frednesberg

Kingo Houses, at Elsinore, Denmark

Sydney Opera, at Sydney, Australia

JOSEPH ALLEN STEIN

(April 10, 1912 – October 6, 2001) was an American architect and a major figure in the establishment of a regional modern architecture in the San Francisco Bay area in the 1940s and 1950s during the early days of the environmental design movement.

In 1952 he moved to India, and became head of the department of architecture at the Bengal Engineering College in Calcutta. He worked in New Delhi from 1955 onwards, starting with another American architect, Benjamin Polk and even after retirement in 1995, continued to design for the architecture firm he founded

WORKS:

India Habitat Cente

India International Center

Indian Institute of Management

Triveni Kala Sangam

ZAHA HADID

She is an Iraqi-British architect. She received the Pritzke Architecture Prize in 2004—the first woman to do so—and the Stirling Prize in 2010 and 2011.

Her buildings are distinctively neofuturistic, characterised by the "powerful, curving forms of her elongated structures with "multiple perspective points and fragmented geometry to evoke the chaos of modern life". She is currently professor at the University of Applied Arts Vienna in Austria.

WORK:

Vilnius Guggenheim Hermitage Museum

HeydarAliyev Cultural Centre in Baku, Azerbaijan

Library and Learning Center

Bergisel Ski Jump, Innsbruck, Austria

Bridge Pavilion in Zaragoza, Spain

Phæno Science Center, Wolfsburg, Germany

COLOUR THEORY

(TO LEARN ABOUT THE BASIC COLOUR AND COLOUR SCHEMES)

COLOUR WHEEL

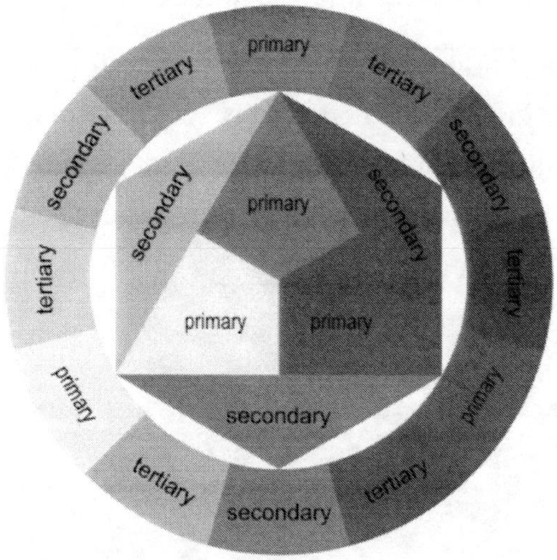

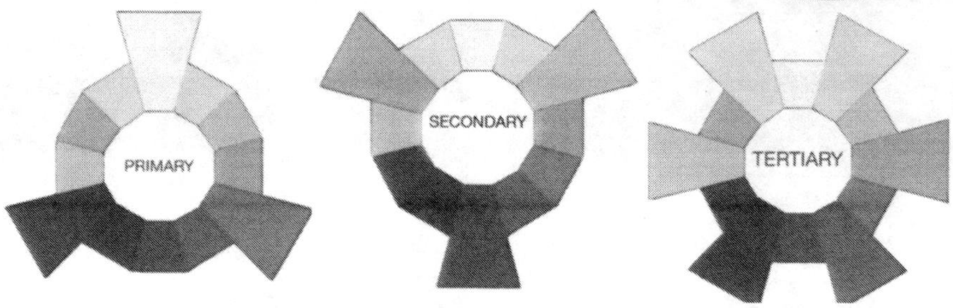

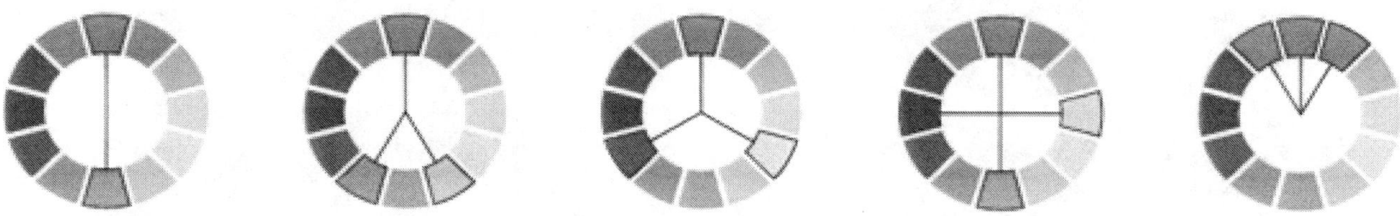

Complements Split-Complements Triad Tetrad Analogous

HUES, TINTS, TONES & SHADES

- **HUE:** - This is what we usually mean when we ask "what color is that?" The property of color that we are actually asking about is "hue". For example, when we talk about colors that are red, yellow, green, and blue, we are talking about hue. Different hues are caused by different wavelengths of light.
- **TINT:** - A tint is the mixture of a color with white, which increases lightness.
- **SHADE:** - A **shade** is the mixture of a color with black, which reduces lightness.
- **TONE:** - A tone is produced either by mixing with grey ,or by both tinting and shading.

COLOR THEORY

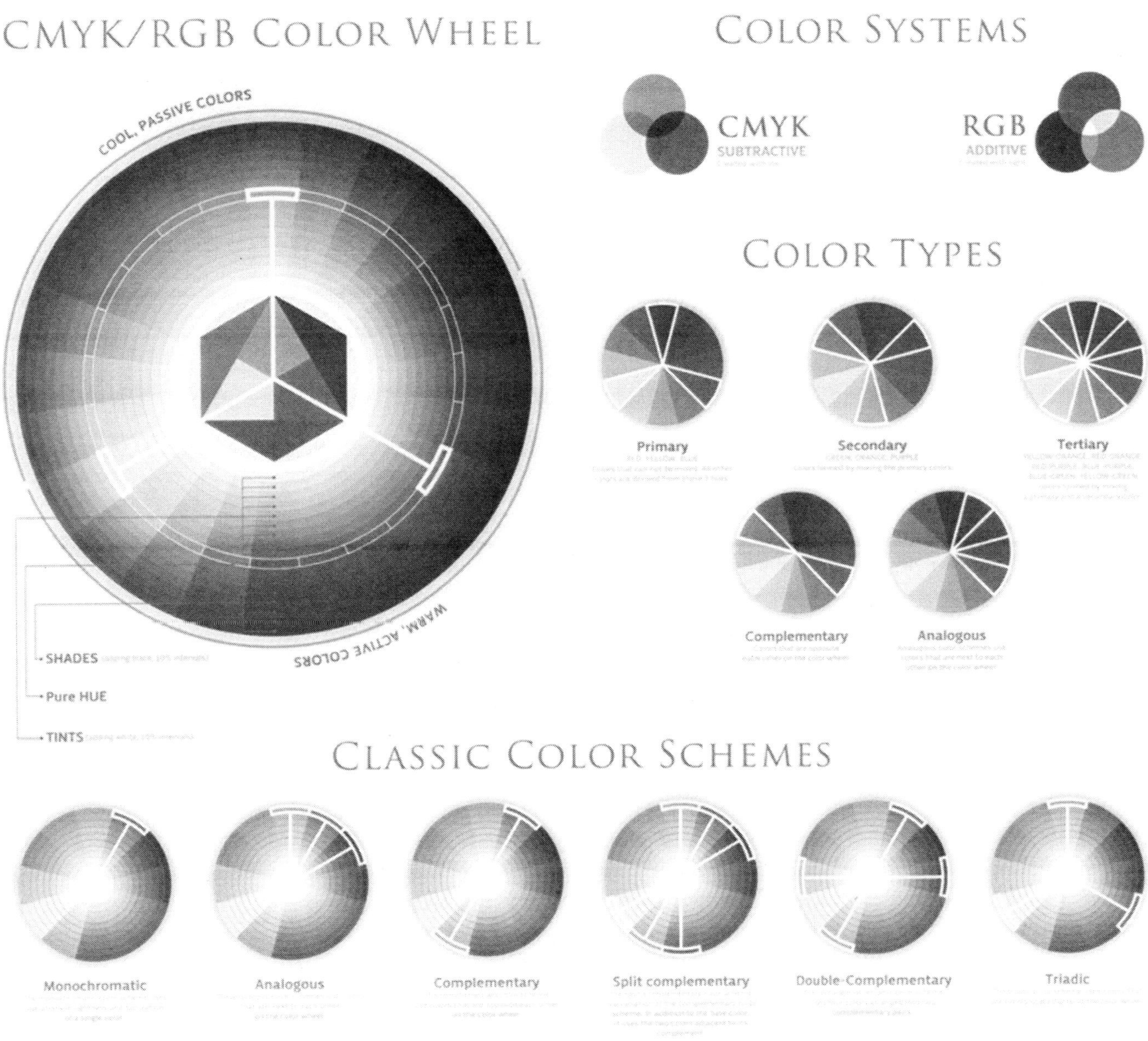

PSYCHOLOGICAL PROPERTIES OF COLORS

1. RED. Physical

Positive: Physical courage, strength, warmth, energy, basic survival, 'fight or flight', Stimulation, masculinity, excitement.

Negative: Defiance, aggression, visual impact, strain.

2. BLUE. Intellectual

Positive: Intelligence, communication, trust, efficiency, serenity, duty, logic, Coolness, reflection, calm.

Negative: Coldness, aloofness, lack of emotion, unfriendliness.

3. YELLOW. Emotional

Positive: Optimism, confidence, self-esteem, extraversion, emotional strength, Friendliness, creativity.

Negative: Irrationality, fear, emotional fragility, depression, anxiety, suicide.

4. GREEN. Balance

Positive: Harmony, balance, refreshment, universal love, rest, restoration, Reassurance, environmental awareness, equilibrium, peace.

Negative: Boredom, stagnation, blandness, enervation.

5. VIOLET. Spiritual

Positive: Spiritual awareness, containment, vision, luxury, authenticity, truth, quality.

Negative: Introversion, decadence, suppression, inferiority.

6. ORANGE.

Positive: Physical comfort, food, warmth, security, sensuality, passion, Abundance, fun.

Negative: Deprivation, frustration, frivolity, immaturity.

7. PINK.

Positive: Physical tranquility, nurture, warmth, femininity, love, sexuality, Survival of the species.

Negative: Inhibition, emotional claustrophobia, physical weakness.

8. GREY.

Positive: Psychological neutrality.

Negative: Lack of confidence, dampness, depression, hibernation, lack of energy.

9. BLACK.

Positive: Sophistication, glamour, security, emotional safety, efficiency, substance.

Negative: Oppression, coldness, menace, heaviness.

10. WHITE.

Positive: Hygiene, sterility, clarity, purity, cleanness, simplicity, sophistication, efficiency.

Negative: Sterility, coldness, barriers, unfriendliness, elitism.

11. BROWN.

Positive: Seriousness, warmth, Nature, earthiness, reliability, support.

Negative: Lack of humor, heaviness, lack of sophistication.

GENERAL AWARENESS AND ARCHITECTURAL AWARENESS

(GAIN MORE KNOWLEDGE ABOUT GENERAL AND ARCHITECTURE WORLD)

Animal, Tallest	Giraffe
Archipelago, Largest	Indonesia
Bird, Fastest	Swift
Bird, Largest	Ostrich
Bird, Smallest	Humming Bird
Bridge, Longest Railway	Huey P. Long Bridge, Louisiana (U.S.A.)
Building, Tallest in the World	Burj, Dubai (UAE)
Canal, Longest Irrigational	The Kalakumsky Canal
Canal, Longest	Suez Canal
Capital, Highest	La Paz (Boliva)
City, Biggest in Area	Mount Isa Australia
City, Largest in Population	Tokyo
City, Costliest	Tokyo
City, Highest	Van Chuan (China)
Continent, Largest	Asia
Continent, Smallest	Australia
Country, Biggest (Area)	Russia
Country, Largest (Population)	China
Country, Largest (Electorate)	India
Creature, Largest	Blue Whale
Delta, Largest	Sunderban (Bangladesh & India)

Desert, Largest (World)	Sahara (Africa)
Desert, Largest (Asia)	Gobi
Dam, Largest	Grand Coulee Dam (U.S.A.)
Dam, Highest	Hoover Dam (U.S.A.)
Diamond, Largest	The Cullinan
Dome, Largest	Astrodome, in Housten (U.S.A.)
Epic, Largest	Mahabharat
Irrigation Scheme, Largest	Lloyd Barrage, Sukkur (Pakistan)
Island, Largest	Greenland
Sea, Largest	Mediterranean sea
Lake, Deepest	Baikal (Siberia)
Lake, Largest (Artificial)	Lake Mead (Boulder Dam)
Lake, Highest	Titicaca (Bolivia)
Lake, Largest (Fresh water)	Superior
Lake, Largest (Salt water)	Caspian
Library, Largest	United State Library of Congress, Washington D.C.
Mountain Peak, Highest	Everest (Nepal)
Mountain Range, Longest	Andes (S. America)
Museum, Largest	British Museum, London
Ocean, Largest	Pacific
Palace, Biggest	Vatican (Italy)

Park, Largest	Yellow Stone National Park (U.S.A.)
Peninsula, Largest	Arabia
Place, Coldest (Habitated)	Verkhoyank (Siberia)
Place, Dryest	Iqique (In Atacama Desert, Chile)
Place, Hottest	Azizia (Libya, Africa)
Place, Rainiest	Mausinram (Meghalaya, India)
Planet, Biggest	Jupiter
Planet, Brightest	Venus
Planet, Smallest	Mercury
Plateau, Highest	Pamir (Tibet)
Platform, Longest	Kharagpur (India)
Railway, Longest	Trans-Siberian railway
Railway Station, Longest	Grand Central Terminal, Chicago (U.S.A.)
River, Longest	Nile (Africa)
River, Largest	Amazon (S. America)
Sea-bird, Largest	Albatross
Star, Brightest	Sirius
Statue, Tallest	Statue of Motherland, Volgagrad (Russia)
Telescope, Largest Radio	New Mexico (U.S.A.)
Tramway, World's first	New York
Tunnel, Longest (Railway)	Tanna (Japan)
Tunnel, Longest (Road)	Mont Blanc Tunnel between France and Italy
Volcano, Highest	Ojos del Salado
	(Andes, Ecuador)
Volcano, Most Active	Maunaloa (Hawail-U.S.A.)
Wall, Longest	Great wall of China
Waterfall, Highest	Angel (Venezuela)
Water, Lowest body	Dead Sea
Longest river (India)	Ganges
Longest river (World)	Nile
The longest tributary river of India	Yamuna
The longest river of the south	Godavari
Highest mountain peak	Godwin Austin (k2)
Largest lake (Fresh water)	Wular lake (Kashmir)
Highest Dam	Tehri Dam on Bhagirathi River
Largest Mosque	Jama Masjid, Delhi
Longest Road	Grand Trunk Road
State with longest coastline	Gujarat
Largest railway route	Dibrugarh in Assam to Kannyakumari in Tamil Nadu
Longest tunnel	Jawahar tunnel (Jammu & Kashmir)
Longest national highway	NH-7 which runs from Varanasi to Kanyakumari
Longest Dam	Hirakod Dam (Orissa)
Longest River Bride	Mahatma Gandhi Setu, Patna
Longest populated city	Mumbai (1.60 crore)
Largest Museum	National Museum, Kolkata

Largest Delta	Sunderban Delta, W. Bengal
Largest Dome	GolGumbaz, Bijapur (Karnataka)
Largest man-made Lake	GovindVallabh Pant Sagar (Rihand Dam)
Largest Desert	Thar (Rajasthan)
Highest Tower	Pitampura Tower, Delhi
Smallest State (Area)	Goa
Smallest State (Population)	Sikkim
Highest Waterfall	Gersoppa waterfall (Karnataka)
Longest Electric railway line	From Delhi to Kolkata via Patna
Densest populated State	West Bengal
Largest cave temple	Kailash temple, Ellora (Maharashtra)
Largest animal Fair	Sonepur (Bihar)
Highest Gateway	BulandDarwaza, FatehpurSikri (Agra)
Biggest Hotel	Oberal –Sharaton (Mumbai)
Largest State (Area)	Rajasthan
Largest State (Population)	Uttar Pradesh
Place of heaviest rainfall	Mausinram (Meghalaya)
Largest cantilever span bride	Howrah Bridge (Kolkata)

Largest forest state	M.P.
Highest straight gravity Dam	Bhakra Dam
Longest Railway Platform	Kharagpur (W. Bengal)
Largest Stadium	Salt lake (YuvaBharti), Kolkata
Largest Port	Mumbai
Highest Lake	Devatal (Garhwal)
Largest Lake (Saline water)	Chika lake, Orissa
Highest Award	Bharat Ratna
Highest Gallantry Award	Paramveer Chakra
Largest Gurudwara	Golden Temple, Amritsar
Deepest river valley	Bhagirathi &Alaknanda
State with longest coastline of South India	Andhra Pradesh
Longest river which forms estuary	Narmada
Largest Church	Saint Cathedral (Goa)
Longest Beach	Marina Beach, Chennai
Highest Battle field	Siachin Glacier
Highest Airport	Len (Laddakh)
Largest river island	Majuli (Brahmaputra river, Assam)
Largest Planetarium	Birla Planetarium (Kolkata)

ARCHITECTURE AWARENESS (PART-1)

Name of the Building
Place
Name of the Architect

1. **Asiad Village**
   New Delhi
   Raj Rewal
2. **Asian Games Residential**
   New Delhi
   Raj Rewal
3. **Assembly Hall**
   Chandigarh
   Le Corbusier
4. **Bahai Temple (Lotus Temple)**
   New Delhi
   FariburzSaabha
5. **Bharat Bhawan**
   Bhopal
   Charles Correa
6. **Belgian Embassy**
   New Delhi
   SatishGujral
7. **Buddha Jayanti Gardens**
   New Delhi
   M.M Rana
8. **Chandigarh**
   Chandigarh
   Le Corbusier
9. **Chanakya Theater**
   New Delhi
   P.N Mathur
10. **ChashmaShahi**
   Kashmir
   Shahjahan
11. **Connaught Place**New Delhi
   Edwin Lutyens
12. **CMC Building**
   Mumbai
   RasikBahl&Vinod Gupta
13. **DLF Centre**
   Connaught Placc
   Hafeez Contractor
14. **Dulles Airport**Washigton D.C
   Eero Saarinen
15. **Eiffel Tower**
   Paris
   Stephen Sauvestre
16. **Falling Waters**
   USA
   Frank LLyod Wright
17. **Fransworth House**
   USA
   Mies Vander Rohe\
18. **Guggenheim Museum**
   USA
   Frank LLyod Wright
19. **Hall of Nations (PragatiMaidan)**
   New Delhi
   Raj Rewal
20. **High Court**
   Chandigarh
   Le Corbusier
21. **Gujrat High Court**Ahemdabad
   Bimal Patel
22. **Hotel Cidade De Goa**Panaji(Goa)
   Charles Correa
23. **Hotel Mugal Sheraton**
   Agra
   The Design Group
24. **Ahamdavad Ni Gufa**
   Ahemdabad
   Balkrishna V. Doshi
25. **Hong Kong Bank**
   Hong Kong
   Norman Foster
26. **India International Centre**
   New Delhi
   Joseph Allen Stein

27. **IIT, Kanpur**
Kanpur
A.P Kanvinde

28. **IIM, Ahemdabad**
Ahemdabad
Louis Kahn

29. **IIM Banglore**
Banglore
B.V Doshi

30. **Hotel Park**
New Delhi
Bose Brothers

31. **Jantar Mantar**
Jaipur
Jai Singh

32. **Indra Gandhi Indoor Stadium**
NewDelhi
Sharat Das

33. **Jawaharlal Nehru Stadium**
New Delhi
C.P Kukreja

34. **LIC Building**
Connaught Place
Charles Correa

35. **Louvre Pyramid**
Paris
I.M Pei

36. **Mahabalipuram Temples**
Mahabalipuram
Pallavas

37. **Memorium Arch**
USA
Eero Saarinen

38. **NDMC Building**
New Delhi
Kuldeep Singh

39. **NDMC Indoor Stadium**
New Delhi
Satish Grover

40. **North &South Block**
New Delhi
Herbert Baker

41. **New Secretariat**
Kolkata
Habib Rehman

42. **Parliament Annxe**
New Delhi
F.W Benjamin

43. **Parliament House**
New Delhi
Herbert Baker

44. **Pinjore Garden**
Haryana
Fidai Khan

45. **Rajiv Gandhi Bhavan**
New Delhi
Sikka

46. **Rajiv Gandhi Memorial**
SriperumbudurK.T
Ravindran

47. **Rashtrapati Bhawan**
New Delhi
Edwin Lutyens
(Viceroy's Residence)

48. **SanchiStupa**
NearBhopal
Ashoka

49. **Sri Ram Centre**
New Delhi
Shivnath Prasad

50. **Shakti Sthala**
New Delhi
RajendraBhan

51. **Sitaram Bharti Institute**
New Delhi
SumeetGhosh

52. **STC Building**
New Delhi
Raj Rewal

53. **Statue of Liberty**
USA
Eugene

54. **Sun Temple**
Konark
NarsinghDev

55. **Sydney Opra House**
Sydney

Jon Utzon

56. **TajBengal**
Kolkata
The Design Group

57. **Taj Mahal**
Agra
Ustad Isa

58. **Teen Murti Bhawan**
Jodhpur
M.M.Rana

59. **The Auditorium**
MIT ,Massachusetts
EeroSarrinen

60. **The Chapel,**
MIT ,Massachusetts
EeroSarrinen

61. **The White House**
Washington D.C
James Hoban

62. **Triveni Kala Sangam**
New Delhi
J.A Stein

63. **TWA Terminal** New York
Eero Saarinen

64. **JFK Airport**
New York
Eero Saarinen

65. **VidhanSabha**
Banglore
P.W.D Karnataka

66. **World Trade Centre**
New York
Minoru Yamasaki

67. **World Habitat Centre**
New York
J.A Stein

68. **Victoria Terminus**
Mumbai
F.W Stevens

69. **Jawaharlal Nehru Kala Kendra**
Jaipur
Charles Correa

70. **Kanchanjanga Apparments**
Mumbai
Charles Correa

71. **Tara Apparments**
New Delhi
Charles Correa

72. **HirandhiniGardens**
Mumbai
Hafeez Contractor

73. **White hall**
London
Inigo Jones

74. **Brooklyn bridge**
New York
John A. Roembling

ARCHITECTURE AWARENESS (PART-2)

Q1. What is the standard parking Bay for a four wheeler?

- 3m x 5m

Q2. The Terms 'Transom '& 'Mullion' are used in?

- Window Frames

Q3. 'Asphalt' is used in construction for?

- Damp Proofing

Q4. What do different lines represent?

- Vertical lines – Stability
- Horizontal lines – Relaxation
- Curved lines – speed
- Wavy lines – Rhythm
- Criss -cross lines – confusing

Q5. White color is a mixture of how many colors?

- 7

Q6. What is vanishing Point?

- End point

Q7. What was the main characteristic of Indus – valley civilization?

- Drainage System

Q8. Which color of Marble when expose to Sun will be hottest?

- Black

Q9.Surki is made of?

- Well burnt Bricks

Q10. What is the weight and Volume of Ordinary Cement Bag?

- Volume – 0.034m3
- Weight- 50 kg

Q11. Central Building Research Institute is located in?

- Roorkee

Q12. What is the minimum height for an air-conditioned room?

- 2.4 m clear height

Q13. What is the minimum height of a Room?

- 3m

Q14. What is the minimum width of staircase in Residence?

- 1m

Q15. What is the minimum Plinth height of a Building?

- 30 cm

Q16. What is the minimum height of Parapet walls and Handrails?

- 0.9m or 3ft

Q17. Why do we shade a Drawing?

- To show shadow

Q18. What is the minimum height of a chair?

- 0.4m

Q19. Who was the last Mughal emperor?

- Bahadur shah Zafar

Q20. What is the minimum height of a Table?

- 0.75m

Q21. What is similar name for word "Arch"?

- Curve

Q22. What is the minimum height of a door?

- 2.1m

Q23. What is General height of a window?

- 1.5 m

Q24. Who is famous architect of kanchanjunga apartments?

- Charles Correa

Q25. What is the similar word for Arcade?

- Covered Walkway

Q26. The city of Agra was founded by?

- Sikander Lodi

Q27. What is Balcony?

- Projection

Q28. Generally the type of Bricks used for Permanent Construction?

- First class bricks

Q29.Exterior walls are generally painted with?

- Cement Paints

Q30. In Buildings linoleum is generally used for?

- Flooring

Q31. First – Class Bricks are?

- Well- burnt

Q32. What are Distempers?

- Water Paints

Q33. 'INTEL', the world renowned company manufactures?

- Microprocessor chips

Q34. The First Mughal Building to have been built entirely of Marble is?

- TajMahal

Q35. How many spokes does the 'chakra' in Indian National Flag contains?

- 24

Q36. Who is Architect of 'JeevanBharti Building' in New Delhi?

- Charles Correa

Q37. 'Ajanta Caves 'are situated in?

- Maharashtra

Q38. Weight of a Good – Brick is about?

- 3kg

Q39.The cement used for general construction work is?

- Portland cement

Q40. The Hard wood is?

- Kail

Q41. Which Indian Singer is also an Architect?

- Remo Fernandez

Q42. 'The Fountain- head' a story about an architect is written by?

- Ayn Rand

Q43. 'The Fountain- head' is a story about which architect?

- Frank Lloyd Wright

Q44. Usually Door and Window frames are made of?

- Teak

Q45. Thinner used in Paints is usually?

- Turpentine oil

Q46. Which Surface can be distempered?

- Masonry walls

Q47.The size of Kitchen should not be less than?

- 6.0m^2

Q48. Single story houses normally have load bearing walls of thickness?

- 1 Bricks

Q49. The Desirable depth of a wardrobe for hanging clothes is?

- 0.6mt or 2 ft

Q50. Which Indian Architect has been awarded 'Premium –Imperial' the alternative Nobel in Japan?

- Charles Correa

Q51. Measurement of brick?

- 230mm x 115mm x 75mm

Q52.The 'World Trade Centre Building' in New York is designed by?

- Minoru Yamasaki

Q53. Corbett National Park is located in which state?

- Uttaranchal

Q54. The TajMahal was designed by a Persian Architect?

- Ustad Ahmad Lahauri

Q55. The architecture of the city of Cochin in Kerala reflects the influence of?

- British, Portuguese&Dutch

Q56. Laurie Baker is associated with?

- Low cost housing

Q57.Brick Walls are comparatively weaker and less durable than?

- Stone Walls

Q58. From where did the advent of French start?

- Pondicherry

Q59.Panels walls are meant for?

- Decorations

Q60.In English Bond brick courses consist of?

- Stretchers and Headers alternatively.

Q61. Bitumen is used in the building for?

- Water proofing

Q62. Which monument was built in memory of a British monarch?

- Victoria Memorial

Q63. In which Indian city would you find the mosque with "Shaking Minarets"?

- Ahmadabad

Q64. Ellora in Aurangabad (Maharashtra) is famous for ancient caves representing Buddhism, Hinduism and Jainism. Of these, the largest number pertains to?

- Hinduism

Q65. Master plan of Independent Delhi was charted by?

- Ram Sharma

Q66. RashtrapatiBhawan has been designed in which style?

- Classical

Q67. The common material used for water supply is?

- Cast Iron

Q68.Which variety of glass is heat resistant?

- Pyrex Glass

Q69.Which Civilization used stone completely?

- Mesopotamia

Q70. The Art of Gardening is called?

- Horticulture

Q71.One Hectare is approximately equal to?

- 10,000.0mt^2

Q72. Who completed the construction of "QutabMinar" at Delhi?

- Iltutmish

Q73.Who built the "Tower of Victory" at Chittorgarh?

- RanaKumbha

Q74.Who designed the Memorial of Rajiv Gandhi at Perumbudur?

- K.T. Ravindran

Q75. Moti Masjid in Agra was built by?

- Shahjahan

Q76. Banaras Hindu University was founded by?

- Madan Mohan Malviya

Q77. HussainDoshiGufa is situated in?

- Ahmadabad

Q78. Which Indian city has the maximum number of historical monuments?

- Delhi

Q79. The Famous Rock Garden is located at?

- RashtrapatiBhawan , New Delhi

Q80. The Famous Rock Garden is located at?

- Chandigarh

Q81. Lingraj Temple located at?

- Bhuvneshwar

Q82. The Great Pyramid, one of the Seven Wonders of the World is in?

- Egypt

Q83.Charles De Garlle airport is at?

- Paris

Q84. The Headquarters building of International labor organization?

- Geneva

Q85. The Headquarters building of UNO is located at?

- New York

Q86. The Headquarters building of WHO is located at?

- Switzerland

Q87. "The sphinx" is in?

- Egypt

Q88. The First Pyramid was built by?

- King Djoser (Cheops Type)

Q89. The Deepest Lake in the world is?

- Baikal

Q90. Nandlal Bose is Famous for?

- Paintings

Q91. In which state of India the Famous Sun temple of Modhera is situated?

- Gujarat

Q92.Sun Temple of konark is located at?

- Madhya Pradesh

Q93.In which year the Sir J.J Collage of Art, Mumbai was established?

- 1857

Q94. Full Form of "J.J" in Sir J.J Collage of Art?

- James jeejeebhoy

Q95.IBM of computer memory is?

- 1024 KB

Q96. Which is the hardest stone?

- Granite

Q97. Mesopotamia is now refers?

- Iraq

Q98. Mannekenpis is a ?

- Sculpture of young Boy

Q99. The famous Painting "The starry Nights " was Painted by?

- Vincent Vangogh

Q100. The Famous Building Birds nest in Beijing is

- Olympic Stadium

Q101. Mickey Mouse was designed by?

- Walt Disney

Q102. Warli art is a type of?

- Tribal Art

Q103. Edward Munch is?

- Painter , Graphic Artist

Q104. Michel Angelo is Famous for?
- Sculptures, Paintings, poems, architecture, engineer of high renaissance.

Q105. Pieta is a Famous?
- Sculpture

Q106.Pakhwaj is a?
- Musical instrument

Q107. RabindraNath Tagore was awarded Nobel Prize in which year?
- 1913

Q108. Music Created by RabindraNath Tagore is known as?
- RabindraSangeet

Q109. The Sistine chapel is situated at?
- Rome

Q110.Mount Mary church is situated at?
- Bandra, Mumbai

Q111. What is the other Name of Indus – valley civilization?
- Harappa

Q112. Red Fort is built by which Mughal Emperor?
- ShahJahan

Q113. Salimchistti was a?
- Sufi saint

Q114. The Sculptures of Henry Moore are?
- Abstract

Q115. DilipChhabria was a?
- Automobile Designers

Q116. Lust for life is a biography of?
- Vincent Vangogh

Q117. Paint Ravi Shankar is associated with?
- Tabla, Music

Q118. V. Shanta Ram is associated with?
- Movie or Film making

Q119.Mahatma Gandhi was born in which year?
- 1869

Q120. Charminar at Hyderabad is a?
- Mosque

Q121. BFA stands for?
- Bachelor of Fine Arts

Q122. Largest island?
- Green Land

Q123. The City of Jaisalmar is densely formed with Thousands of?
- Courtyard Houses

Q124. White Hall is in?
- London

Q125.Kanha National park is in?
- Madhya Pradesh

Q126. Diameter of GolGumbaz, largest Dome in India?
- 144 ft

Q127. Which City is Most Famous?
- NewYork

Q128. Famous IbadatKhana is in?
- Fatehpurisikri

Q129.Which town plan may be related to Lutyens?
- Delhi

Q130. Pinjore and Surajkundis in?

- Haryana

Q131. Which city of India is known as Venice of the east?

- Alleppey, kerela

Q132. National Emblem of India's Replica Ashoka Pillars are at?

- Sarnath

Q133. Ranthambhore National Park is in?

- Rajasthan

Q134. Which Hill Station is named after a Governor?

- Dalhousie

Q135. Ootacamand is Famous hill station is in which state?

- TamilNadu

Q136. Where was the First T.V Centre of India setup?

- Delhi

Q137. Bhakra Dam is on which River?

- Satluj River

Q138. Writer Builder is in?

- Kolkata

Q139.India House is located at?

- London

Q140.Hirakund Dam is on?

- Mahanadi River

Q141. Lingraj Temple is in?

- Bhubaneswar

Q142.National Modern Art Gallery is in?

- Delhi

Q143.National library of India is situated at?

- Kolkata

Q144.Taj Mahal at Agra was completed by ShahJahan in which year?

- 1653 (took 22 years to complete)

Q145. The Outline of the Plan of QutabMinar?

- Is different on Each Floor

Q146.India First Rocket on launcher station is in?

- Konark

Q147. Indian Institute of Petroleum is in?

- Dehradun

Q148.National Institute of Oceanography?

- Goa

Q149.Tower of victory of Rajasthan?

- Chittorgarh

Q150. Sanchi in M.P. is Famous For?

- Buddhist stupa

Q151.The Film and Movie institute is in ?

- Pune

Q152. Salarjung Museum is in?

- Hyderabad

Q153. Le Corbusier is from?

- France

Q154. Free standing rock cut rath is in?

- Mahabalipuram

Q155. Why Bulanddarwaza was built?

- Victory over Khandesh

Q156. JahazMahal of Mandu belongs to which age?

- Industrial

Q157. Talkatora Swimming Pool built for Asiad had which material?

- Fiber Glass Domed Roof

Q158. The First ship yard Building is located in?
- Cochin

Q159. Largest Football stadium with capacity 1,50,000 in world is in ?
- Spain

Q160. Abbay is Theatre in island?
- Dublin

Q161.Niagra in the Canada is?
- Water Fall

Q162. MeditterianSea is connected by Red Sea through which canal ?
- Suez

Q163. Mahatma Gandhi founded Sabarmati Ashram at?
- Ahmedabad

Q164. Paris is situated on which river?
- Siene river

Q165. Headquarters of Red Cross is in?
- Geneva

Q166.Rome is situated on which river?
- Tiber

Q167. Kala- Hari is in?
- South Africa

Q168. Makrana is a type of?
- Marble

Q169. For good bricks, what is the percentage of Silica in the Earth?
- 60 %

Q170. India's largest Stadium in Delhi is?
- Jawaharlal Nehru Stadium

Q171. Which U.SPresident was also an architect?
- Thomas Jefferson

Q172. Which was the first city to have underground railway station?
- London

Q173. Who was the Architect of Empire State Building?
- William Fredrick Lamb

Q174. The structure of Golden Gate Bridge is?
- Suspension

Q175. HUDCO is an organization of?
- Housing and Urban Development

Q176. Statue of liberty is situated in?
- America

Q177.Who was the Architect of flatiron Building?
- Daniel Burnham

Q178. Who was the Architect of Eiffel tower ?
- Stephen Souvestre

Q179.The well- known work of Leonardo Da Vince?
- Monalisa

Q180.The Author of Harry Potter is?
- J.K. Rowling

Q181.Sydney opera House was Designed by?
- John Utzon

Q182.Which City is located on Rhine River ?
- Germany , Austria , Switzerland , Franch&Liechnenstein

Q183. Rourkela Steel plant is collaborated with in?
- Germany

Q184. Highest LakeinIndia ?
- Wular

Q185. Which was the Capital of MauryaDynasty?

- Patliputra , Bihar

Q186. Indira Gandhi Rajasthan Canal Project completed in which year ?

- 1 January , 1987 and took 28 years

Q187. Where did Aryans settle First ?

- Indus Valley

Q188. Approximately length of Grand Trunk Road?

- 1500 Miles

Q189. Port city of Harappa Civilization?

- Lothal

Q190. Capital of Pakistan occupied Kashmir?

- Muzaffrabad

Q191. Early name of Bangkok?

- Krungthep

Q192. Largest desert is?

- Sahara

Q193. Khajuraho temple is situated at?

- Madhya Pradesh

Q194.ShekhSalimchisti is at?

- Agra

Q195.Tomb of sher shah suri is at?

- Sasaram , Bihar

Q196. Sun Temple Destroyed by?

- Mohammad Gajni

Q197.Pratap Singh Museum is at?

- Srinagar

Q198.Central Drug Research institute is at?

- Mumbai

Q199.Birla- Planetarium is at?

- Kolkata , Jaipur , Hyderabad , Chennai , Delhi

Q200. Narora Atomic Plant is at?

- Uttar Pradesh

Q201.Mount Abu is at?

- Rajasthan

Q202. Badrinath and kedarnath is at?

- Uttarakhand

Q203. India largest Indoor Stadium?

- Indira Gandhi Stadium

Q204.Indian institute of Petroleum is at?

- Dehradun

Q205.Charles correa is?

- Indian Architect

Q206. Edwin Lutyens is an?

- English Architect

Q207. Indian First RocketLauncher is at ?

- Thumba

Q208. MusumelicCentury is at ?

- Karnataka

Q209. Indus-valley people have trade relationship with ?

- Mesopotamia

Q210. The largest Foot-Ball Stadium is?

- Salt lake stadium , Kolkata (1,20,000)

Q211. Punjab was reorganized on linguistic Basis in year?

- 1966

Q212. Marose state was renamed as Karnataka in year ?

- 1979

Q213. National Integration Day?

- Octobar,31

Q214. Air force Day ?

- October,8

Q215. Reserve Bank in India was setup in year ?

- 1934

Q216. The First 5 years plans started in which year ?

- 1951 TO 1952

Q217. Life insurance corporation in india was established in which year ?

- 1956

Q218. All Indaia – Radio was renamed as Aakashwani in which year ?

- 1957

Q219. Radio – Broadcast started in India in which Year ?

- 1927

Q220. T.V was started in India as an Eperimental service in which year ?

- 15,September,1959

Q221. The PIN is introduced in which year?

- 1972

Q222. PIN stands for?

- Post index no.

Q223. In which year Rabindranath Tagore won the Nobel Prize for Literature ?

- 1913

Q224. In which year Mother Teresa was Awarded "BharatRatna"?

- 1980

Q225. Common wealth Day celebrated on?

- 24 May

Q226. Jesus – Christ was crucified on?

- 29 A.D

Q227.French Revolution took place in year ?

- 1789 A.D

Q228. Bismillah-khan is?

- Shehnai player

Q229. Todar Mal was a Finance minister of which Mughal Emperor ?

- Akbar

Q230. Who carried away the Famous Peacock Throne from the India?

- Nadirshah

Q231. The First Governor General of free India?

- Raj Gopalchari

Q232. Who was known as Iron man of India?

- SardarVallabhBhai Patel

Q233.Who formed AryaSamaj?

- Swami DhyanandSaraswati

Q234.Arya-Bhatt was?

- Indian Mathematician

Q235.Mulana Abdul kalamAazad was born in state?

- Mecca

Q236.First governor of Reserve Bank of India?

- C.D Deshmukh

Q237. Who introduced the concept of 5 years plans in India?

- Jawaharlal Nehru

Q238.The rupee was minted in 1542 during the Rule of which Emperor?

- Sher- ShahSuri

Q239.The leader of India's First Antarctica Expedition?

- S.Z. Quasim

Q240.The Pioneer of Atomic Energy in India was?

- Homi Jahangir Bhabha

Q241.The First man to walk in space?

- Alexicileonov

Q242. Geetanjali was written by which author?

- RabindraNath Tagore

Q243.Who has written the book "Death of a city"?

- Amrita Pritam

Q244. Arthshashtra was written by?

- Kautilya

Q245. Author of Mother India?

- Katherine Mayo

Q246. QutabMinar is largely cladded with?

- Red Sand Stone

Q247. Natural Shadow less light is available from which direction in India?

- North

Q248. In which place in India can we find cave Temples of Three faiths?

- Ellora

Q249.Horizontal Sun shades are required to protect windows on which facades of a building?

- South

Q250. The Summer Sun in Northern Hemisphere rises from ?

- North- east

Q251. Place of winds is located in?

- Rajasthan

Q252. Which city in India lies in cold and Dry Region?

- Leh

Q253. Which type of Roof will keep the Room Cooler?

- Concrete Slab with Cement Plaster

Q254. The City, where canals are used as Transportation channel is ?

- Venice

Q255. Who has famous but has not designed any building?

- Pablo Picasso

Q256. Winters Sun in the Northern Hemisphere rises from ?

- South – East

Q257. A House named " Antilia" is recently built in Mumbai for Whom ?

- MukeshAmbani

Q258. Which one of the following Material is generally used in Exterior cladding of high rise buildings ?

- Aluminium

Q259.Temple city of India?

- Madurai

Q260. Which Cladding Material is the best suited for sound insulation inside an auditorium?

- Timber Tiles

Q261. Heat gain in buildings is best resisted by?

- Cavity Walls

Q262. The color of a well baked brick is ?

- Red

Q263.What is "Green Architecture"?

- Where building material used have consumed least energy

Q264. Cavity walls are best suited against?

- Heat

Q265.The Parliament House, New-Delhi is designed by?

- Herbert Baker and Edwin Lutyens

Q266. Arc de Triomphe is a Famous monument found in?

- Paris

Q267.The stair handrail should be?

- Corrugated

Q268. Maximum insulation is offered by?

- Timber

Q269. Plaster of Paris is used for?

- Walls

Q270. A red rose viewed through a Green colored glass, will appear?

- Purple

Q271.The Marble used for the construction of TajMahal is?

- Makrana Marble

Q272. MP VidhanSabha is designed by?

- Charles Correa

Q273. Eiffel Tower is built in?

- Steel

Q274. On the top of RashtrapatiBhawan, New-Delhi, one will find a?

- Stupa Form

Q275. Red Square is in?

- Moscow

Q276.Victoria Memorial is situated at?

- Kolkata

Q277. City of Lakes?

- Udaipur

Q278. Award Connected with Architecture?

- Aga Khan

Q279. Shahjahanabad is presently known as?

- Old Delhi

Q280. Color of light emitted by Fluorescent Bulb?

- White

Q281. The city of Bhubaneswar was designed by?

- Koeingsberges

Q282. Which marble will reflect more radiant heat?

- White Marble

Q283. Ozone layer around the Earth prevents penetration of?

- U.V Rays

Q284. Cement is made out of?

- Limestone

Q285. A white colored Building interiors looks larger because?

- It reflects more light

Q286. Which color is most Tranquilizing?

- Blue

Q287.Matri Mandir is situated in?

- Auroville

Q288. The famousPadmanabhapuram palace is located in state of?

- Tamil Nadu

Q289. Tansen lived during the times of?

- Akbar

Q290. Henry Moore was a?

- Sculptor

Q291. Petronas Twin Towers are located at?

- Malaysia

Q292. Pentagon is?

- The Headquarters of the Department of defence of United States of America

Q293.What is the function of Victoria Terminal building?

- Railway Station

Q294. Stonehenge is situated in?

- Great Britain

Q295. New Guggenheim Museum is designed by?

- F.L Wright

Q296. The Dome of RashtrapatiBhawan is influenced by?

- Stupa

Q297. Which are used to make an Igloo?

- Ice blocks

Q298. SatishGujral is?

- Well known architect

Q299.What is Jantar Mantar?

(Yantra - instruments, mantra - formulae)

Q300. FatehpurSikri is built with?

- Red Sand Stone

Q301. Birju Maharaj is a well known?

- Kathak Dancer

Q302. Amrita Shergil was known for her contribution in field of?

- Painting

Q303.Which finish imparts a glossy look to walls?

- Distemper

Q304. Buckingham Palace & Big Ben is in?

- United kingdom

Q305. Who is the architect of Falling Water house?

- F.L Wright

Q306. The Great wall of China was built by?

- Shithe Hwang Ti

Q307. Jantar-Mantar was created by?

- Jai Singh

Q308. Mill owner's Association Building in Ahemdabad was designed by?

- B. V Doshi

Q309. Who is the Architect of Bharat Bhawan, Bhopal?

- Charles Correa

Q310.Banaras Hindu University was founded by?

- Madan Mohan Malviya
-

Q311. Who built Moti Masjid in Delhi?

- Aurangzeb

Q312. Pinjore Garden has been designed by?

- Fidai khan

Q313.Who designed theShakiSthala?

- RajendraBhan

Q314. JamaMasjad in Delhi was built by?

- DaraShikoh

Q315. Tower of victory at Chittorgarh was built by?

- Rand Kumba

Q316. Chaistya cave at karleis known for one of the finest specimens of?

- Sculpture

Q317. Billing's Gate is?

- London's Fish Market

Q318. Anand Bhawan was the house of which Famous Indian Family ?

- Nehru Family

Q319. Corbett National park is in which state ?

- U.P

Q320.The use of Kharoshti in ancient Indian Architecture is the result of India's contact with ?

- Greece

Q321.There was a sharp class division at Harappa and Mohenjo-Daro, This is clear from the?

- Different types of Dwelings Excavated

Q322. Universities in the Presidency towns in India were established in ?

- 1857

Q323. Who built charminar of Hyderabad?

- Sultan Muhammad QuliQutub Shah

Q324. BibikaMaqbara is a Mausoleum of the wife of ?

- Aurangzeb

Q325. In which city is Petronas Tower situated?

- Kuala Lumpur

Q326. Chrysler Building in New York was completed in which year?

- 1930

Q327. Ajanta Caves situated in Maharashtra were built during the period of?

- Gupta

Q328. Alag committee relates to?

- Civil Servants

Q329. The country which is called the land of the Rising Sun is?

- Japan

Q330. The country which known as the "Sugar Bowl of the world" is?

- Cuba

Q331. Australia was discovered by?

- James Cook

Q332. Which is National Flower of China?

- Narcissus

Q333. The Earlier name of Sri Lanka was?

- Ceylon

Q334. "Last Judgment" was the First Painting of an Italian Painter named Michael Angelo. Where is this painting?

- Sistine Chapel

Q335. New York is popularly known as the city of?

- Frederick Auguste Bartholdi

Q336. Who is the Father of Geometry?

- Euclid

Q337. The Famous Dilwara Temples are located in?

- Rajasthan

Q338. Thakurbari in Kolkata is the ancestral Home of?

- RabindraNath Tagore

Q339. In which Indian City would you find the Mosque with "Shaking Minarets"?

- Ahemdabad

Q340.Saint Peter Cathedral (Rome) was built during?

- 1541-1561

Q341. Taj Mahal is the typical example of?

- Indo- Persian Architecture

Q342. Which city was the Summer Capital during British Raj?

- Shimla

Q343.Where is the world's largest Panoramic Sculptural relief located?

- Mahabalipuram , Chennai

Q344. Which Foreign influence is seen in the Rock cut Architecture of India?

- Persian

Q345. What is used in Pencils?

- Graphite

Q346. Grand Central Terminal, Park Avenue,Newyork is the world's?

- Largest Railway Station

Q347. The 2010 Men's Hockey world cup held in?

- India

Q348.Der Neue Zollhof was designed by which architect (Dusseldorf, Germautly)?

- Frank O Gehry

Q349. Which architect designed Bonnefanten Museum (Maastricht, The Netherlands)?

- Aldo Rossi

Q350. The Dome over the Pantheon is of?

- Concrete

Q351. The Empire state Building is in which material?

- Steel

Q352. Where is Khajuraho?

- Bhopal

Q353. Soil is composed of?

- Water + Air + Mineral

Q354. "Less is Bore". Who said this in response to Mies Vander Rohe's famous Dictum, " Less is More"?

- Robert Venturi

Q355. Gateway of India is situated at?

- Mumbai

Q356. The Washington Monument is in which material?

- Stone

Q357. The Sydney opera house is made of?

- Prestressed Concrete

Q358. Which architect designed the Carson, Pirie, Scott Building (Chicago, Illinois)?

- **Louis Sullivan**

Q359. Which architect designed the Centre of Science and Industry (Columbus, Ohio)?

- AratalIsozaki

Q360. Which architect Designed the SagradaFamilia (Barcelona, Spain)?

- Antonio Gaudi

Q361. Which architect Designed the Bank of China (Honkong, china)?

- I M Pei

Q362. Which Architect designed the Getty Centre (Los Angeles, California)?

- Richard Meier

Q363.Which architect was part of the team that designed centre Pompidou (Paris, France)?

- Richard Rogers

Q364. RathYatra is a major Festival of?

- Puri

Q365. The World Telecommunication Day is observed on?

- May 17

Q366. Ranbaxy Company is being acquired by a company of?

- Japan

Q367. Blindness is caused by the deficiency of?

- Vitamin – A

-

Q368. The Term butterfly stroke is referred to which game?

- Swimming

Q369. The First Kanshi Ram khel Ratna Award was given to?

- Praveen Kumar

Q370. In the 15th Asian Games India Bagged the largest Number of Medals in?

- Shooting

Q371. Which country's Government report is known as Yellow Book?

- France

Q372. Which architect designed the Kimball Art Museum (Fort Worth, Texas)?

- Louis Khan

Q373. Which architect designed the Kaufman desert house (Palm Springs, California)?

- Richard Neutra

Q374. In which city is the Country's largest stadium located?

- Kolkata

Q375. When Nepal was declared a Secular Nation?

- 2006

Q376. Joint SAARC University of eight SAARC Nations will be established in?

- New Delhi

Q377. India won its first tri series against Australia in?

- Brisbane

Q378. Olympic torch relay began in?

- 1952

Q379. Guggenheim Museum (New York City)?

- Concrete

Q380. Which Architect Designed Taliesin (Spring Green, Wisconsin)?

- Frank Lloyd Wright

Q381. Which Architect Designed the Harwood-Stone House (Northampton, Massachusetts)?

- TullioInglese

Q382. In which city was the First Engineering College set up?

- Roorkee

Q383. Radha Mohan Cup is associated with?

- Polo

Q384. The captain of Indian Hockey Team who won Asia Cup 2007 was?

- PrabodhTirkey

Q385. The Robie House was designed by which Architect (Chicago, Illinois)?

- PeterEisenman

Q386.Which Architect designed the Wexner Centre (Columbus, Ohio)?

- PeterEisenman

Q387. Which Architect designed Villa Savoye (Poissy, France)?

- Le Corbusier

Q388. "Future Shock" is written by whom?

- Alvin Toffler

Q389. Who wrote "The wonder that was India"?

- A.L Basham

Q390. Who wrote "The Valley of Dolls"?

- Jacqueline Suzaun

Q391. Who was the architect of "PrarthanaSamaj"?

- MahadevGobindRanade

Q392. The Seat of International Court of Justice is at?

- Hauge

Q393.The Meenakshi Temple is situated at?

- Madurai

Q394. Sarnathis associated with Lord Buddha because he ?

- Preached his first Summon there

Q395. What does Tensile structure mean ?

- Flexible material such as Fabric membranes supported by a system of steel cables with Rigid Frame work.

Q396. In soil, clay is good for what?

- Acoustical Mare

Q397. Longest Casting Building Material Available?

- Rock

Q398. Rammed Earth is category of?

- Old and New Material

Q399. Commonly used Roof Material?

- Slate

Q400. Stone from Medieval to Modern Times?

- Granite

Q401. Hut is an example of?

- Thatch structure

Q402. Which Civilization used stone completely?

- Mesopotamia

Q403. Ice is used for Constructing?

- Igloo

Q404. Sound Travel Faster in?

- Steel

Q405. Who discovered X- Rays?

- Rontgen

Q406. Excessive consumption of Alcohol Destroy?

- Liver

Q407. Specific Gravity of Milk is measured by?

- Lactometer

Q408. Paper is mainly made of?

- Bamboo

Q409. The term "Grand slam" is used in ?

- Badminton

Q410. Lady Ratana Tata Trophy is associated with?

- Women's Hockey Championship

Q411. The Term "Fauna" is used in?

- Plants life

Q412. Oldest oil Refinery in India?

- Digboi

Q413. How much Quantity of Methyleisocynative gas leaked from Union Labaider Bhopal on Night of 23 December 1984?

- 40 Tones

Q414.What were the main characteristics of the Indus Valley Civilization?

- Town Planning and Drainage System

Q415. To which age the Indus Valley Civilization belongs?

- Neolithic Age

Q416. Which metals were mostly used to make the tools and weapons of Harappan Civilization?

- Copper and bronze

Q417. Which metal was not known to the Harappan people?

- Iron

Q418. What was the main occupation of the people of the Indus Valley Civilization?

- Trade

Q419. In which culture the earliest evidence of silver in India is found?

- Harappan culture

Q420. Which soil was used to make bricks in Indus Valley Civilization?

- Alluvial soil

Q421. In which civilization the cotton was cultivated first?

- Indus valley civilization

Q422. Which was the most famous building in Harappa?

- The Granary

Q423. In Harappa how many granaries have been found?

- Six

Q424. In which of the Harappan city rice husks were found?

- Lothal and Rangpur

Q425. When was the Battle of Plassey, a decisive British East India Company victory over the Nawab of Bengal and his French allies, establishing Company rule in South Asia which expanded over much of the Indies for the next 190 years?

- 23 June 1757

Q426. The territory of Porus who offered strong resistance to Alexander was situated between which rivers?

- Jhelum and Chenab

Q427. Which religions' sacred books are called as Tripitakas?

- Buddhists

Q428. The use of Kharoshti in ancient Indian architecture is the result of India's contact with which country?

- Greece

Q429. What is the material used in construction of Indus valley civilization?

- Bricks

Q430. The Ochterlony Monument was built in 1848 by Sir David Ochterlony to commemorate his victory in the Nepal War (1814 – 1816). What was it renamed as after India achieved independence?

- Shaheedminar

Q431. Everyone knows 'The TajMahal'. It was built by the Emperor Shah Jahan, but for whom?

- MumtazMahal

Q432. Where is the world's largest panoramic sculptural relief located?

- Mahabalipuram

Q433. In which place in India can we find cave temples of three faiths?

- Ellora

Q434. Which foreign influence is seen in the rock cut architecture of India?

- Persian

Q435. Who Invented the First Adhesive Tape?

- Richard Gurley Drew

Q436. Who Invented Metal Can Opener?

- Ezra J. Warner

Q437. Who Invented Coca Cola Drink?

- John Stith Pemberton

Q438. Who Invented Escalator?

- Jesse Wilford Reno

Q439. Who Invented The World Wide Web?

- Sir Timothy John

Q440. Who Invented The Windshield Wiper Cleaner?

- Mary Anderson

Q441. Who Invented Bakelite Plastic?

- Leo Hendrik Baekeland

Q442. Who Invented Electric Street Car?

- Thomas Davenport

Q443. **Who Invented the Blood Bank?**

- Charles Richard Drew

MATERIAL & TEXTURE

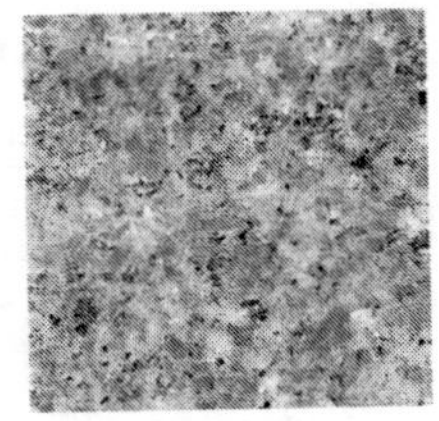

Granite: Granite, the hard igneous rock Granite is a very hard crystalline, igneous or metamorphic rock primarily composed of feldspar, quartz and lesser amounts of dark minerals.

a. Natural granite is rough in texture.

b. Polished granite is smooth and glossy in texture

Lime stone (**Limestone** is a sedimentary rock composed largely of the mineral calcite (calcium carbonate: CaCO3).

Marble (**Marble** is a metamorphic rock resulting from the metamorphism of limestone, composed mostly of calcite (a crystalline form of calcium carbonate, CaCO3). It is extensively used for sculpture, as a building material, and in many other applications. The word 'marble' is colloquially used to refer to many other stones that are capable of taking a high polish) marble.

Pebbles (A **pebble** is a class of rock with a particle size of 4 to 64 millimeters based on the Krumbein phi scale of sedimentology. A rock made predominately of pebbles is termed a conglomerate)

Mosaic (**Mosaic** is the art of decoration with small pieces of colored glass, stone or other material. It may be a technique of decorative art, an aspect of interior decoration or of cultural and spiritual significance as in a cathedral. Small tiles or fragments of pottery or of colored glass or clear glass backed with metal foils are used to create a pattern or picture.)

Terrazzo (Terrazzo workers create attractive walkways, floors, patios, and panels by exposing marble chips and other fine aggregates on the surface of finished concrete or epoxy-resin)

Kota stone (It is a type of lime stone,

Steel Chequered

Kadappa Brushed Finish. (available in different colors)

Glass Block

Glass Block Wall Panel

Corrugated Plastic Sheets

Corrugated Aluminium Sheet

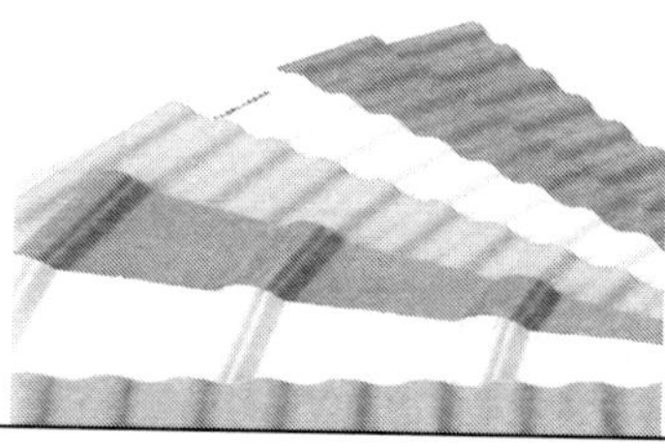

Wallpaper

Mangalore Roof Tile

Brick Wall

Wood

Grass

Wood Veneer

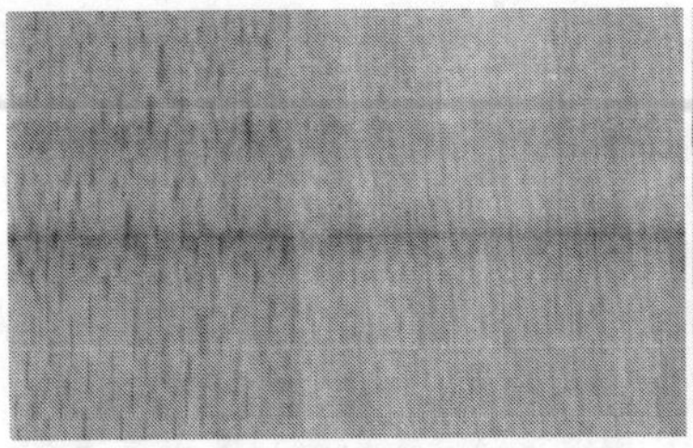

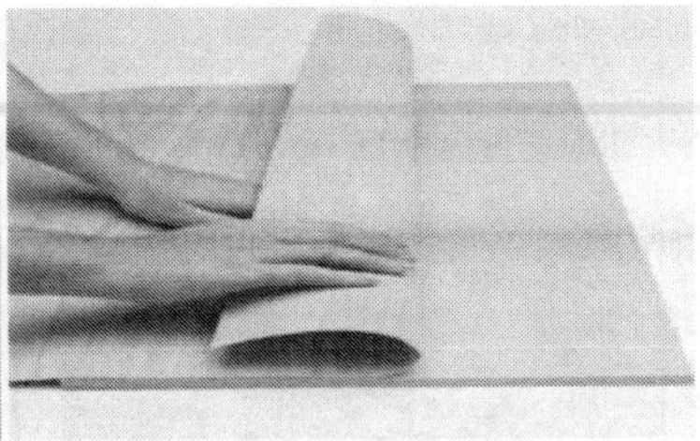

Fabric

Carpet

ORIENTATION OF ROOMS AND BUILDINGS

ORIENTATION OF A BUILDING

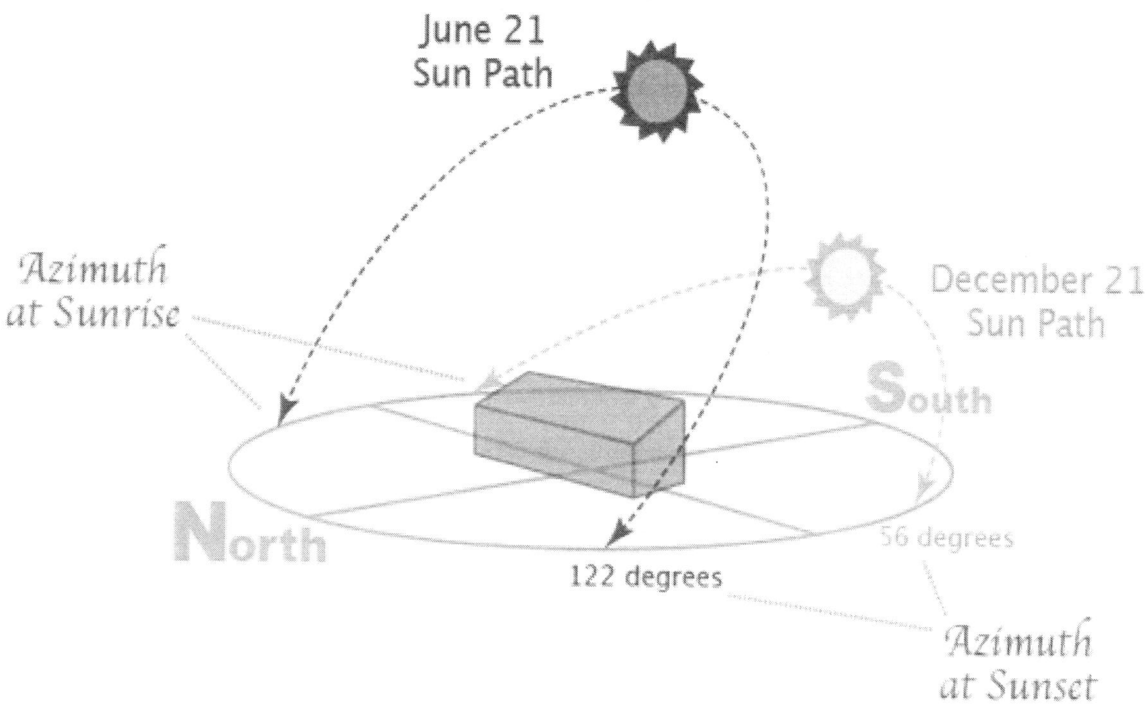

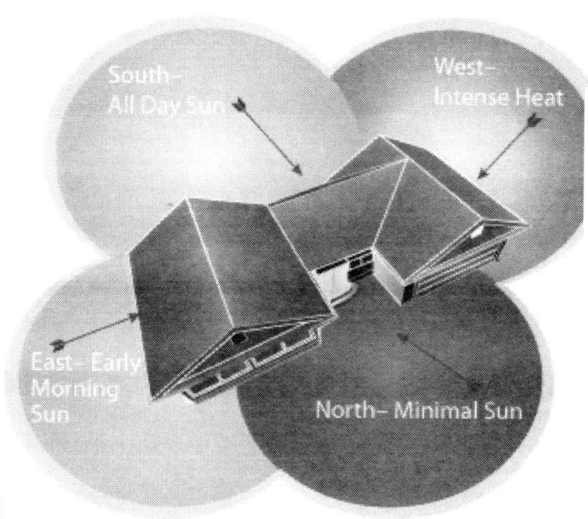

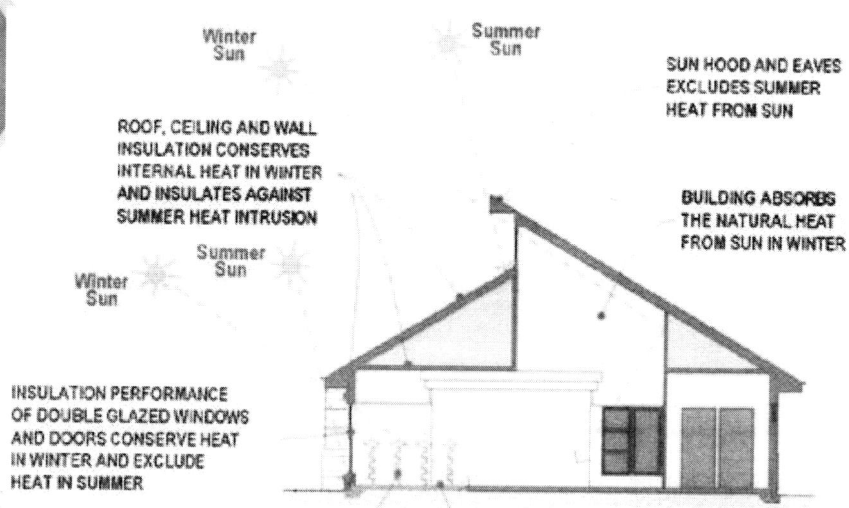

ORIENTATION OF ROOMS IN A BUILDING

ACC TO VASTU

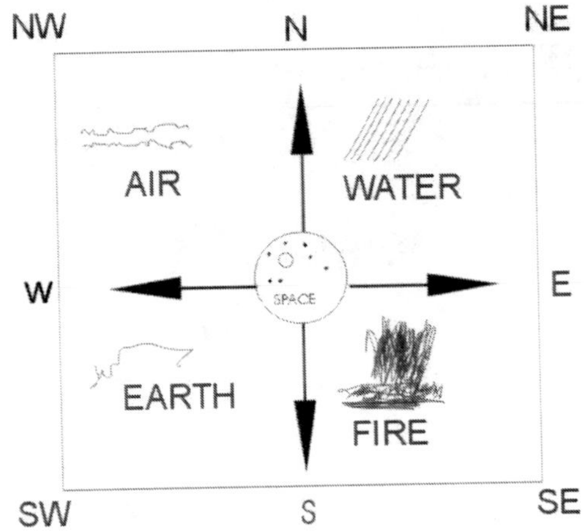

NW

- Granary & Cow Shed
- Washing Place
- Septic Tank
- Guest Bedroom
- Toilet
- Dining & Study Room
- Room for the Elder Child
- Parking

N

- Treasury
- More Open Space
- Living Room
- Bathroom
- Entrance
- Avoid Bedrooms

NE

- Entrance
- Temple / Meditation Room
- Porch
- Balcony / Verandah
- Underground Water Tank
- Avoid Toilet, Kitchen, Septic Tank

W

- Dinning Room
- Overhead Water Tank
- Children's Bedroom
- Study Room
- Toilet / Septic Tank
- Avoid Cellar

Center

- Open space
- More Light & Air
- Ideal for Tulsi Plant

E

- Bathrooms
- More Open Space
- Guest Room
- Living - Room
- Study Room

SW

- Master Bedroom
- Wardrobes
- Dressing Room
- Heavy Items
- Staircase Block
- Overhead Watertank
- Cash Box
- Avoid Cellar / Well

S

- Bedroom - Sleep with head towards south
- Staircase Block
- Provision Room
- Store - Room
- Avoid Cellar / Well

SE

- Kitchen - face east & cook
- Electric Meter
- Store Room for Oil, Ghee etc.
- Tulsi- Plant
- Avoid Cellar / Well

MATHEMATICS FORMULAE

Formulas & Definitions

Definitions

$=$	is equal to	$\perp$	is perpendicular to
$\neq$	is not equal to	$\parallel$	is parallel to
$\approx$	is approximately equal to	$\sim$	is similar to
$>$	is greater than	$\cong$	is congruent to
$<$	is less than	$\ncong$	is not congruent to
$\geq$	is greater than or equal to	$\pm$	plus or minus
$\leq$	Is less than or equal to	$\overline{AB}$	line segment points A and B
π	≈ 3.14	$\overleftrightarrow{AB}$	line containing points A and B
$\angle$	angle	$m(\overline{AB})$	length of $\overline{AB}$
$m\angle$	measure of angle	AB	length of $\overline{AB}$
⊾	right angle	$\lvert\overline{AB}\rvert$	length of $\overline{AB}$
$\triangle$	triangle	$\frac{a}{b}$ or $a:b$	ratio of a to b

Abbreviations for Units of Measurements

	U.S.		Metric	
Distance	in.	inch	m	meter
	ft.	foot	km	kilometer
	mi.	mile	cm	centimeter
			mm	millimeter
Volume	gal.	gallon	L	liter
	qt.	quart	mL	milliliter
	oz.	ounce	cc	cubic centimeter
Mass/Weight	lb.	pound	g	gram
	oz.	ounce	kg	kilogram
			mg	milligram
Temperature	°F	degree Fahrenheit	°C	degree Celsius

Time	sec.	second
	min.	minute
	hr.	hour
Speed	mph	miles per hour

Conversions for Units of Measurement

	U.S. Standard		Metric
Length	12 inches = 1 foot 3 feet = 1 yard 5280 feet = 1 mile	Length	10 millimeters = 1 centimeter 100 centimeters = 1 meter 1000 meters = 1 kilometer
Volume (Liquid)	8 ounces = 1 cup 2 cups = 1 pint 2 pints = 1 quart 4 quarts = 1 gallon	Volume	100 milliliters = 1 liter 1000 liters = 1 kiloliter
Weight	16 ounces = 1 pound 2000 pounds = 1 ton	Weights	1000 milligrams = 1 gram 100 grams = 1 kilogram

Time
60 secdonds = 1 minute
60 minutes = 1 hour
24 hours = 1 day

Formula Sheet

Note to Student: You may use these formulas throughout this entire test. Feel free to use this Formula Sheet as needed during your testing time.

Rectangle

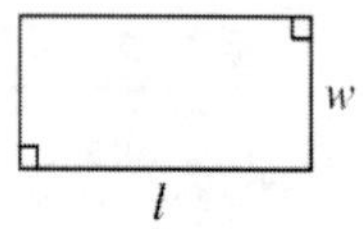

Perimeter $P = 2l + 2w$

$P = 2(l + w)$

Area $A = lw$

Parallelogram

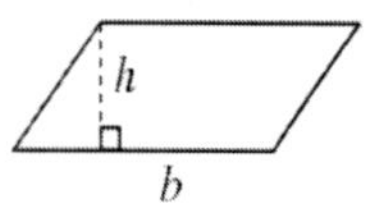

Area $A = bh$

Circle

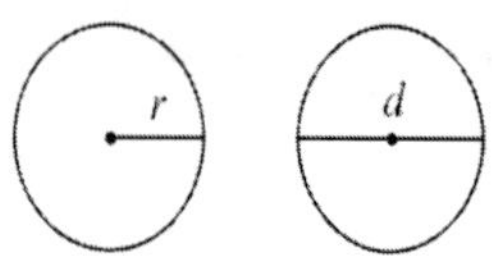

Circumference $C = 2\pi r$

$C = \pi d$

Area $A = \pi r^2$

Pythagorean Theorem

$a^2 + b^2 = c^2$

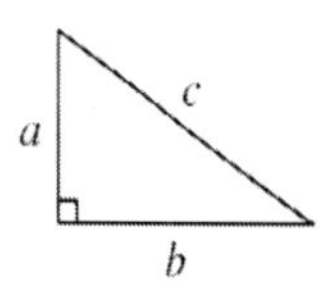

Trigonometric Ratios

$\sin x = \frac{a}{c}$

$\cos x = \frac{b}{c}$

$\tan x = \frac{a}{b}$

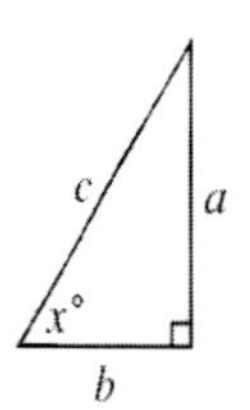

Triangle

Area $A = \frac{1}{2}bh$

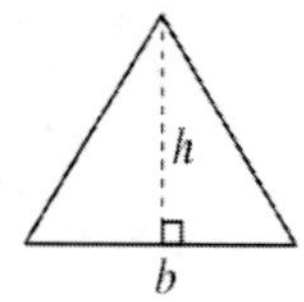

Trapezoid

Area $A = \frac{1}{2}h(b_1 + b_2)$

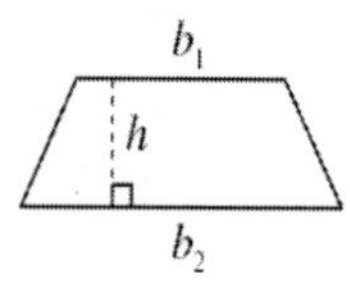

Rectangular Solid

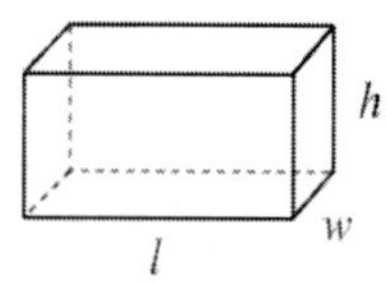

Volume $V = lwh$

Surface Area $SA = 2lw + 2lh + 2hw$

Cylinder

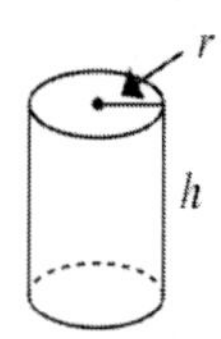

Volume $V = \pi r^2 h$

Cone

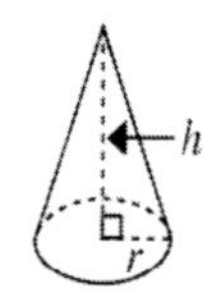

Volume $V = \frac{1}{3}\pi r^2 h$

Other Necessary Information

1 quart ≈ 0.95 liters

1 inch = 2.54 centimeters

1 pound ≈ 0.45 kilograms

$°F = \frac{9}{5}C + 32$

$°C = \frac{5}{9}(F - 32)$

Area of a Rectangle or a Parallelogram

$A = bh$

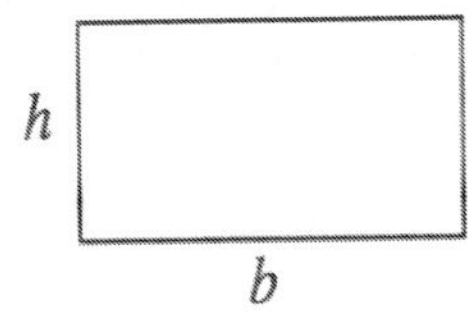

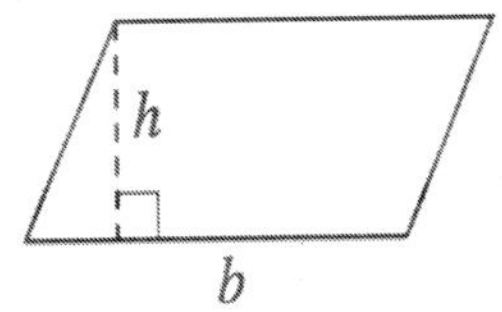

Area of a Triangle

$A = \frac{1}{2} bh$

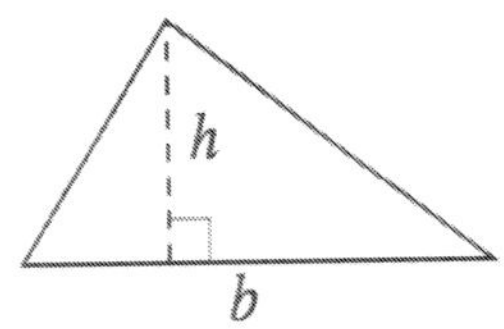

Area of a Trapezoid

$A = \frac{1}{2} h(b_1 + b_2)$

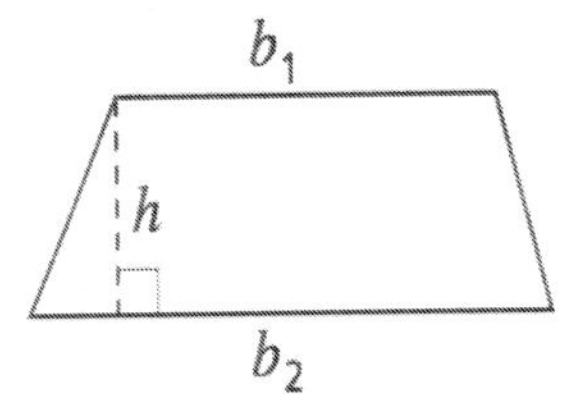

Area of a Circle and Circumference of a Circle

$A = \pi r^2$

$C = 2\pi r$

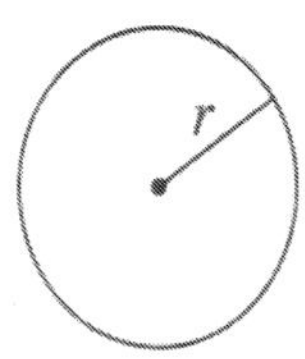

Length of an Arc of a Circle and Area of a Sector of a Circle

$s = \frac{m}{360} C$

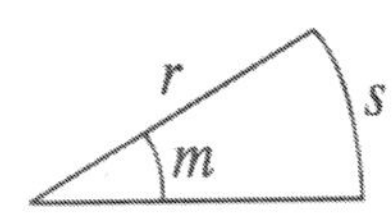

$A_{sector} = \frac{m}{360} \pi r^2$ where m is the angle measure in degrees

Volume of a Prism or a Cylinder

$V = Bh$

where B is the area of the base

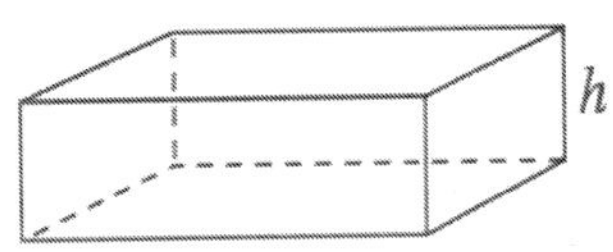

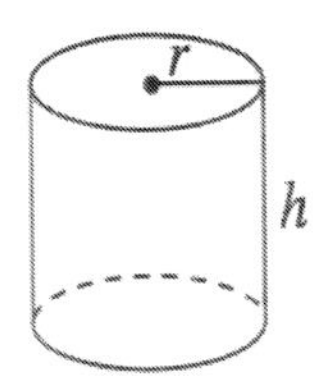

Pythagorean Therorem

$a^2 + b^2 = c^2$

Distance Formula

$d = \sqrt{(x_2 - x_1)^2 + (y_2 - y_1)^2}$

Quadratic Formula

$x = \frac{-b \pm \sqrt{b^2 - 4ac}}{2a}$

Trigonometric Relations

$\sin\theta = \frac{\text{opposite}}{\text{hypotenuse}}$ $\cos\theta = \frac{\text{adjacent}}{\text{hypotenuse}}$ $\tan\theta = \frac{\text{opposite}}{\text{adjacent}}$

Cube

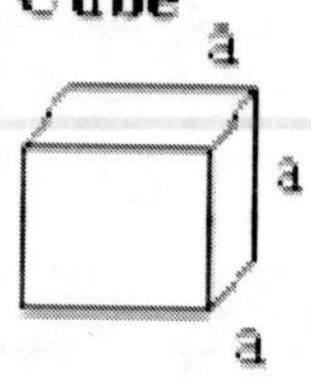

Surface Area $= 6a^2$

Lateral Surface Area $= 4a^2$

Sphere

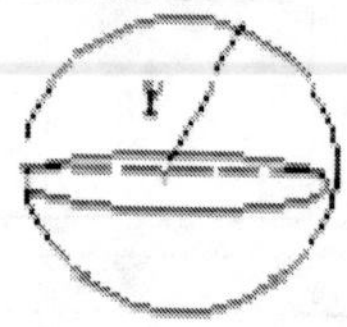

Surface Area $= 4\pi r^2$

Rectangular Prism

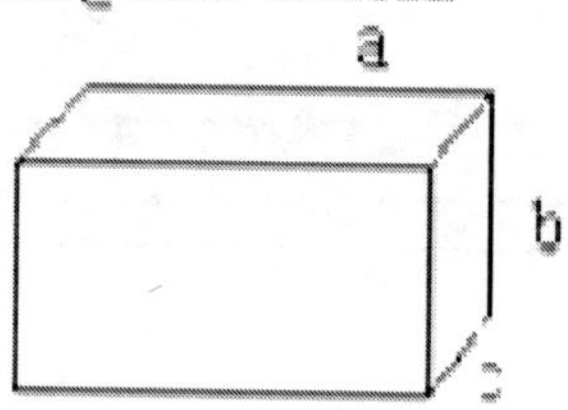

$S = 2ab+2bc+2ac$

$= 2(ab+bc+ac)$

Lateral $S = 2ab+2bc$

$= 2(ab+ac)$

Triangular Prism

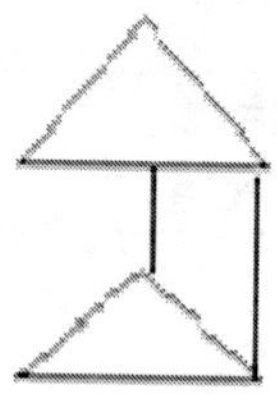

S = Perimeter of base x height + 2(Area of base)

Lateral S = Perimeter of base x height

Cylinder

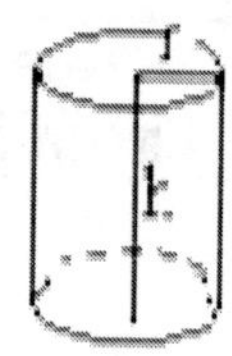

$S = 2\pi r^2 + 2\pi rh$

Lateral $S = 2\pi rh$

Cone or Right Circular Cone

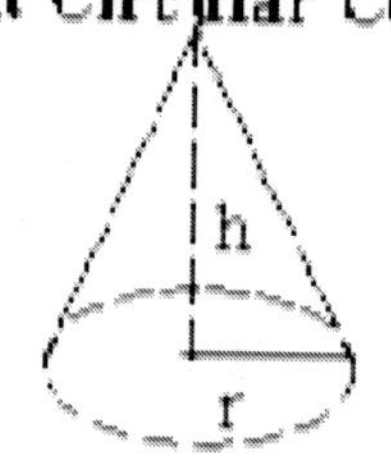

$S = (1/2)\, C \times l + \pi r^2$

$= (1/2)\, 2\pi r \times l + \pi r^2$

$= \pi r l + \pi r^2$

Lateral $S = (1/2) C \times l = \pi r l$

C = Circumference of the base

l = slant height

Pyramid

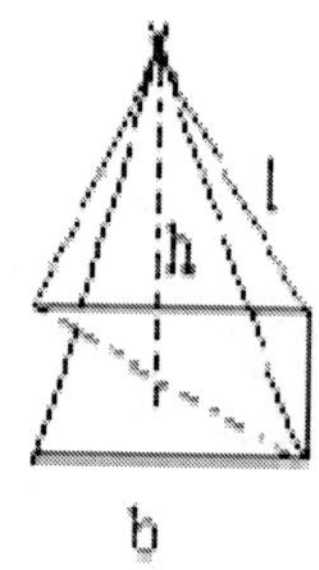

$S = (1/2) lP + B$

Lateral $S = (1/2) lP$

l = slant height

P = Perimeter of the base

B = Area of the base

h = length of height

kwiznet.com

MATHS QUESTIONS

Q1. If the length of the diagonal AC of a square ABCD is 4.2 cm then the area of the square is?

i. 10.42 cm2

ii. 7.92 cm2

iii. 9.00 cm2

iv. 8.82 cm2

Q2. The lengths of diagonals of a rhombus are 24cm and 10cm respectively. What is the area of the rhombus?

i. 240 cm2

ii. 140 cm2

iii. 120 cm2

iv. 100 cm2

Q3. Find the costs of carpeting a square room of side 8 meters with carpet at the rate of Rs.44 per meter square?

i. Rs. 4216

ii. Rs. 2816

iii. Rs. 5000

iv. Rs. 3422

Q4. A room is 8 meters long and 4 meters wide. How many paving stones each measuring

2.5dm X 2dm are required to pave its fl oor?

i. 700

ii. 720

iii. 640

iv. 810

Q5. Volume of a cube is 512m3, fi nd its surface area?

i. 200 m2

ii. 384 m2

iii. 354 m2

iv. 468 m2

Q6. The surface area of cube is 150sq.m. Find its volume?

i. 64 m3

ii. 125 m3

iii. 68 m3

iv. 96 m3

Q7. Find the area of a triangle, whose sides are 15, 16, 17 m respectively.

i. 109.98 m2

ii. 110.20 m2

iii. 114.10 m2

iv. 106.25 m2

Q8. The area of a triangle whose base and height are respectively 6.2m and 50cm is?

i. 1.85 m2

ii. 2.15 m2

iii. 1.25 m2

iv. 1.55 m2

Q9. The cost of carpeting room 6m broad with a carpet at Rs. 4.50 sq.m is Rs.135. Find the length of the room?

i. 6 m

ii. 7 m

iii. 8 m

iv. 5 m

Q10. How many bricks 20cm X 25 cm will be required to pave the fl oor of a room 6m X 5m?

i. 700

ii. 800

iii. 600

iv. 750

ANSWERS

1. iv 2. iii 3. ii 4. iii 5. ii 6. ii 7. i 8. iv 9. iv 10. iii

Q11. Find the radius of a circle whose area is equal to the sum of the area of three circles with radius 1m, 8m, 4m respectively?

i. 18 m

ii. 9 m

iii. 10 m

iv. 7 m

Q12. The difference between the circumference and the radius of a circle is 37 meters. Find the diameter of the circle.

i. 18 m

ii. 14 m

iii. 24 m

iv. 17 m

Q13. The circumference of a circular piece of land is 2200m. Find its area in hectares?

i. 50 hectares

ii. 40.5 hectares

iii. 60 hectares

iv. 38.5 hectares

Q14. 66 cm3 of silver is drawn into a wire of 1mm in diameter. Calculate the length of wire in meters.

i. 67 m

ii. 84 m

iii. 20 m

iv. 56 m

Q15. A semi circular shaped window has diameter of 63 cm. Calculate its perimeter.

i. 174 cm

ii. 178 cm

iii. 162 cm

iv. 200 cm

Q16. The length of a room is 5.5m & width is 3.75m. Find the cost of paving the fl oor by slabs at the rate of Rs.800/m2.

i. 16500

148

ii. 17900

iii. 16200

iv. 19200

Q17. Calculate the no. of revolutions a wheel of dia 49 cm makes in travelling a distance of 176m?

i. 160

ii. 115

iii. 167

iv. 135

Q18. Calculate the area of largest triangle that can be inscribed in a semi circle of radius 2?

i. 8

ii. 6

iii. 5

iv. 4

Q19. The sides of a triangle are in the ratio of 6:4:3. Its perimeter is 52cm.Calculate its sides?

i. 12 ,8,20

ii. 15,19,10

iii. 7 ,18,15

iv. 24,16,12

Q20. A hectare of land is divided into plots, each 25 meters long and 10 meters broad. Find the number of plots?

i. 25

ii. 50

iii. 40

iv. 60

ANSWERS

11. ii 12. ii 13. iv 14. ii 15. iii 16. i 17. i 18. iv 19. iv
20. iii

Q21. If the diagonal of rectangle is 17 cm long & its perimeter is 46cm.Find the area of the rectangle?

i. 120

ii. 115

iii. 167

iv. 400

Q22. Area of a base of a rectangular tank is 6500 cm2. Volume of water in it is 2.6 m3. What is the depth of this tank?

i. 6m

ii. 5m

iii. 1m

iv. 4m

Q23. A cube has a surface area of 384 cm2. Calculate its volume?

i. 520

ii. 615

iii. 567

iv. 512

Q24. 3 cubes of sides of 4m,6m,8m of each are melted & then converted into 1 cube .What is the side of this new cube?

i. 10.0 m

ii. 9.15 m

iii. 8.67 m

iv. 9.25 m

Q25. Three cubes with sides in the ratio 3:4:5 are melted to form a single cube whose diagonal is $12\sqrt{3}$ cm. The sides of the cubes are?

i. 12 ,8,5

ii. 6,8,10

iii. 7,18,20

iv. 24,16,12

ANSWERS

21. i 22. iv 23. iv 24. iv 25. ii 26. i 27. i 28. iv 29.iv 30. iii

Q26. A cylindrical tube open at both ends is made of metal. The internal diameter of the tube is 11.2 cm &its length is 21 cm .The metal everywhere is 4cm thick. Calculate the volume of metal?

i. 306.24 cm3

ii. 346.44 cm3

iii. 359.33 cm3

iv. 323.43 cm3

Q27.The length of an edge of a hollow cube open at one face is √3 meters. What is the length of largest pole that it can accommodate?

i. 3m

ii. 5m

iii. 2m

iv. 4m

Q28.The slant height of a conical mountain is 2.5 km & the area of its base 1.54 km2. Calculate the height?

i. 2.4 km

ii. 1.5 km

iii. 1.7 km

iv. 3.2 km

Q29. How many bricks each measuring 25cm x 11.25cm x 6cm, will be needed to build a wall 8m x 6m x 22.5 cm?

i. 6225

ii. 7500

iii. 5250

iv. 6400

Q30. How many cubes of 3cm edge can be cut out of a cube of 18cm edge?

i. 310

ii. 250

iii. 216

iv. 324

Q31. The height of right circular cylinder is 14 cm & its curved surface area is 704 cm2. Calculate its volume?

i. 2816 cm3

ii. 1195 cm3

iii. 1670 cm3

iv. 9255 cm3

Q32.A hall is 15m long & 12m broad. If the sum of the areas of the fl oor & the ceiling is equal to the sum of areas of four walls then calculate its volume?

i. 1264 m3

ii. 1250 m3

iii. 1200 m3

iv. 1196 m3

Q33.Calculate the volume of a right circular cylinder whose curved surface area is 2640cm2 & circumference of its base is 66 cm

i. 13860 cm3

ii. 11950 cm3

iii. 16700 cm3

iv. 19255 cm3

Q34.How many cubes of 10 cm edge can be put in a cubical box of 1 m edge?

i. 1100

ii. 1200

iii. 1000

iv. 1150

Q35. In a shower, 5cm rain falls. Calculate the volume of water that falls on 1.5 hectares of ground?

i. 750 m3

ii. 850 m3

iii. 900 m3

iv. 960 m3

ANSWERS

31. i 32. iii 33. i 34. iii 35. i 36. iv 37. ii 38. I 39. Ii 40. I

Q36. The curved surface area of a cylindrical pillar is 264 m2 & its volume is 924m3. Find the ratio of its diameter to its height.

i. 3 : 4

ii. 4 : 3

iii. 3 : 5

iv. 7 : 3

Q37.The cost of the paint is Rs.36.50 per kg. If 1 kg of paint covers 16 sq. feet, how much will it cost to paint outside of a cube having 8 feet each inside?

i. Rs.725

ii. Rs.876

iii. Rs.954

iv. Rs.925

Q38. Calculate the volume of a right circular cone having base radius 70 cm & curved surface area 40040 cm2?

i. 862400 cm3

ii. 825400 cm3

iii. 900670 cm3

iv. 909255 cm3

Q39. The perimeter of one face of a cube is 20 cm. Calculate its volume?

i. 140 cm3

ii. 125 cm3

iii. 115 cm3

iv. 135 cm3

Q40. Calculate the curved surface area of a cone whose slant height & height is 10m & 8m respectively?

i. 60π m 2

ii. 75π m2

iii. 50π m2

iv. 85π m2

Q41. The volume of a rectangle block is 10368dm3. Its dimensions are in the ratio 3:2:1. Calculate its total cost, if its entire surface is polished at 2 paisa/dm2.

i. Rs .34.44

ii. Rs .35.46

iii. Rs .63.36

iv. Rs .48.54

Q42. A power tin has a square base with side 8 cm & height 14 cm. Another tin has a circular base with diameter 8 cm & height 14cm. Calculate the difference in their capacities.

i. 147 cm3

ii. 165 cm3

iii. 192 cm3

iv. 185 cm3

Q43. Calculate the number of coins of radius 0.75 cm & thickness 0.2 cm to be melted to make a right circular cylinder of height 8cm & base radius 3cm.

i. 650

ii. 750

iii. 700

iv. 640

Q44. Calculate the length of canvas 1.1 wide required to build a conical tent of height 14 m & the floor area of 346.5 m2?

i. 565 m

ii. 575 m

iii. 525 m

iv. 590 m

Q45. The radii of two cones are in ratio 2:1, their volumes are equal. Find the ratio of their heights?

i. 1: 4

ii. 4 : 3

iii. 3 : 5

iv. 7 : 8

Q46. Given that the 1 cm3 of marble weights 25 gm, the weight of a marble block 28 cm wide & 5 cm thick is 112 kg. Calculate the length of the block?

i. 22cm

154

ii. 29cm

iii. 32 cm

iv. 40 cm

Q47. The volumes of two cubes are in ratio 8:27. Calculate the ratio of their surface area?

i. 1 : 9

ii. 4 : 9

iii. 3 : 5

iv. 7 : 9

Q48. A boat having a length 3m & breadth 2m is fl oating on a lake. The boat sinks by 1cm when a man gets on it. Calculate the mass of man?

i. 55 kg

ii. 45 kg

iii. 60 kg

iv. 40 kg

Q49. A swimming pool 9m wide &12 m long is 1m deep on shallow side & 4 m deep on deeper side. Calculate its volume?

i. 300 m3

ii. 265 m3

iii. 270 m3

iv. 360 m3

Q50. The surface area of a cube is 600 cm2. Calculate the length of its diagonal?

i. $12\sqrt{10}$

ii. $15\sqrt{9}$

iii. $10\sqrt{3}$

iv. $12\sqrt{6}$

ANSWERS

41. iii 42. iii 43. iv 44. iii 45. i 46. iii 47. ii 48. iii 49. iii 50.

ENGLISH QUESTIONS

Q1. Bespeak: synonym
a. narrate
b. foretell
c. Report
d. recall

Q2. Palpitate: synonym
a. relax
b. force
c. Thrive
d. throve

Q3. Infi nitude: synonym
a. Boundlessness
b. Voraciousness
c. Foresight
d. Hindsight

Q4. Spoiling: synonym
a. Mending
b. Messing up
c. Up- rooting
d. tilling

Q5. Pretence: synonym
a. feigning
b. fi endishness
c. Self- effacer
d. factiousness

Q6. Lowercase: synonym
a. Minuscule
b. Major
c. Moderate
d. Base

Q7. Barge: synonym
a. frigate
b. fl atboat
c. Yacht
d. canoe

Q8. Unaesthetic: synonym
a. Inartistic
b. Basic
c. Actinic
d. quixotic

Q9. Boaster: synonym
a. Low - profi ler
b. Bragger
c. Self- effacer
d. Pretender

Q10. Milieus: synonym
a. Circulars
b. Surrounding
c. Arrangements
d. Apprehensions

Q11. Hornet: synonym
a. Organ
b. a small horn
c. Hornwort
d. Vespid wasp

Q12. Inquisitors: synonym
a. Passers-by
b. Adjudicators
c. Arbitrators
d. Questioners

Q13. Regime: synonym
a. A unit of army
b. discipline
c. Government
d. Freedom

Q14. Surrealist: synonym
a. Fantasizer
b. Dreamer
c. Fiction-Writer
d. Fantsmagoricalist

Q15. Spar: synonym
a. plair
b. fi stcuff
c. chain
d. imprison

Q16. Felon: synonym
a. Criminal
b. innocent
c. Witness
d. Supporter

Q17. Internalization: synonym
a. Reservation
b. Incorporation
c. Rationalization
d. Management

Q18. Overenthusiastic: synonym
a. overzealous
b. moderate
c. penetrating
d. ever ready

Q19. Cozily: synonym
a. pensively
b. restlessly
c. 3snugly
d. awkwardly

Q20. Factious: synonym
a. tranquil
b. turbulent
c. diffi cult to please
d. artifi cial

ANSWERS
Q1 -b, Q2-d, Q3- a, Q4-b, Q5-a, Q6-a, Q7-b, Q8-a, Q9-b, Q10-a, Q11-d, Q12-b, Q13-c,

Q14-d, Q15-b, Q16- a, Q17 - b, Q18-a, Q19- c, Q20-b

Choose the most nearest synonym of the following words

Q21. FIDELITY
a. restlessness
b. disloyalty
c. feeble
d. vagueness

Q22. TENACIOUS
a. intentional
b. obnoxious
c. holding fast
d. collecting

Q23. SURVEILLANCE
a. inattention
b. visibility
c. census
d. prevention

Q24. VOLUBLE
a. serious
b. worthwhile
c. loquacious
d. circular

Q25. STANDING
a. reputation
b. activity
c. long time
d. duration

Q26. ANALOGOUS
a. capable
b. culpable
c. comparable
d. corporeal

Q27. AUGMENT
a. magnify
b. decrease
c. belittle
d. simplify

Q28. EXIGENT
a. treatise
b. expedient
c. urgent
d. miser

Q29. PEDIGREE
a. courage
b. line of ancestry
c. dogs
d. vast

Q30. CANDID
a. anxious
b. experienced
c. outspoken
d. vague

Q31. ATTENUATE
a. Soothe
b. weaken
c. testify
d. appear

Q32. ONUS
a. honest
b. inclination
c. accuse
d. responsibility

Q33. MISPRIZE
a. covet
b. devalue
c. erroneous
d. despise

Q34. WHIMSICAL
a. swift
b. fanciful
c. momentary
d. victorious

Q35. FERVID
a. delightful
b. diffi cult
c. ardent
d. obstinate

Q36. SONOROUS
a. sisterly
b. reassuring
c. resonant
d. repetitive

Q37. SACROSANT
a. sacrifice
b. worship
c. best
d. too important

Q38. DIVULGE
a. refuse
b. reveal
c. look
d. deride

Q39. CENSURE
a. uncertain
b. edit
c. approve
d. purify

Q40. CIRCUITIOUS
a. complete
b. indirect
c. aware
d. obvious

Q41. NASCENT
a. purpose

b. threat
c. emerging
d. quality

Q42. TENACIOUS
a. obnoxious
b. intentional
c. collecting
d. holding fast

Q43. EFFIGY
a. accordition
b. organ
c. charge
d. dummy

Q44. BENIGN
a. tenfold
b. envy
c. malignant
d. kindly

Q45. CITE
a. locate
b. galvanize
c. visualize
d. quote

Q46. EMPIRICAL
a. mathematical
b. verbal
c. royal
d. theoretical

Q47. EFFUSIVE
a. spontaneous
b. peaceful
c. reserved
d. wise

Q48. GENRIC
a. subdued
b. external
c. particular
d. personal

Q49. GREGARIOUS
a. noisy
b. logical
c. solitary
d. helpful

Q50. TRANSIENT
a. emptiness
b. permanent
c. ephemeral
d. clear

ANSWERS
Q21 – c, Q22-d, Q23- b, Q24-b , Q25-a , Q26-c, Q27-a, Q28-c, Q29-b, Q30-c, Q31-b, Q32-b, Q33-d, Q34-b, Q35-b, Q36-c, Q37 -b, Q38-b, Q39- a, Q40-a,Q41-c, Q42-c, Q43-d, Q44 -d, Q45-d, Q46- a, Q47-a , Q48-c , Q49-a, Q50-d

Choose the best Antonyms for the following Words

Q51. SPENDTHIRIFT
a. Extravagant
b. cautious
c. savings
d. miser

Q52. EXPEDIENT
a. mistake
b. impediment
c. delayed
d. illiterate

Q53. BOLSTER
a. depth
b. to strengthen
c. defeat
d. be angry

Q54. OBJECTIVE
a. indecisive
b. apathetic
c. authoritative
d. emotionally involved

Q55. VERITY
a. rarity
b. sanctity
c. falsehood
d. household

Q56. SHALLOW
a. hollow
b. high
c. deep
d. hidden

Q57. DIVULGE
a. intake
b. involve
c. conceal
d. coverage

Q58. ALIVE
a. asleep
b. dead
c. passive
d. drowsy

Q59. EMPIRICAL
a. mathematical
b. verbal
c. royal
d. theoretical

Q60. EXONERATE
a. reimburse

b. forge
c. accuse
d. record

Q61. RETROGRADE
a. concentraining
b. progressing
c. inclining
d. evaluating

Q62. ANALOGUE
a. dull
b. same
c. digital
d. lengthy

Q63. GREGARIOUS
a. glorious
b. antisocial
c. similar
d. anticipating

Q64. PRECARIOUS
a. dangerous
b. safe
c. easy
d. cautious

Q65. DISABLE
a. freed
b. burdened
c. spoil
d. fraud

Q66. ACCORD
a. concord
b. act
c. solution
d. dissent

Q67. ERUDITE
a. ignorant
b. immature
c. unimaginative
d. professional

Q68. DANGLE
a. secure
b. loose
c. mingle
d. hanging

Q69. APPROPRIATE
a. unskilled
b. unqualifi ed
c. unable
d. unsuitable

Q70. ANALOGOUS
a. not capable
b. not culpable
c. not congenial
d. not comparable

Q71. DEBILITATE
a. bedevil
b. animate
c. deaden
d. balmy

Q72. SYNTHETIC
a. affable
b. cosmetic
c. natural
d. plastic

Q73. HAUGHTY
a. cowardly
b. humble
c. scared
d. pitiable

Q74. TRANSIENT
a. permanent
b. certain
c. close
d. carried

Q75. RUTHLESS
a. mindful
b. merciful
c. compassionate
d. majestic

Q76. COMPLIANCE
a. energize
b. take away
c. fresh
d. light

Q77. IRRADIATE
a. fl ight
b. agreement
c. distance
d. clarity

Q78. PAUCITY
a. richness
b. presence
c. surplus
d. scarcity

Q79. ANOMALY
a. desperation
b. regularity
c. equisition
d. registry

Q80. ACQUITTED
a. entrusted
b. freed
c. convicted
d. burdened

Q81. BENIGN
a. wavering
b. peaceful
c. malignant
d. blessed

Q82. LEND
a. borrow

b. pawn
c. hire
d. cheat

Q83. EXHIBIT
a. prevent
b. conceal
c. concede
d. withdraw

Q84. CENSURE
a. augment
b. eradicate
c. enthrall
d. commend

Q85. VIOLENT
a. gentle
b. humble
c. tame
d. harmless

Q86. DEROGATORY
a. roguish
b. immediate
c. praising
d. conferred

Q87. OPTIMUM
a. worst
b. chosen
c. pessimistic
d. minimum

Q88. VIRTUE
a. crime
b. wickedness
c. fraud
d. vice

Q89. CENSURE
a. process
b. penetrate
c. enclose
d. praise

Q90. TRANSTPARENT
a. opaque
b. colored
c. imminent
d. childlike

Q91. CRYPTIC
a. futile
b. candid
c. indifferent
d. famous

Q92. MINOR
a. major
b. tall
c. heavy
d. big

Q93. SURVEILLANCE
a. visibility
b. census
c. prevention
d. inattention

Q94. OVERT
a. shallow
b. secret
c. unwritten
d. deep

Q95.AUGMENT
a. dig out
b. to increase
c. be disturbed
d. keep away

Q96. DEEP
a. superfi cial
b. elementary
c. perfunctory
d. shallow

Q97. OPAQUE
a. covered
b. clear
c. transparent
d. misty

Q98. AUTONOMY
a. submissiveness
b. slavery
c. dependence
d. subordination

Q99. ERRONEOUS
a. curious
b. abrupt
c. accurate
d. dignifi ed

Q100. DEARTH
a. Abundance
b. suffi ciency
c. Extravagance
d. scarcity

ANSWERS
Q51 -d, Q52-a, Q53-a, Q54-c , Q55-a ,
Q56-b, Q57-c, Q58-b,Q59-d, Q60- c, Q61-b,
Q62-a, Q63-b, Q64-b, Q65-c, Q66-d, Q67 -a, Q68-b, Q69- d, Q70-d, Q71-c, Q72-c,Q73-b, Q74 -a,Q75-c, Q76-b, Q77-c,Q78-c,Q79-b, Q80-c,Q81-c, Q82-a,Q83-b, Q84-d,Q85-b,Q86-c,Q87-a,Q88-d,Q89-d,Q90-d, Q91-c,Q92-a,Q93-d,Q94-b,Q95-a,Q96-a,Q97-c, Q98-c,Q99-c,Q100-

3D FIGURES

FOLDED FIGURES

1.

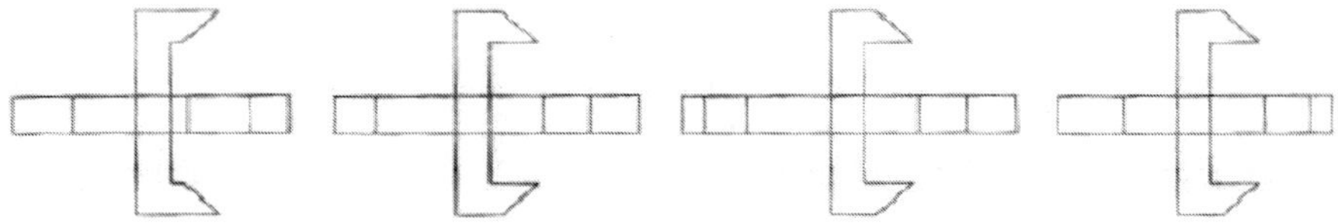

(1) (2) (3) (4)

2.

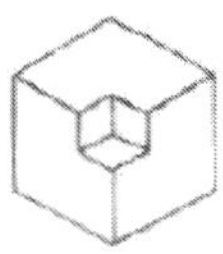

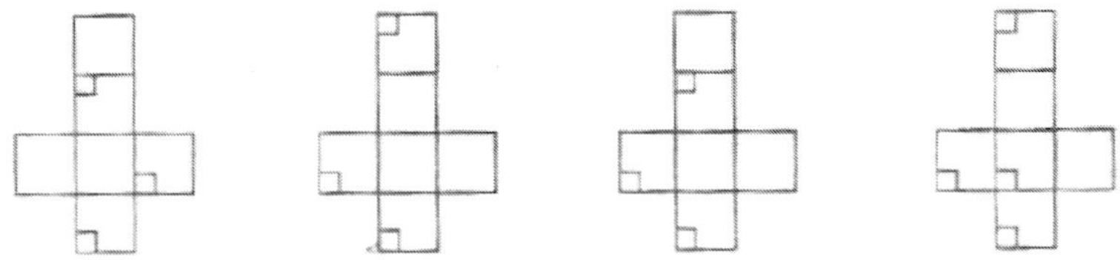

(1) (2) (3) (4)

3.

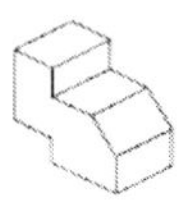

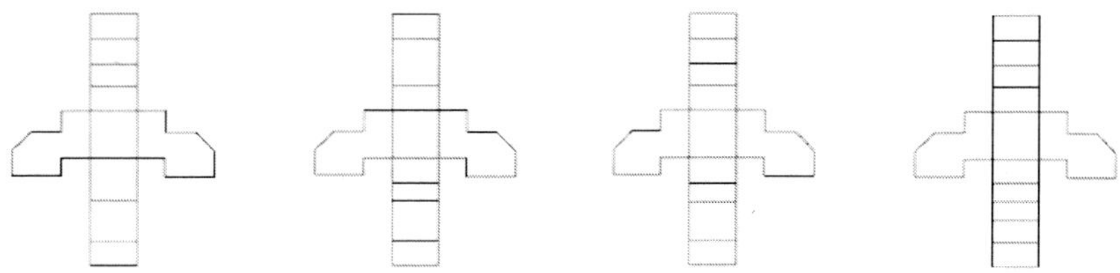

(1) (2) (3) (4)

4.

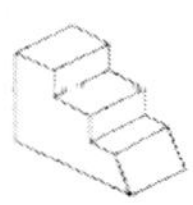

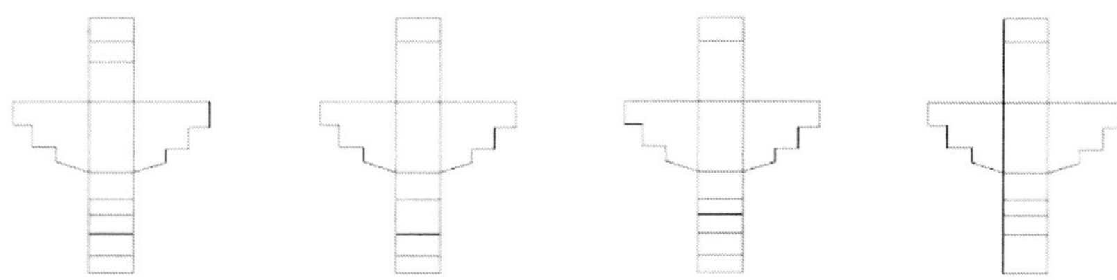

(1) (2) (3) (4)

5.

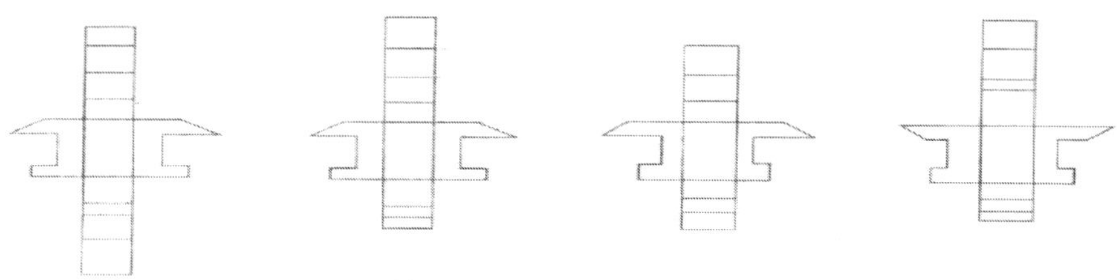

(1) (2) (3) (4)

6.

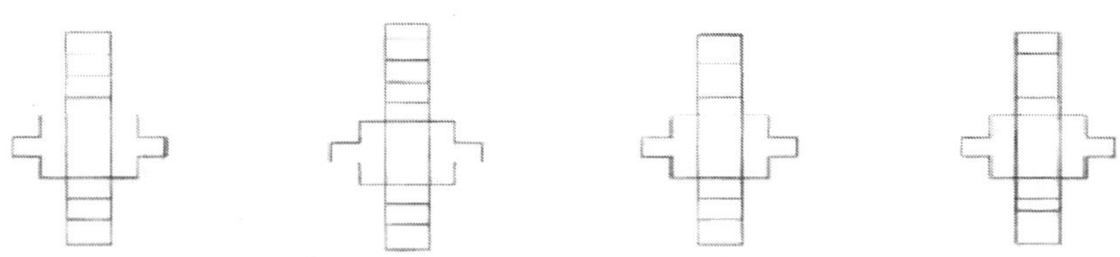

(1) (2) (3) (4)

7.

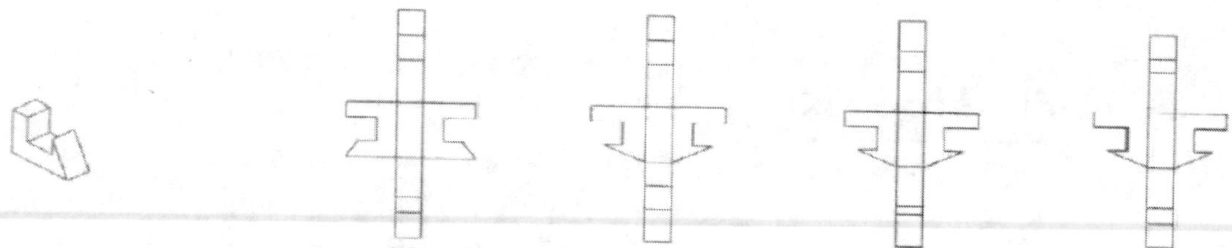

(1) (2) (3) (4)

8.

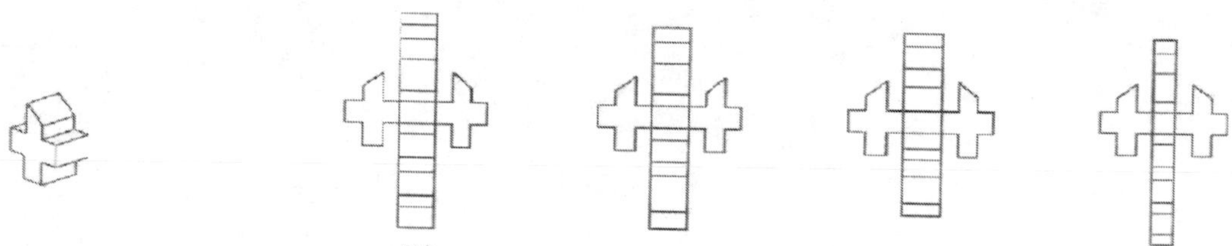

(1) (2) (3) (4)

9.

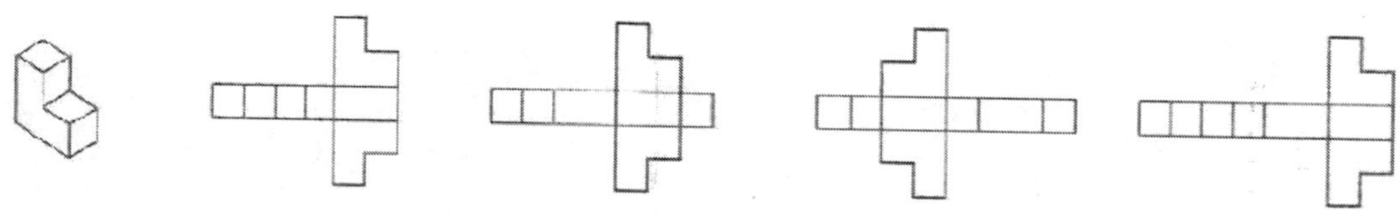

(1) (2) (3) (4)

10.

(1) (2) (3) (4)

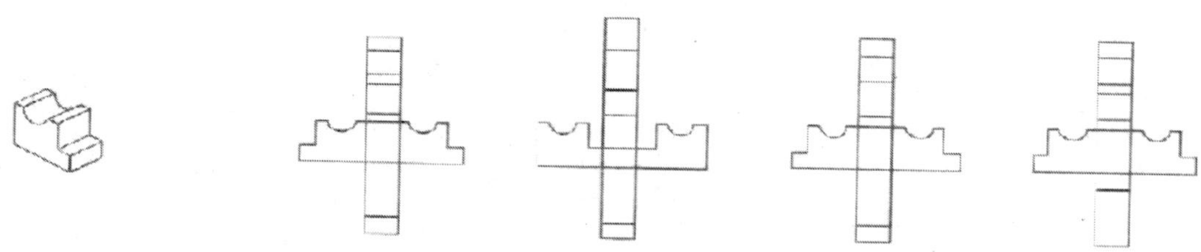

(1) (2) (3) (4)

11.

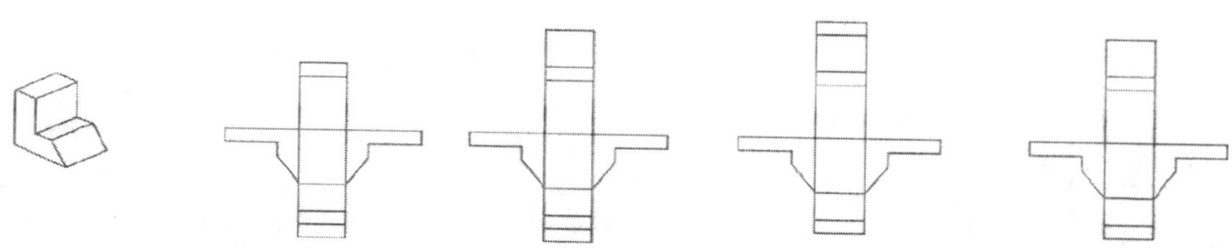

(1) (2) (3) (4)

12.

13.

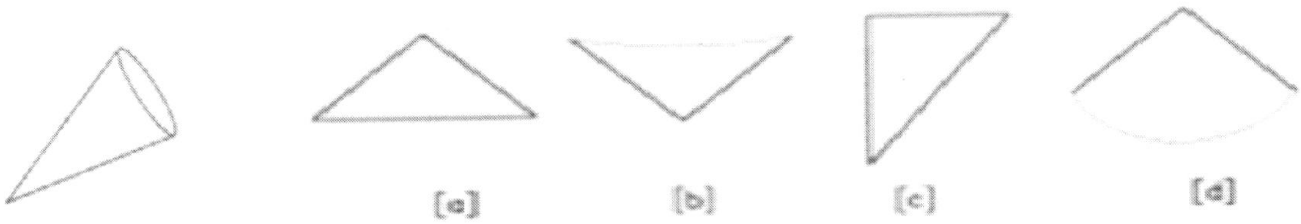

[a] [b] [c] [d]

14.

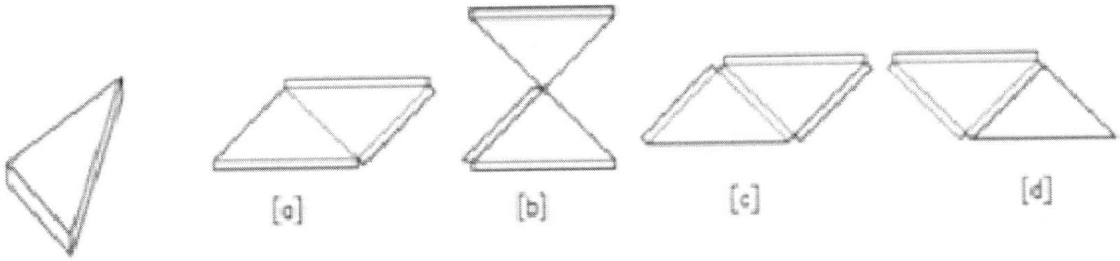

[a] [b] [c] [d]

15.

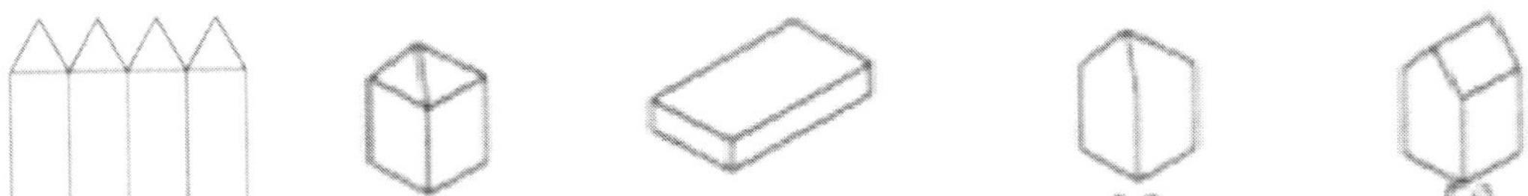

[a] [b] [c] [d]

16.

[a] [b] [c] [d]

17.

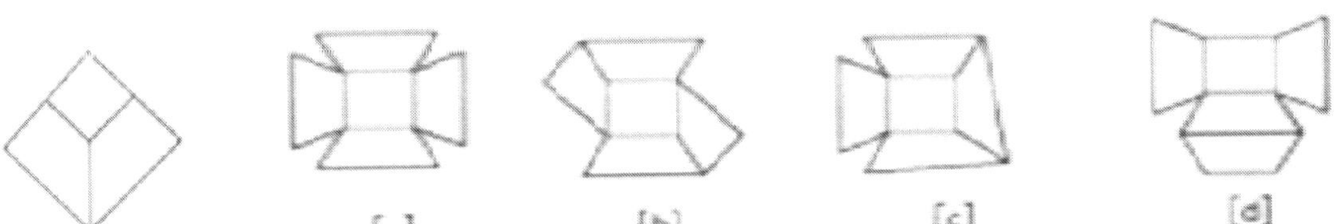

[a] [b] [c] [d]

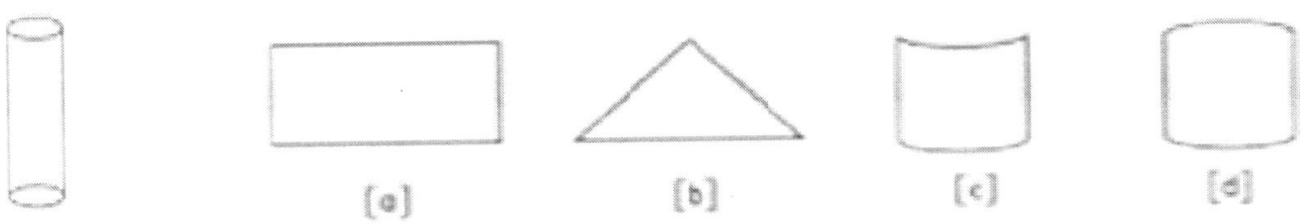

[a] [b] [c] [d]

18.

[a] [b] [c] [d]

19.

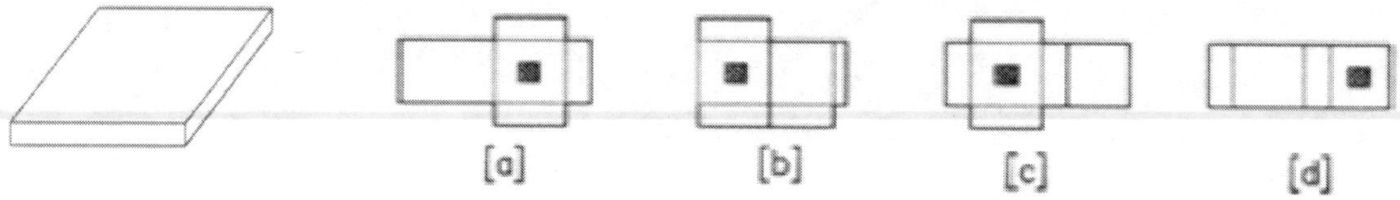

20.

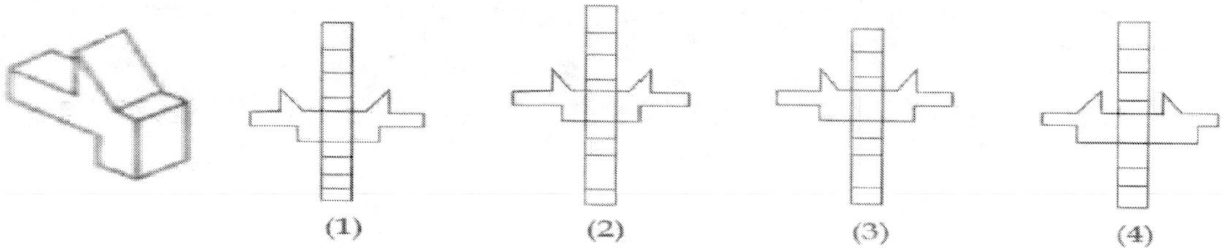

21.

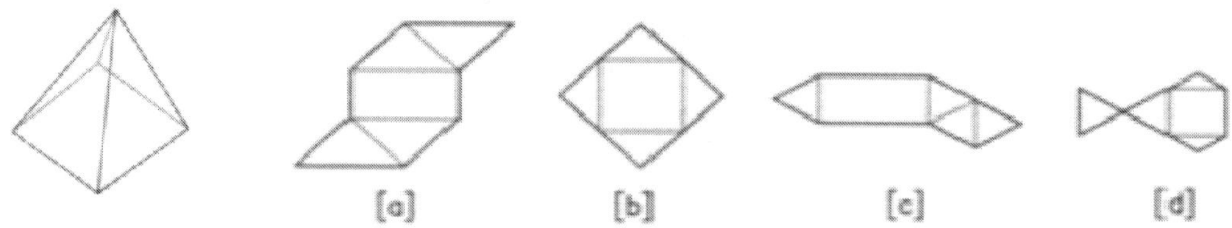

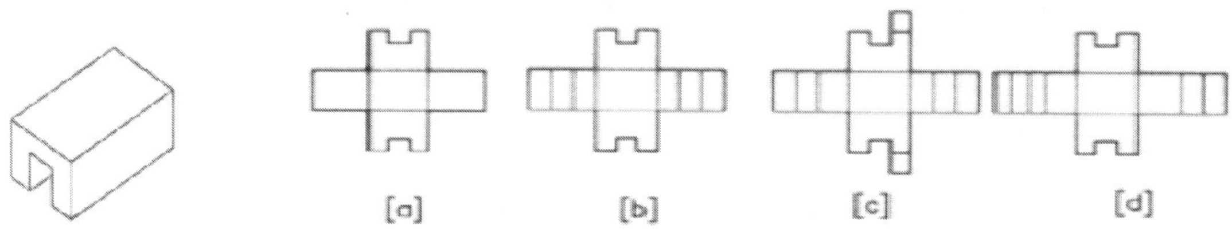

22.

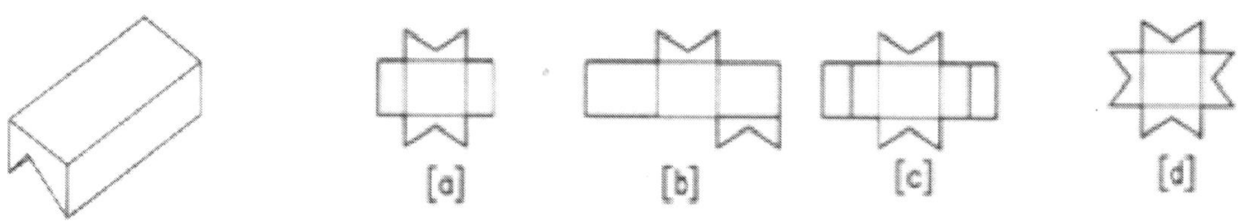

23.

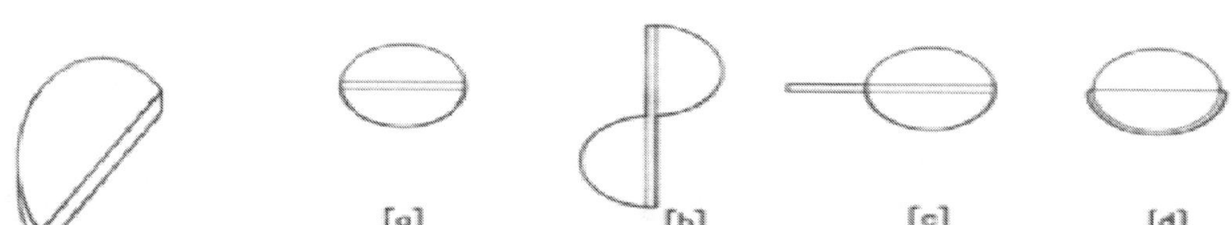

24.

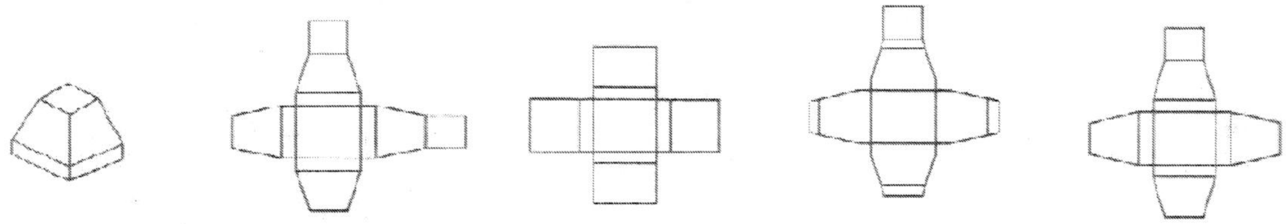

(1) (2) (3) (4)

25.

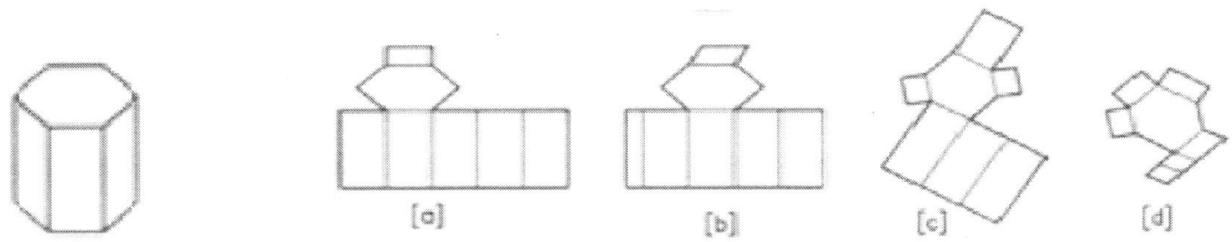

[a] [b] [c] [d]

26.

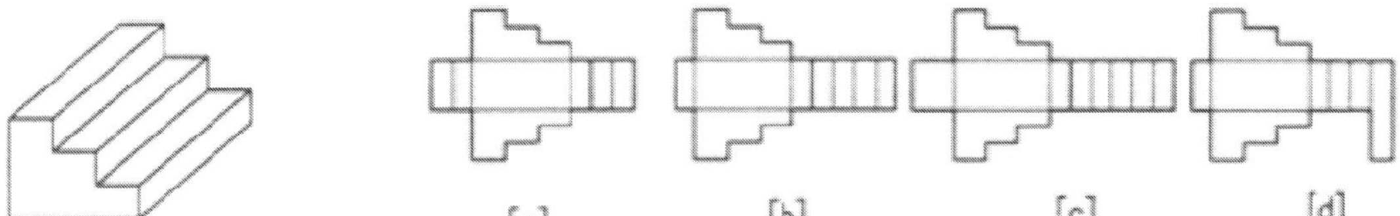

[a] [b] [c] [d]

27.

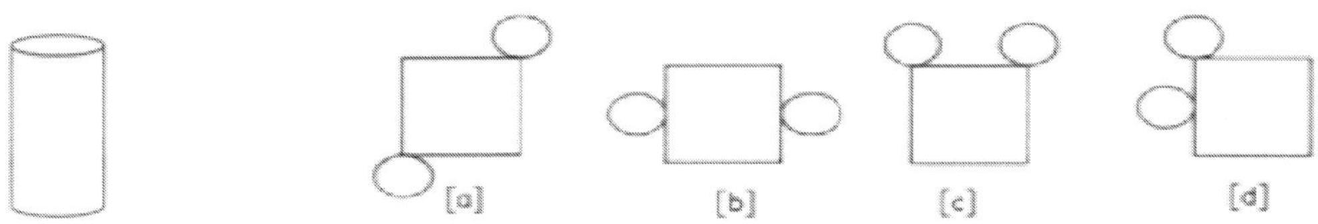

[a] [b] [c] [d]

28.

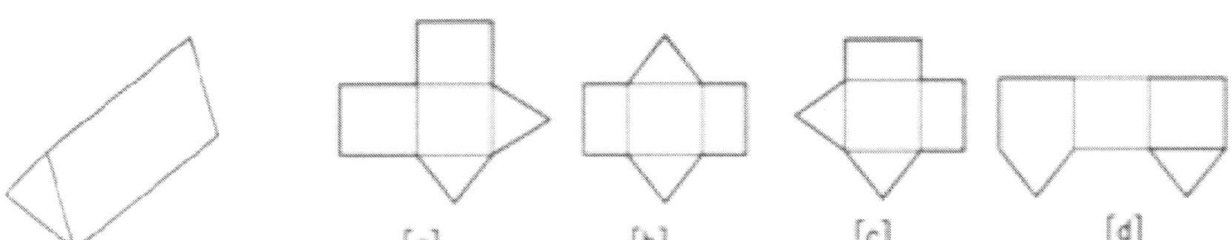

[a] [b] [c] [d]

FRONT ELEVATION

1.

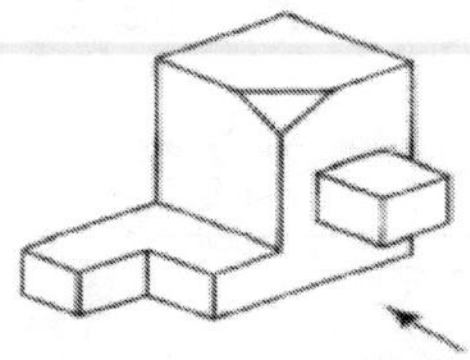

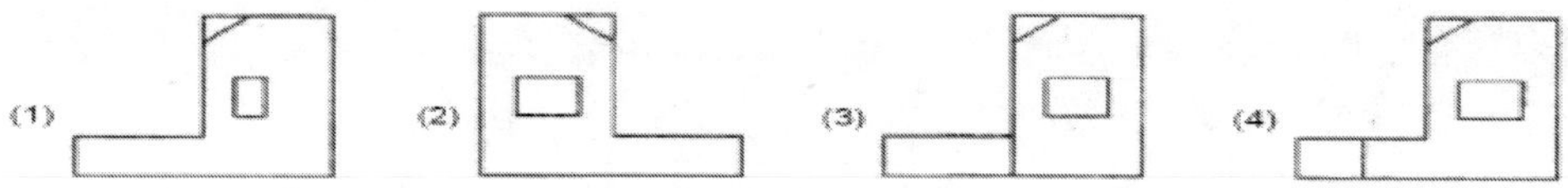

2.

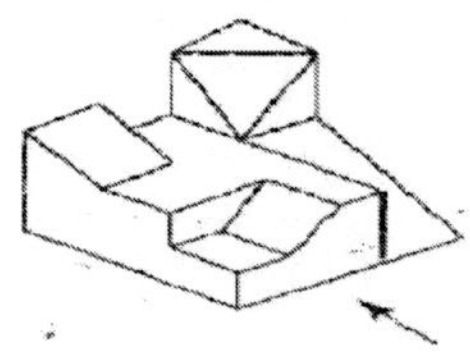

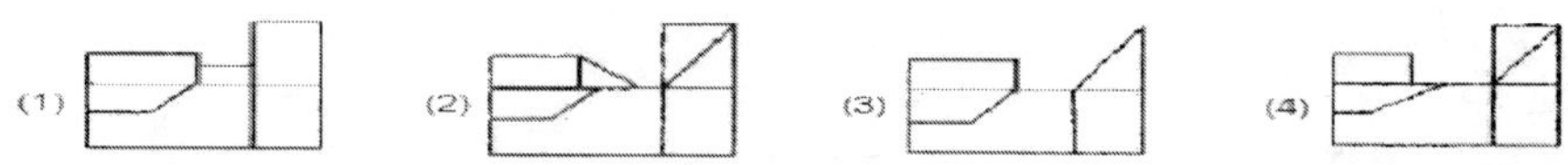

3.

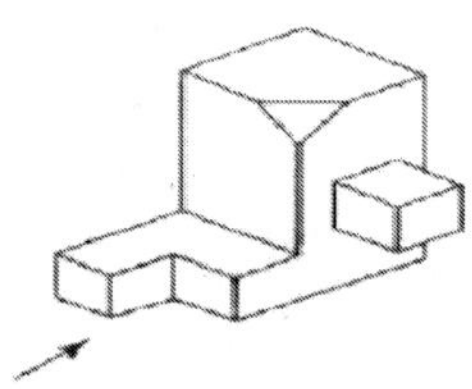

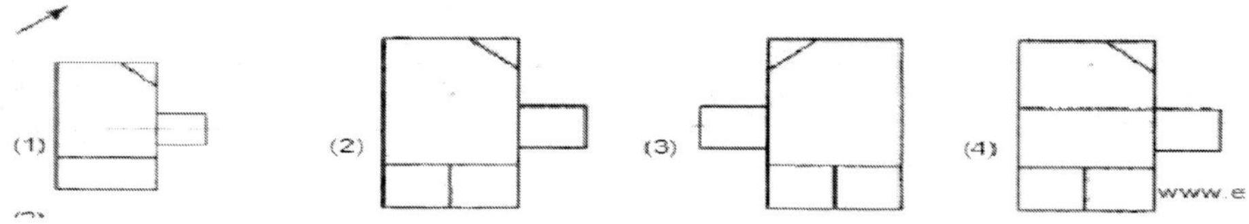

4.

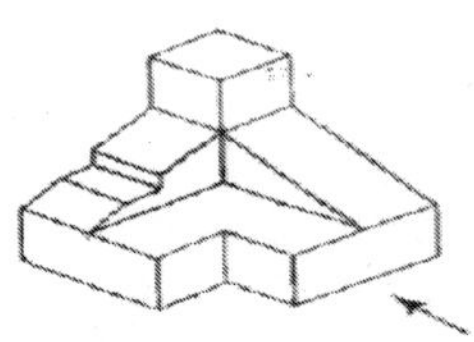

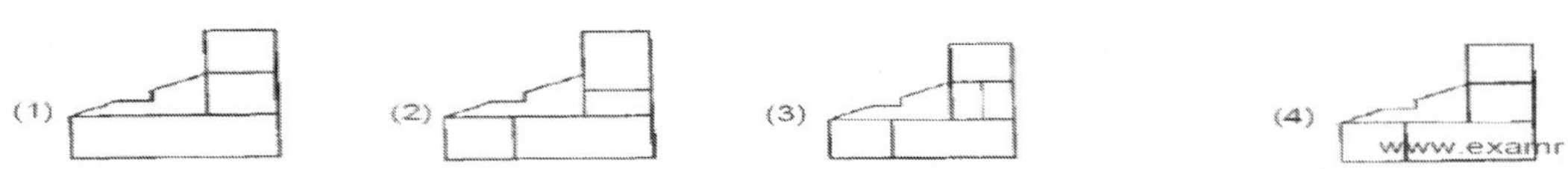

5. 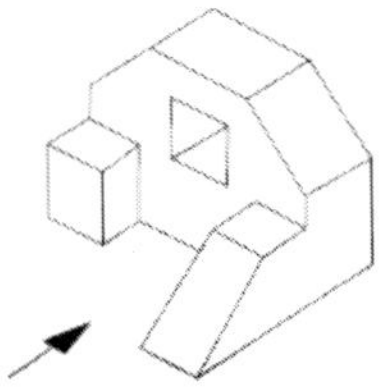

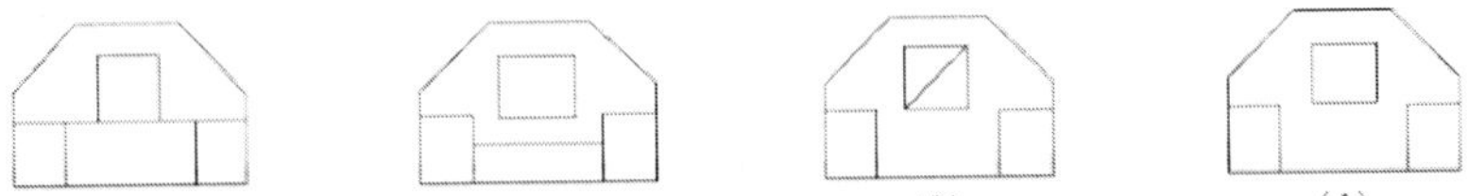

(1) (2) (3) (4)

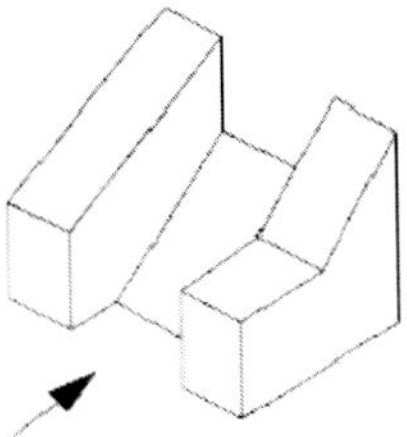

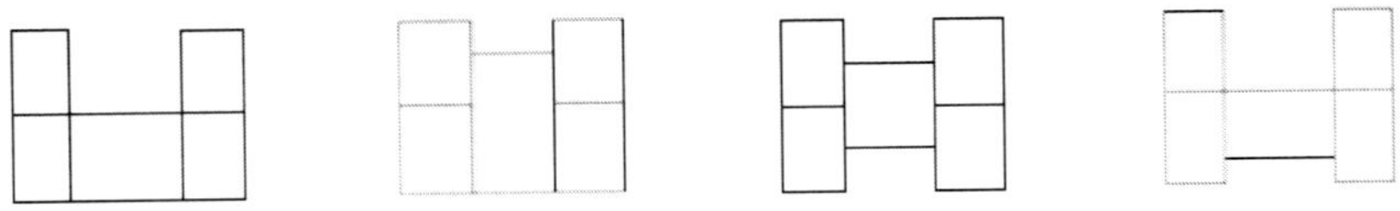

(1) (2) (3) (4)

6. 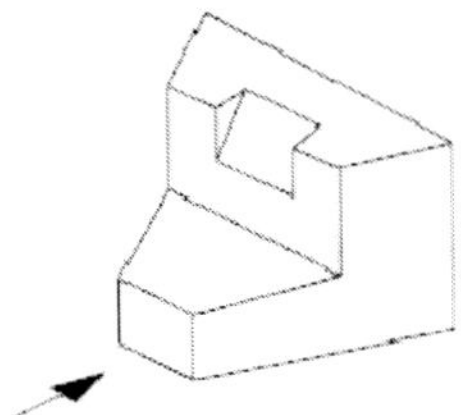

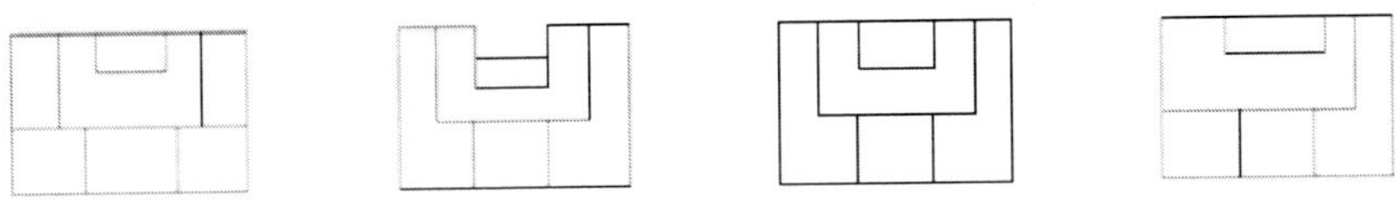

(1) (2) (3) (4)

7. 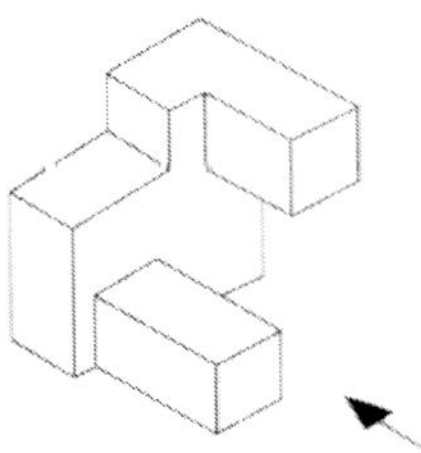

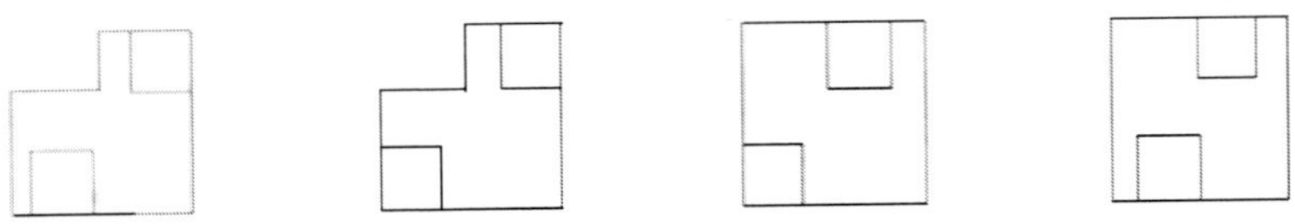

(1) (2) (3) (4)

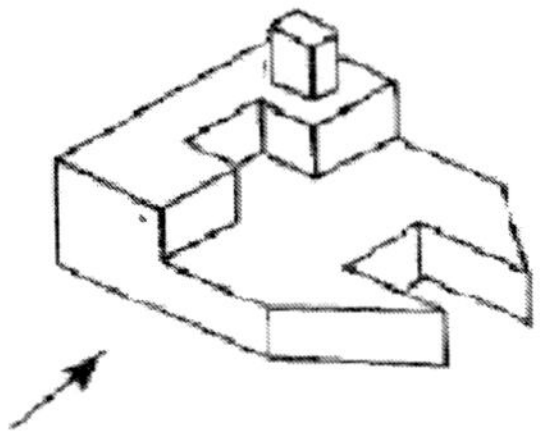

8.

(1) 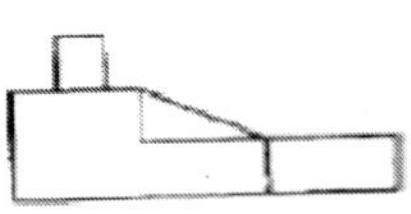 (2) 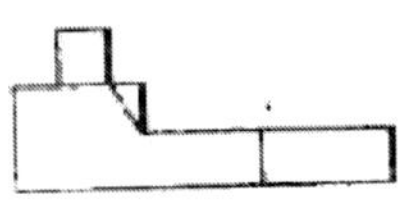 (3) 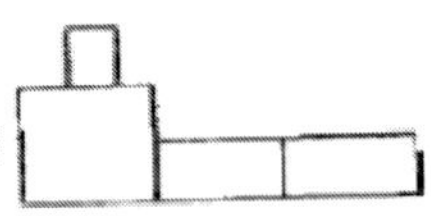 (4) 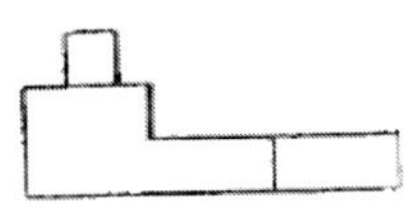

9. 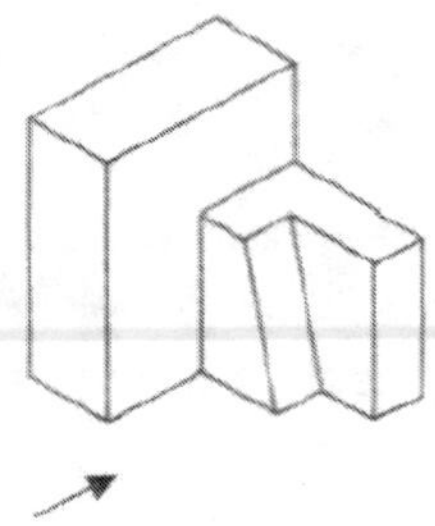

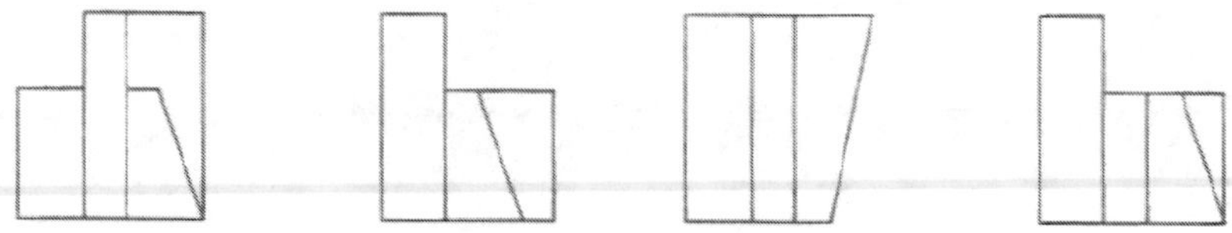

(1) (2) (3) (4)

10. 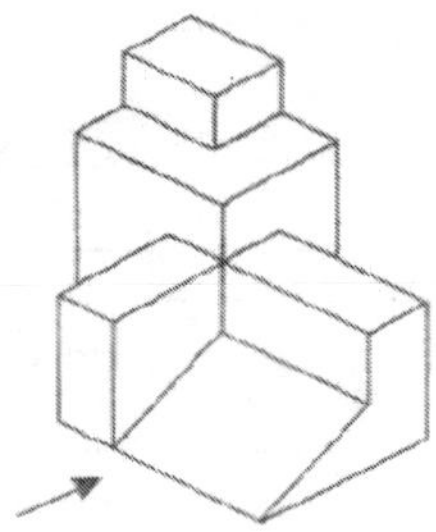

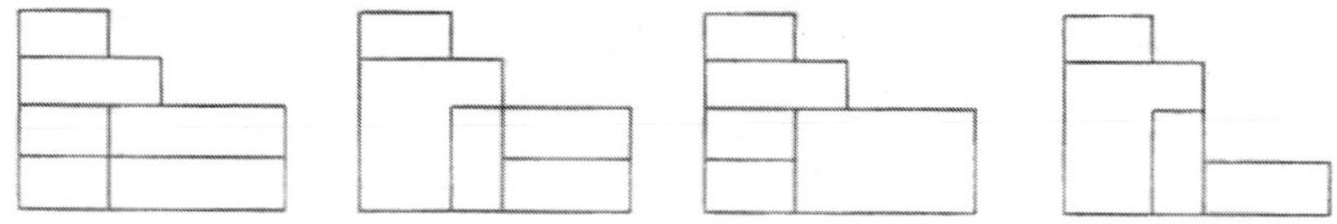

(1) (2) (3) (4)

11. 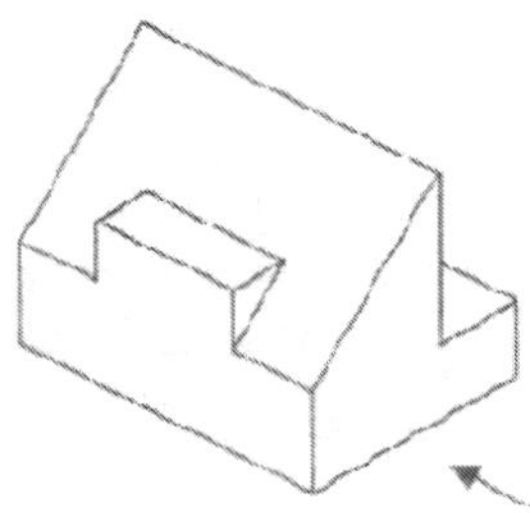

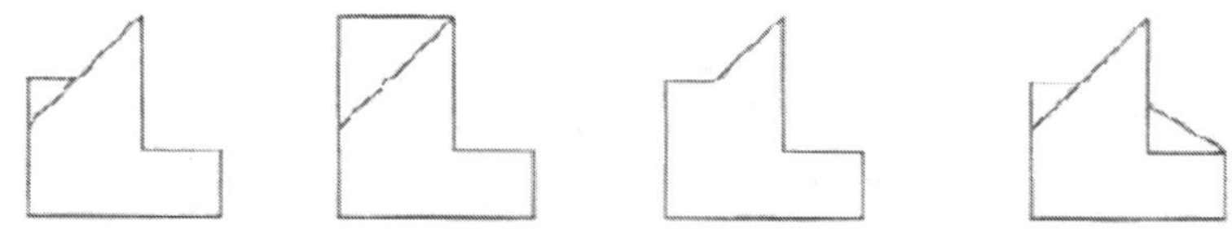

(1) (2) (3) (4)

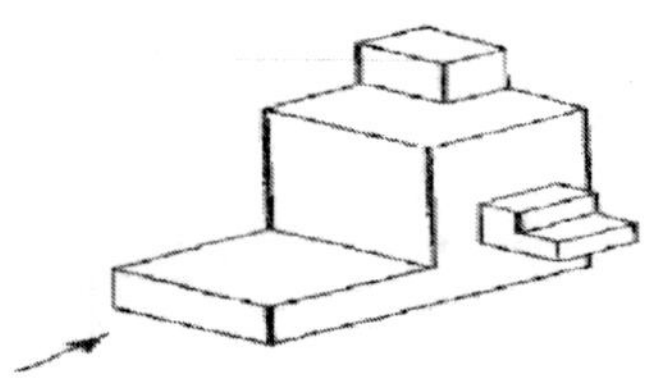

12. 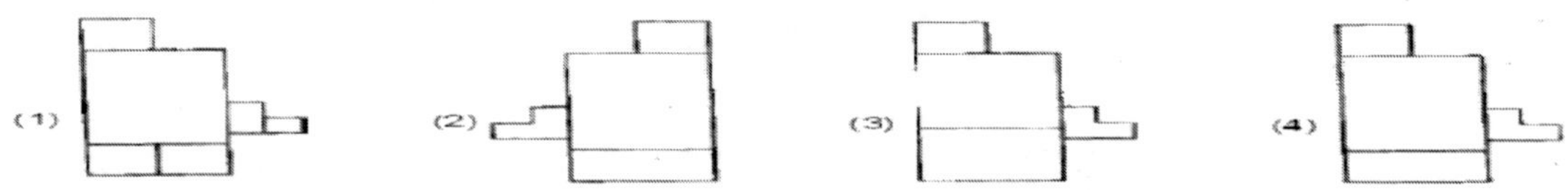

13. 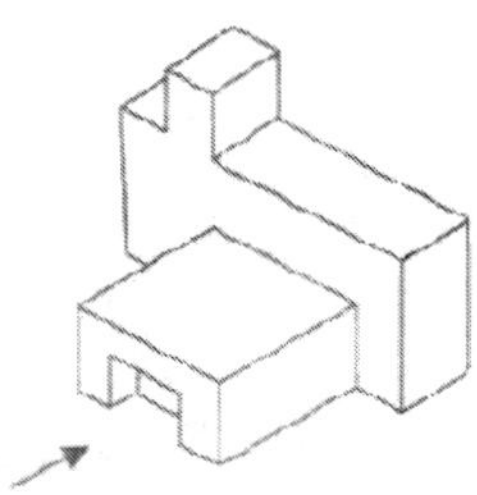

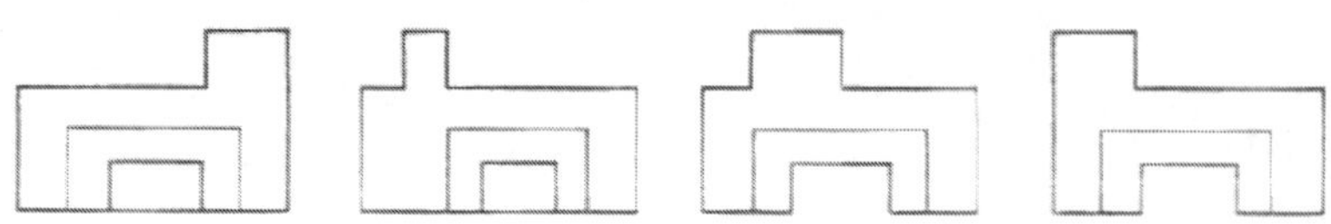

(1) (2) (3) (4)

14. 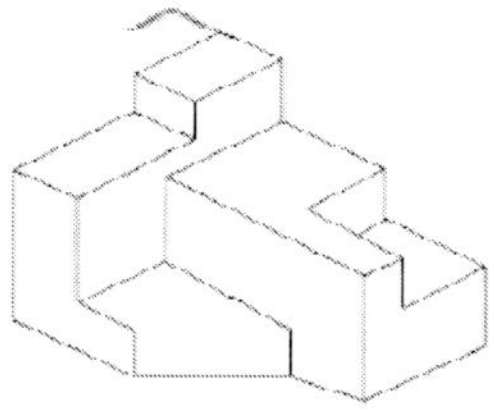

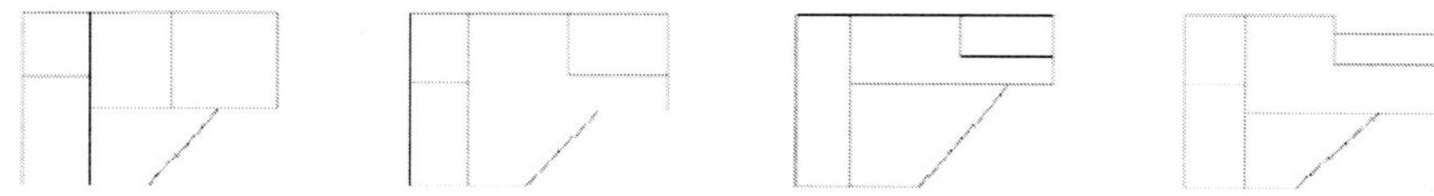

(1) (2) (3) (4)

15. 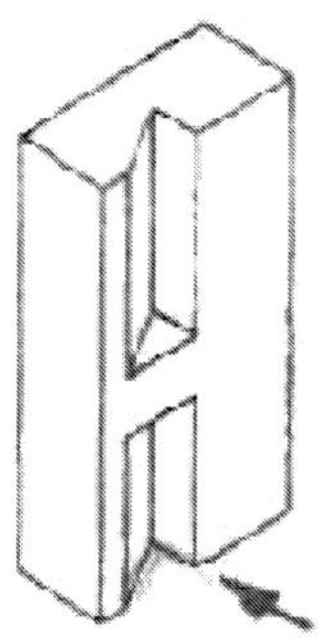

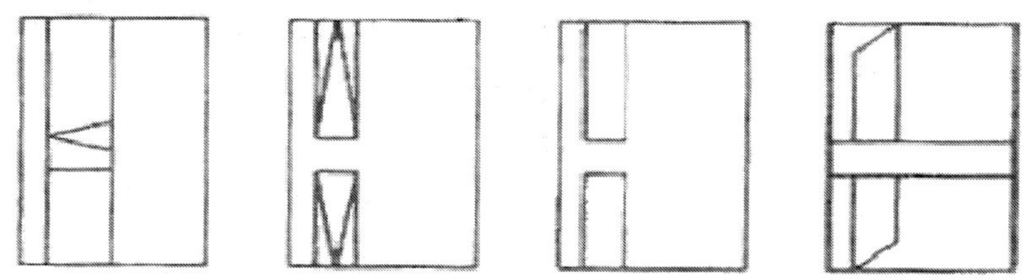

(1) (2) (3) (4)

16. 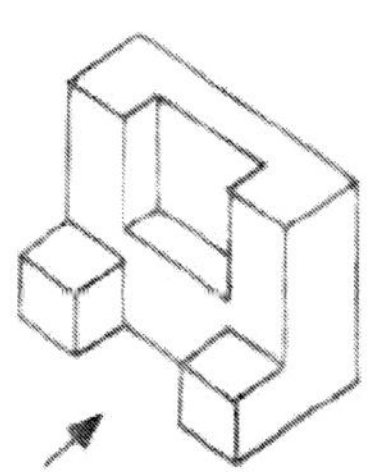

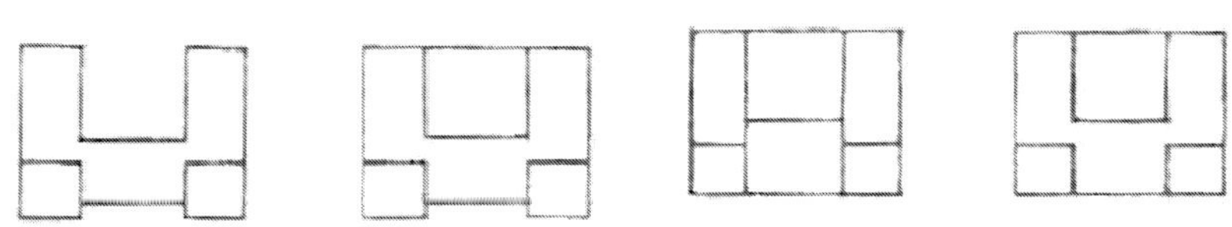

(1) (2) (3) (4)

17. 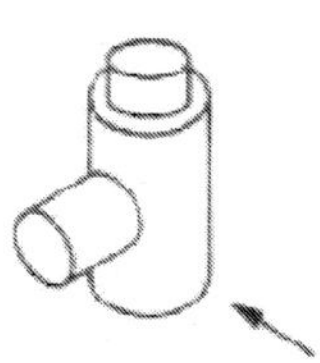

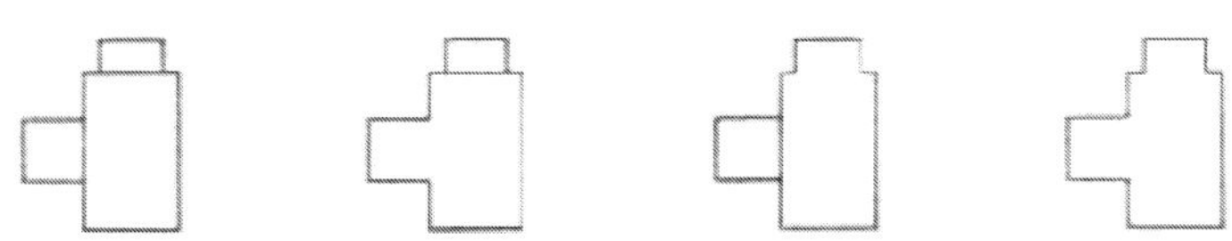

(1) (2) (3) (4)

18. 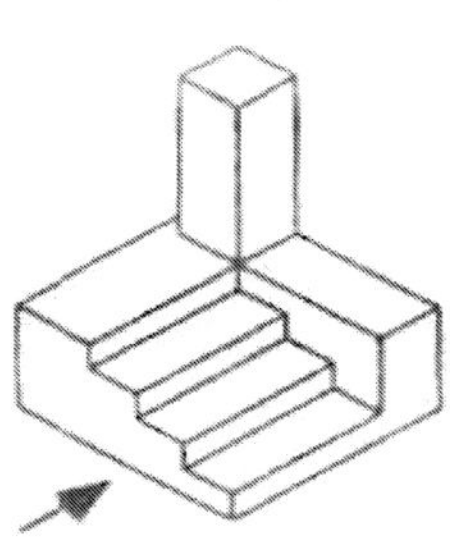

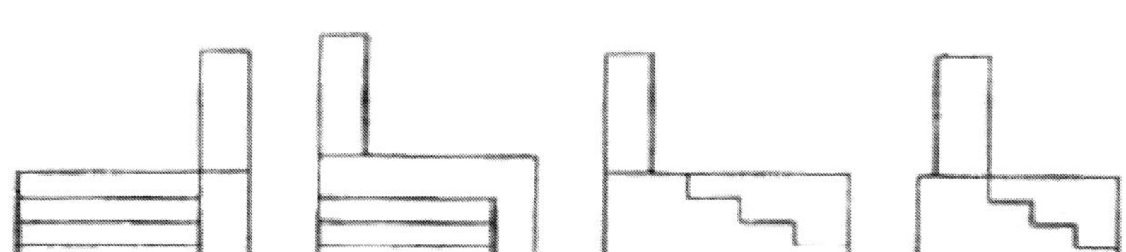

(1) (2) (3) (4)

19. 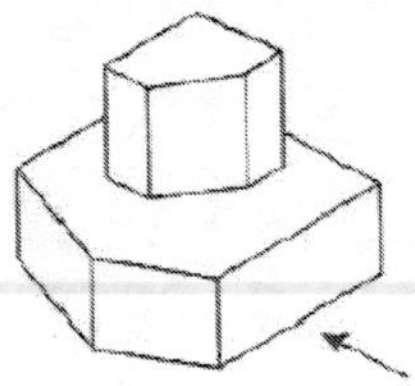

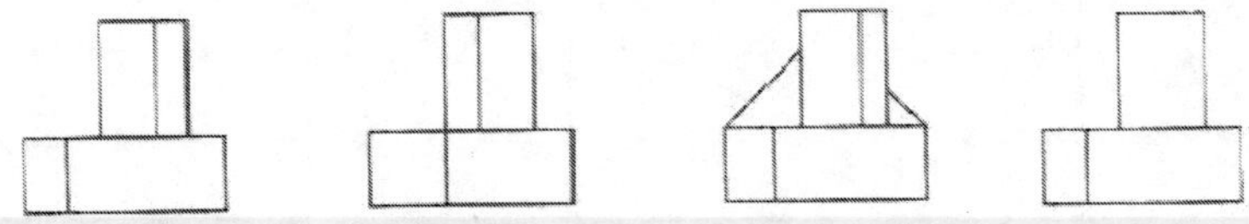

(1) (2) (3) (4)

20. 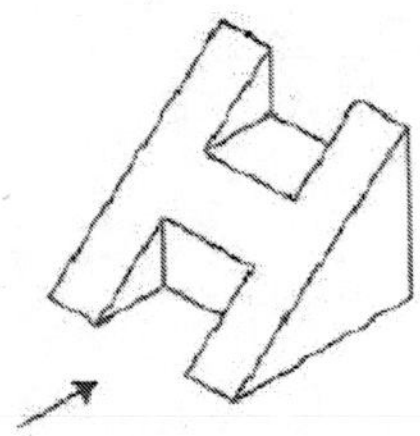

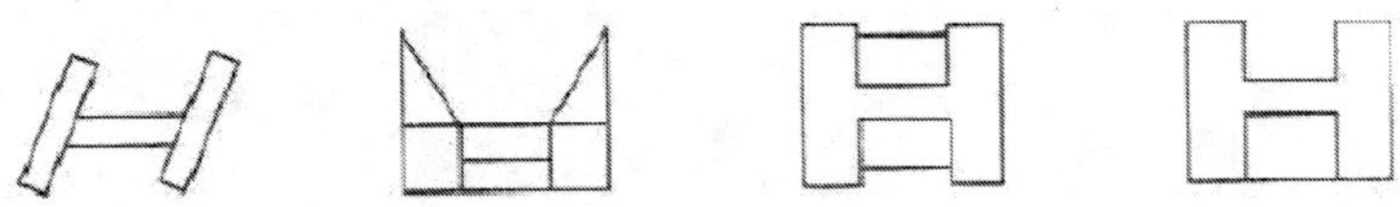

(1) (2) (3) (4)

21. 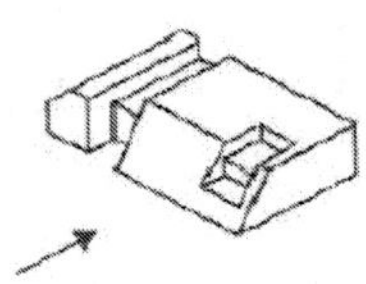

(1) (2) (3) (4)

22. 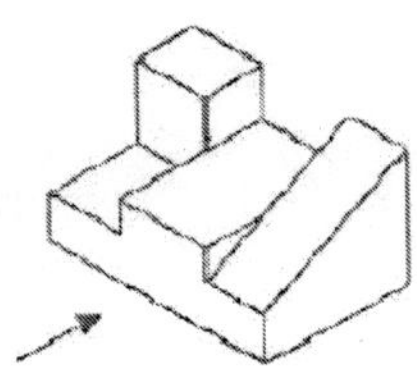

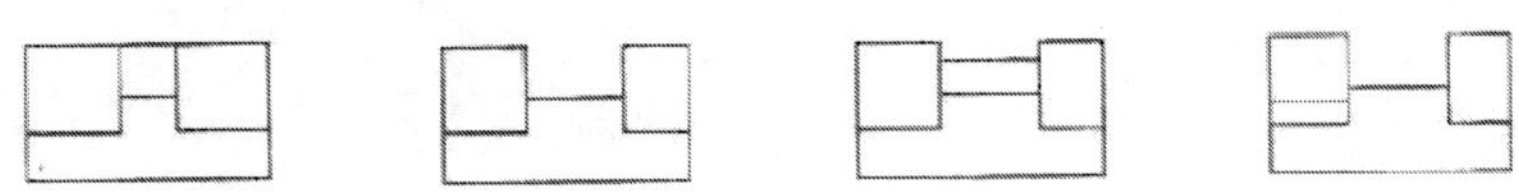

(1) (2) (3) (4)

23. 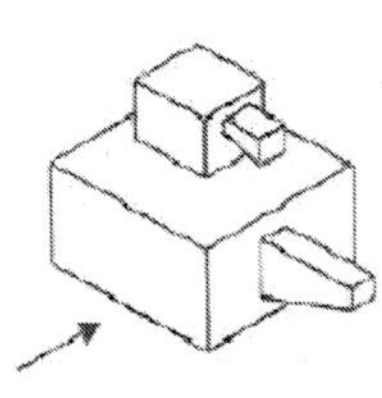

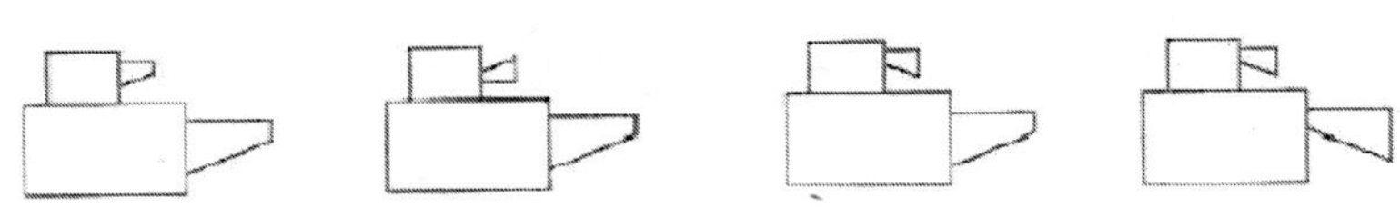

(1) (2) (3) (4)

TOP VIEW

24.

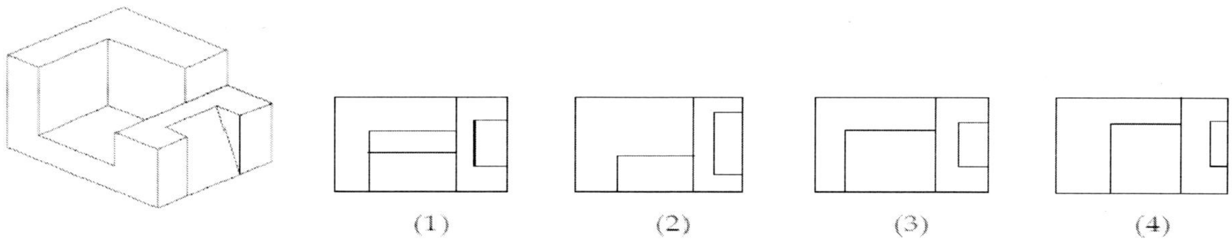

25.

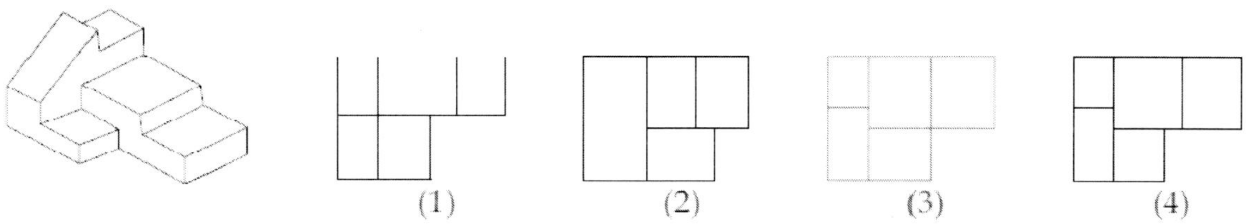

26.

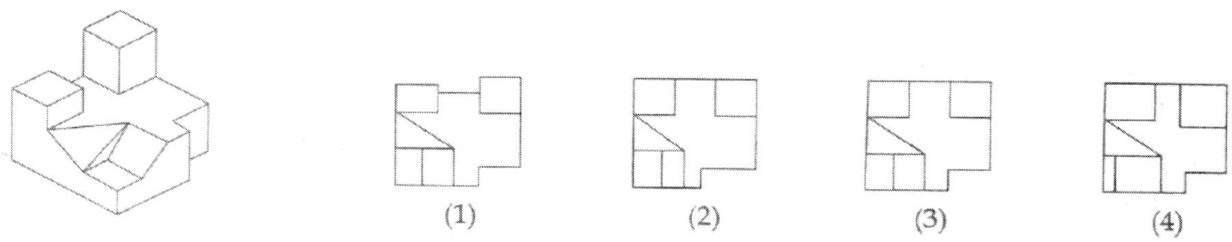

27.

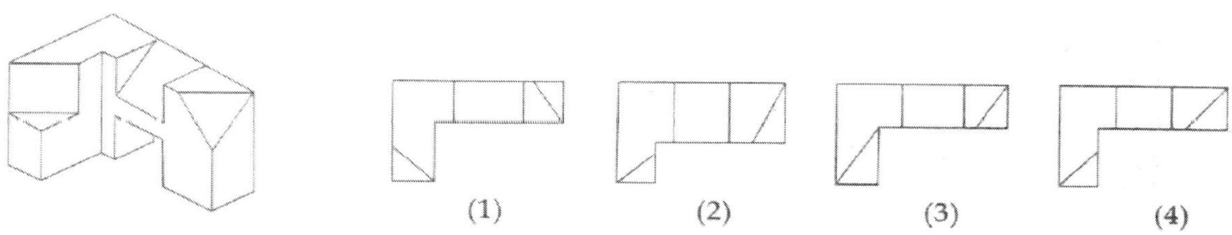

28.

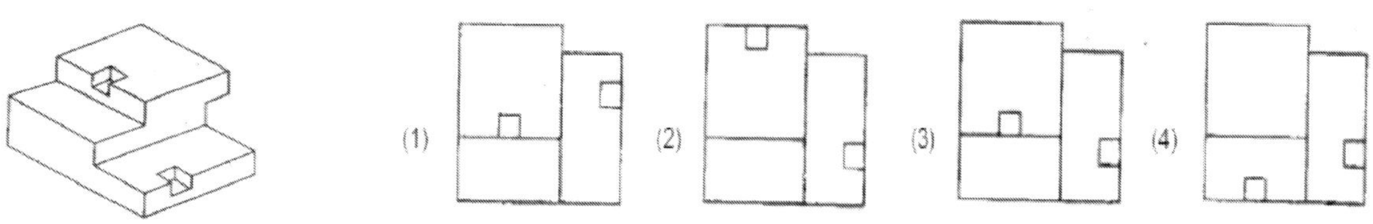

29.

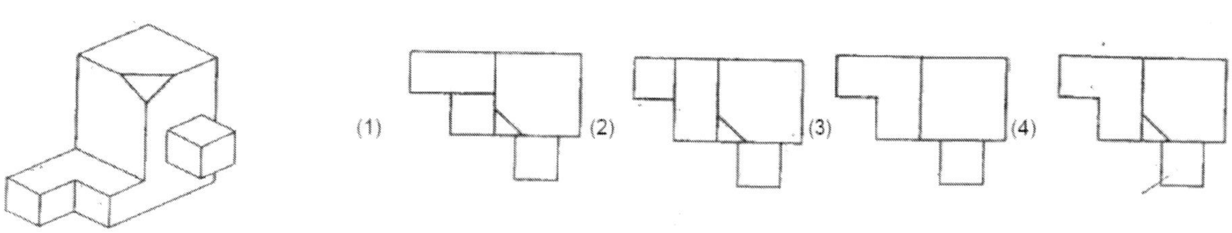

30. 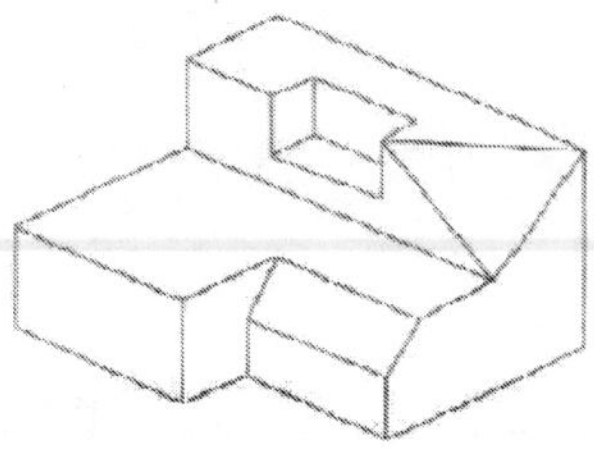

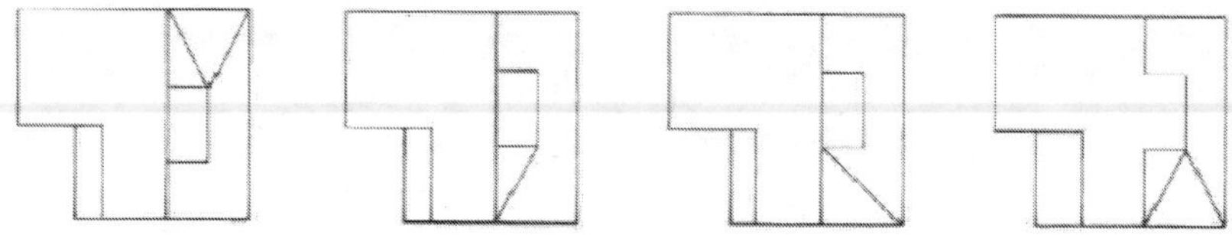

(1) (2) (3) (4)

31. 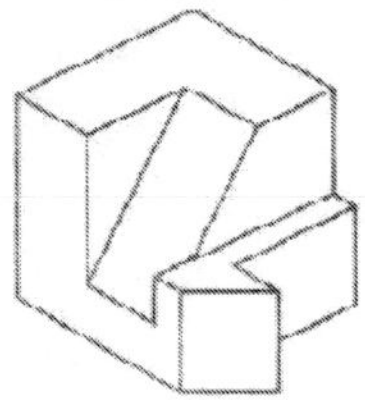

(1) (2) (3) (4)

32. 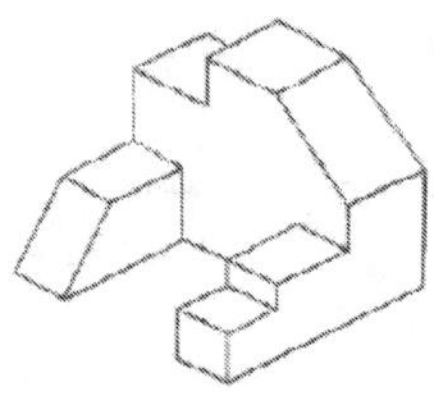

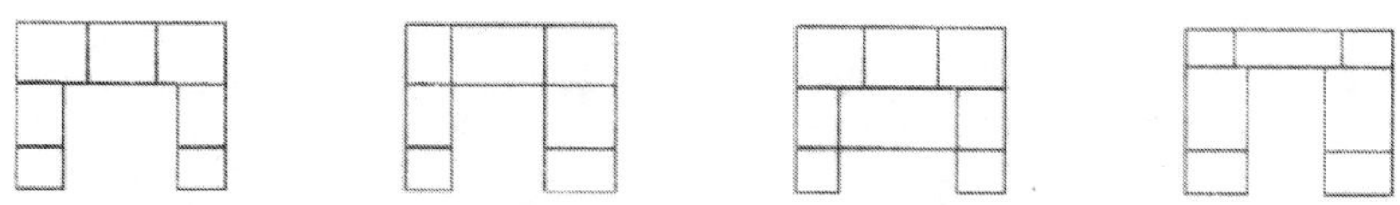

(1) (2) (3) (4)

33. 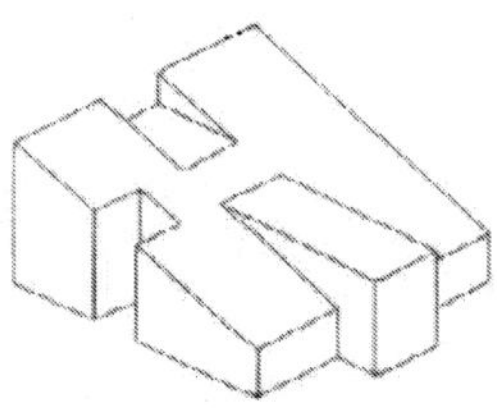

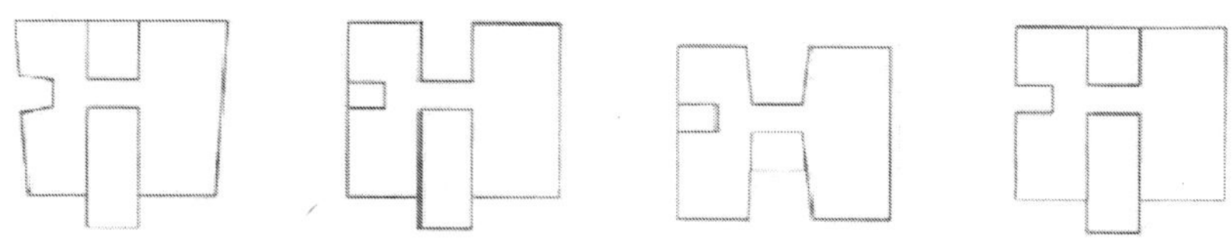

(1) (2) (3) (4)

34. 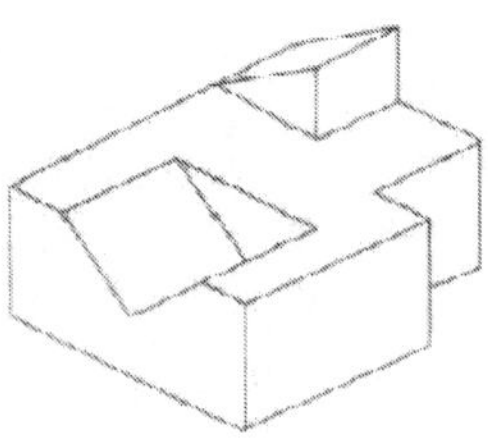

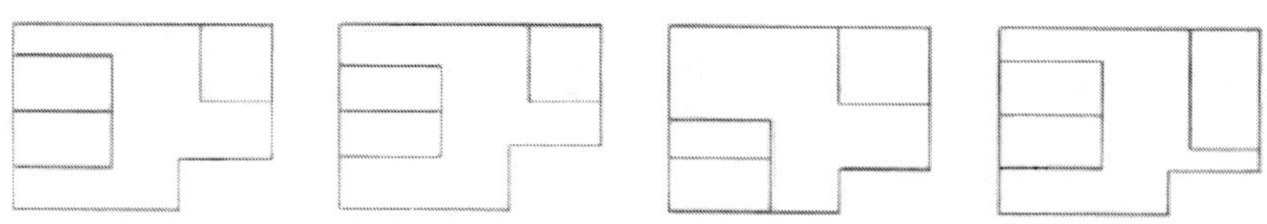

(1) (2) (3) (4)

35. 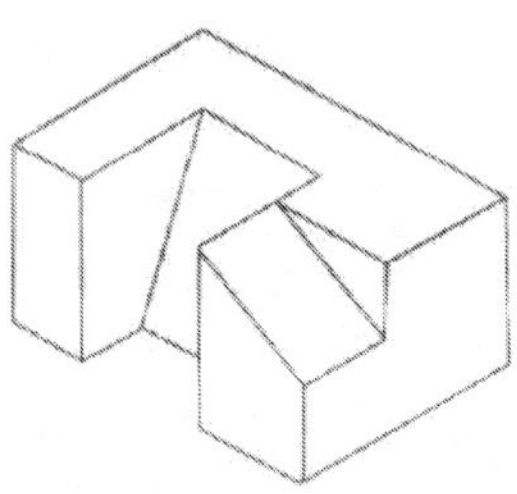

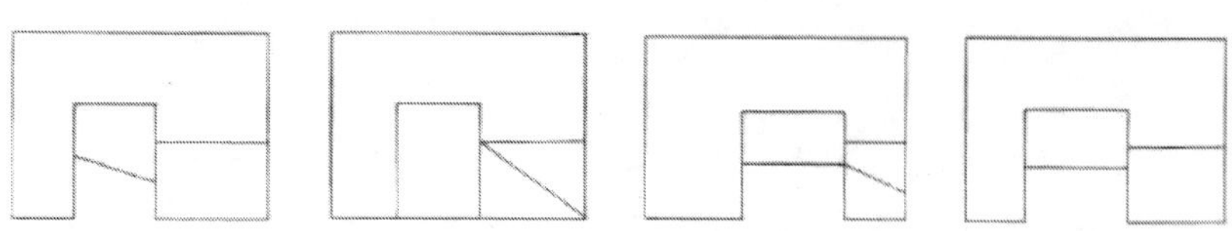

(1) (2) (3) (4)

36. 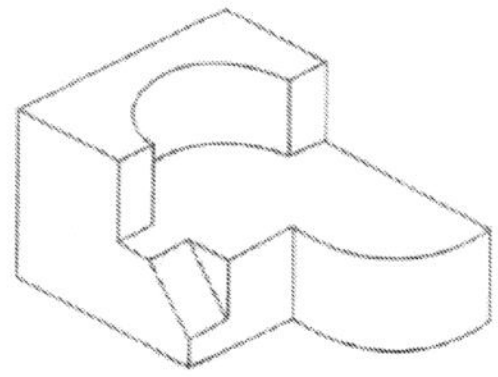

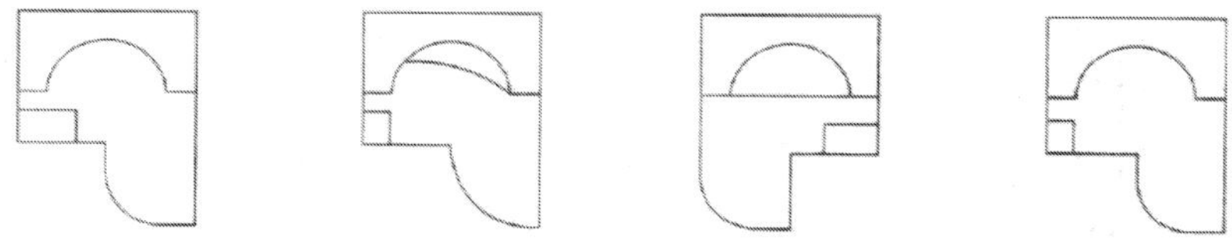

(1) (2) (3) (4)

COUNT THE NO. OF SURFACE

1. 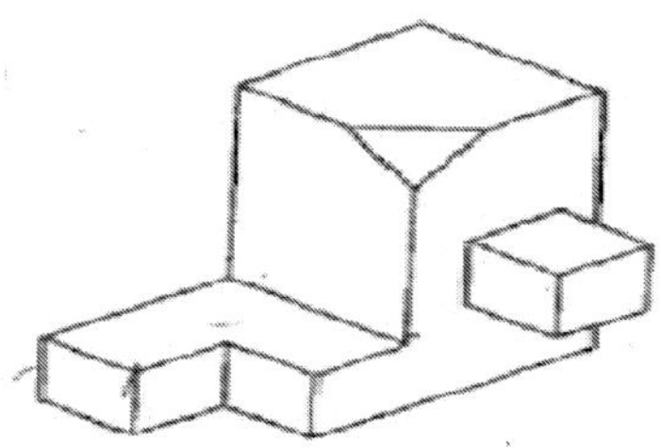

(1) 16 (2) 17 (3) 20 (4) 18

2. 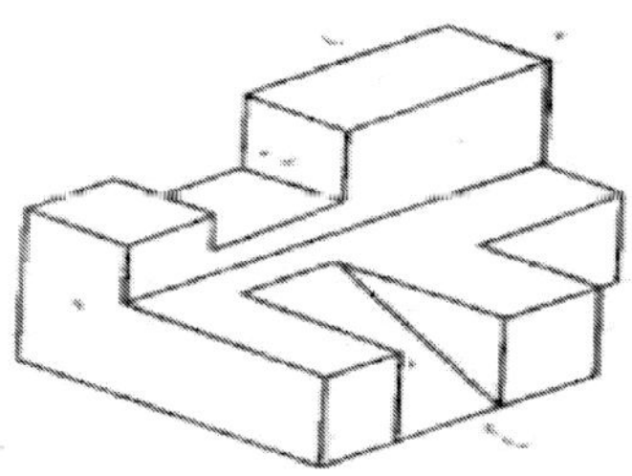

(1) 20 (2) 22 (3) 19 (4) 18

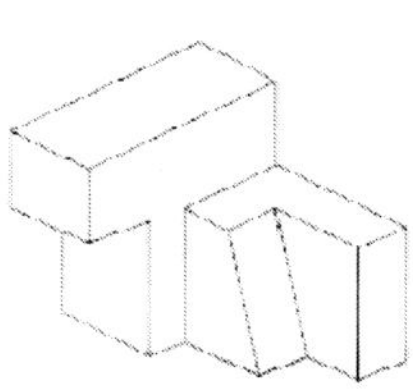

3. (1) 13 (2) 12 (3) 11 (4) 10

4. 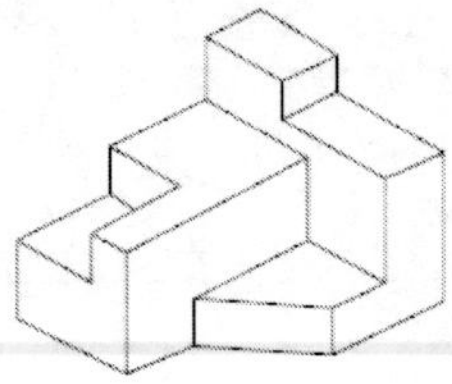

(1) 14 (2) 15 (3) 17 (4) 16

5. 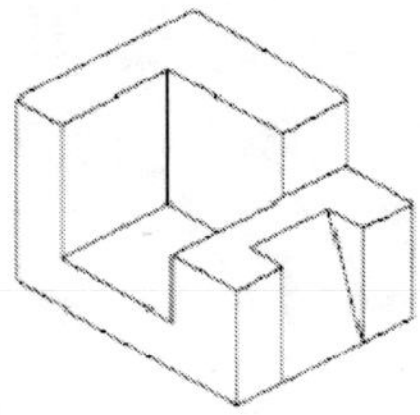

(1) 15 (2) 16 (3) 14 (4) 13

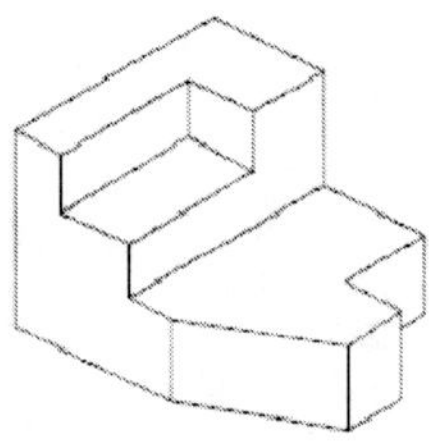

6. (1) 11 (2) 12 (3) 14 (4) 15

7. 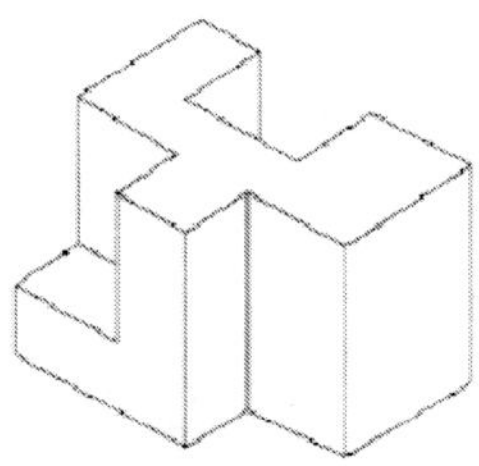

(1) 15 (2) 12 (3) 13 (4) 14

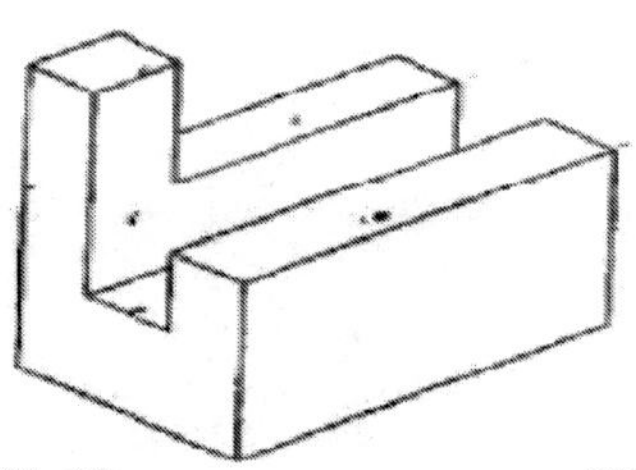

8. (1) 13 (2) 12 (3) 14 (4) 15

9. 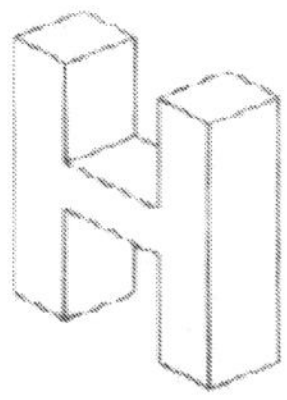

(1) 14 (2) 15 (3) 16 (4) 13

10. 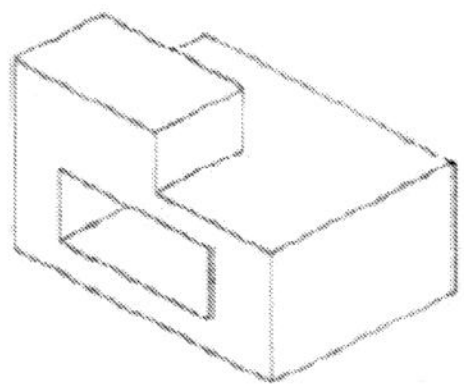

(1) 10 (2) 13 (3) 12 (4) 9

11. 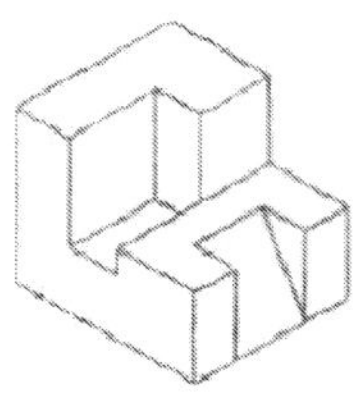

(1) 18 (2) 15 (3) 14 (4) 16

12. 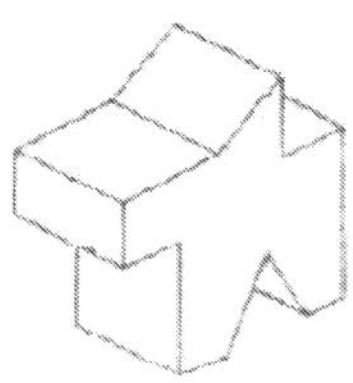

(1) 14 (2) 15 (3) 12 (4) 13

13. 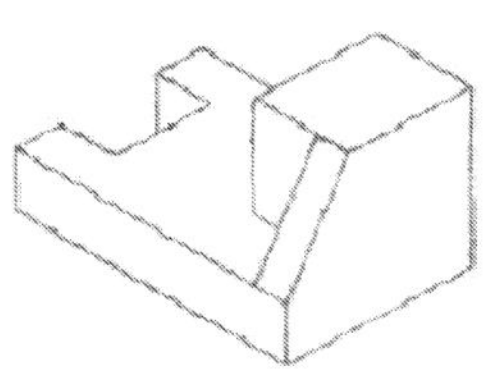

(1) 13 (2) 12 (3) 15 (4) 14

14. 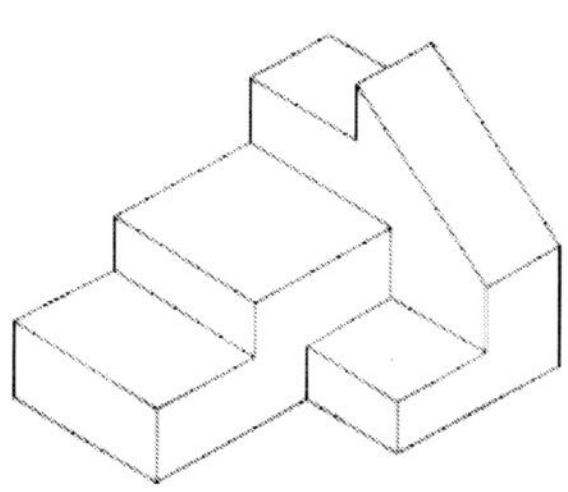

(1) 15 (2) 16 (3) 14 (4) 13

15. 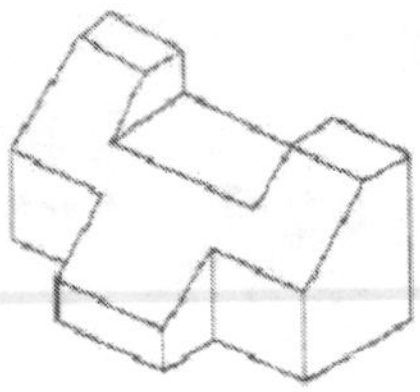

(1) 15 (2) 14 (3) 13 (4) 16

16. 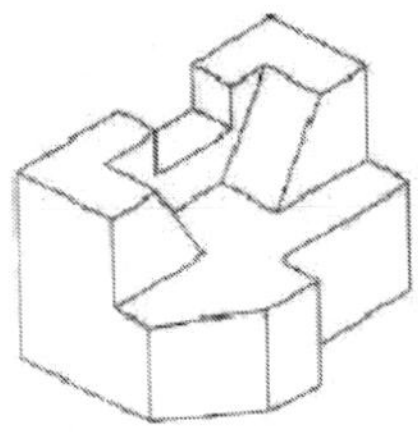

(1) 20 (2) 17 (3) 19 (4) 18

17. 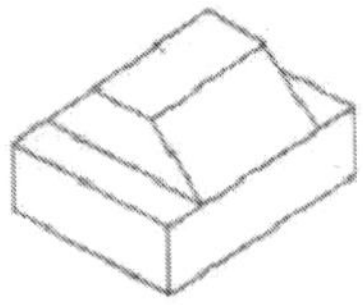

(1) 12 (2) 15 (3) 14 (4) 13

18. 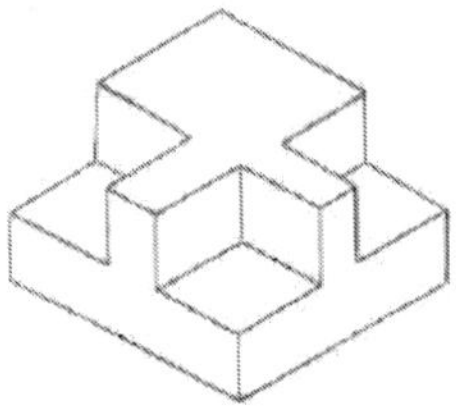

(1) 15 (2) 12 (3) 13 (4) 14

19. 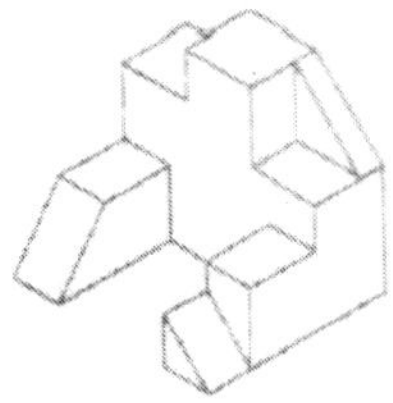

(1) 19 (2) 17 (3) 21 (4) 20

20. 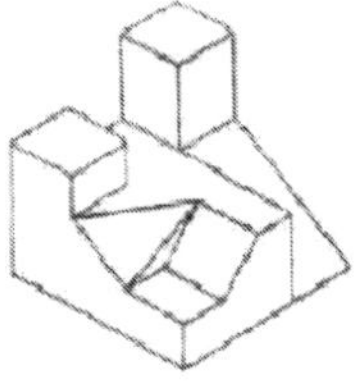

(1) 17 (2) 18 (3) 20 (4) 19

21. 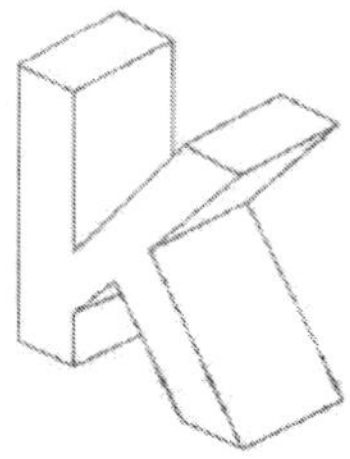

(1) 14 (2) 11 (3) 12 (4) 13

22. 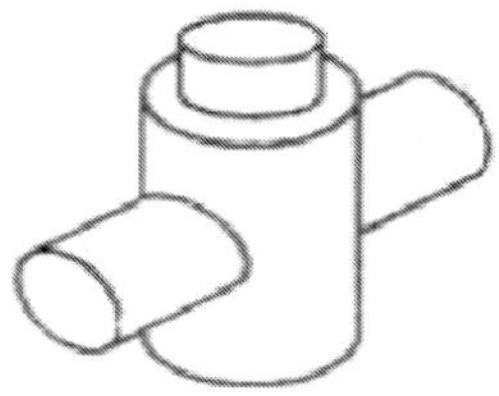

(1) 20 (2) 21 (3) 22 (4) 23

23. 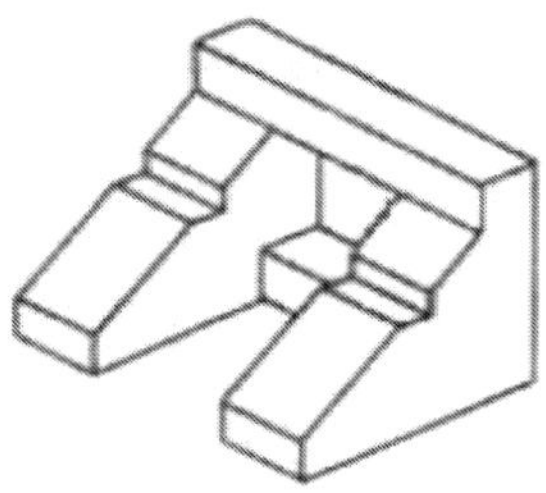

24. 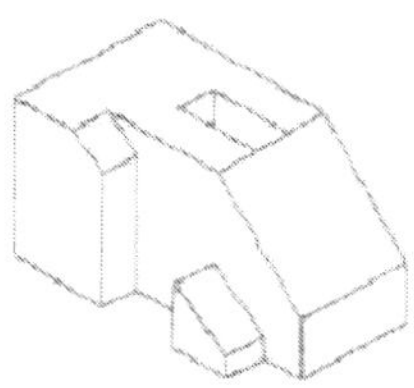

(1) 20 (2) 19 (3) 17 (4) 18

25. 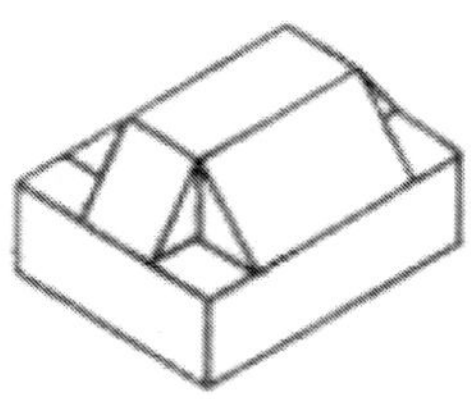

(1) 20 (2) 21 (3) 22 (4) 23

26. 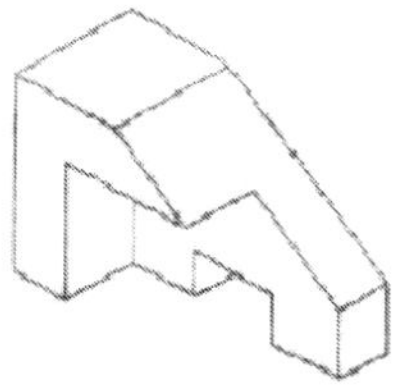

(1) 12 (2) 14 (3) 15 (4) 13

COUNT THE NO. OF SHAPES

1.

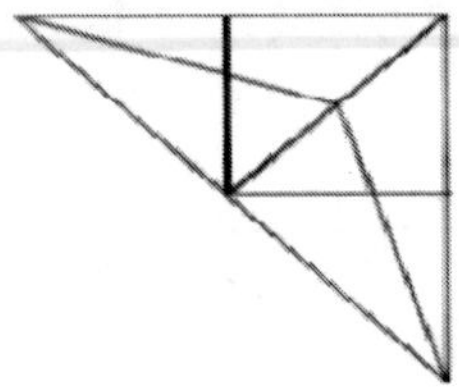

(1) 17 (2) 19 (3) 20 (4) 18

2.

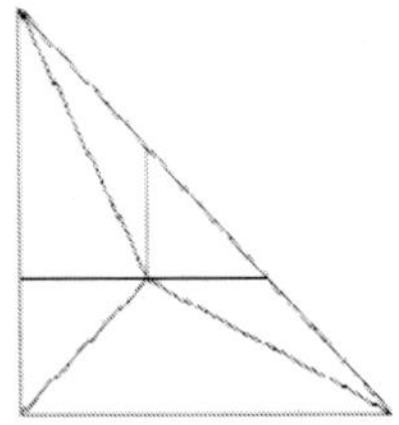

(1) 11 (2) 12 (3) 10 (4) 9

3.

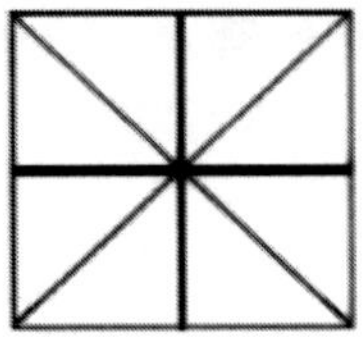

(1) 18 (2) 20 (3) 16 (4) 17

4.

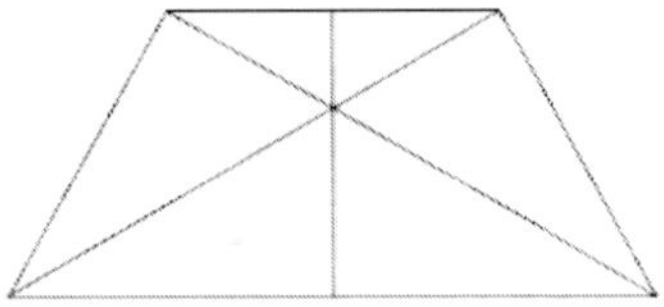

(1) 12 (2) 13 (3) 11 (4) 14

5.

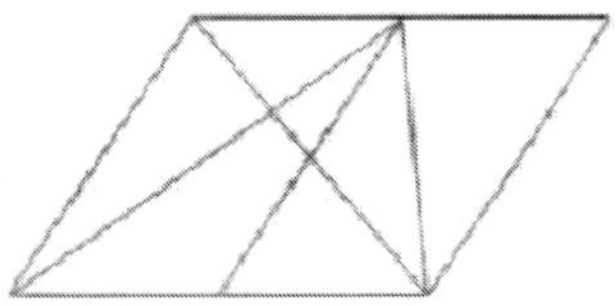

(1) 17 (2) 14 (3) 16 (4) 18

1. 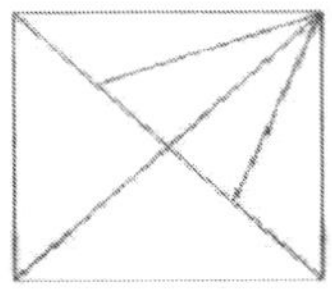

(1) 13 (2) 15 (3) 14 (4) 16

2. 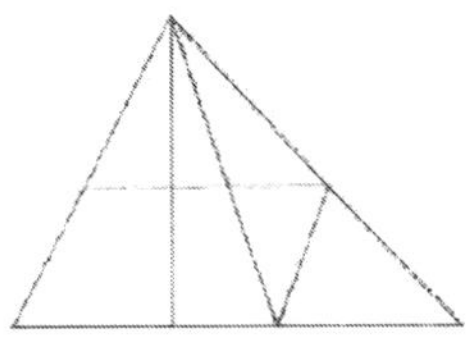

(1) 12 (2) 13 (3) 11 (4) 14

3. 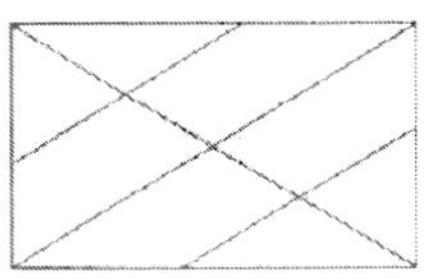

(1) 12 (2) 13 (3) 11 (4) 14

4. 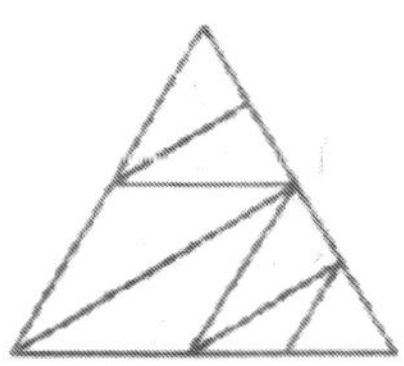

(1) 12 (2) 13 (3) 11 (4) 14

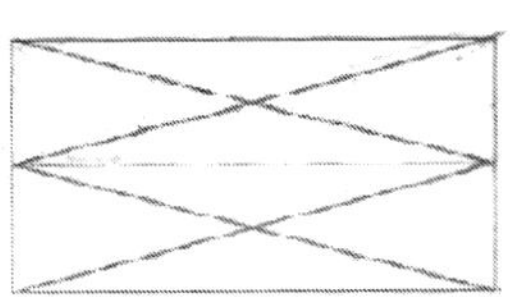

5. (1) 17 (2) 19 (3) 20 (4) 18

Count no. of squares

6.

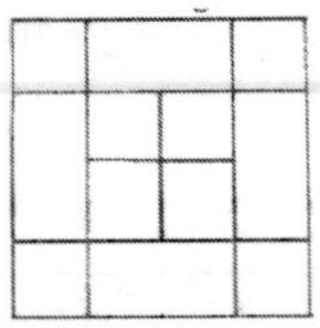

(1) 18 (2) 20 (3) 16 (4) 17

7.

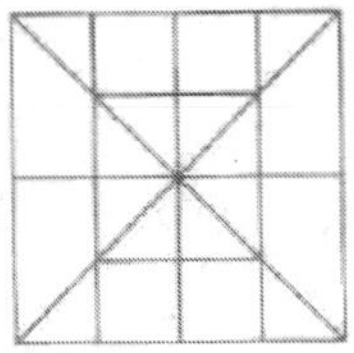

(1) 20 (2) 13 (3) 16 (4) 19

Count no. of rectangles

8.

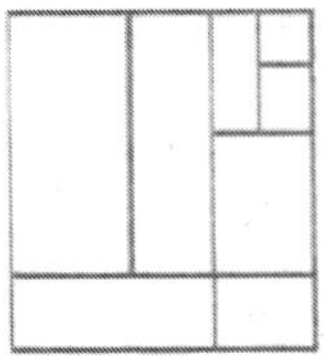

(1) 13 (2) 15 (3) 14 (4) 16

9.

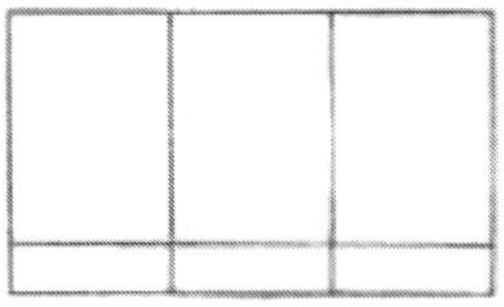

(1) 18 (2) 20 (3) 16 (4) 17

10.

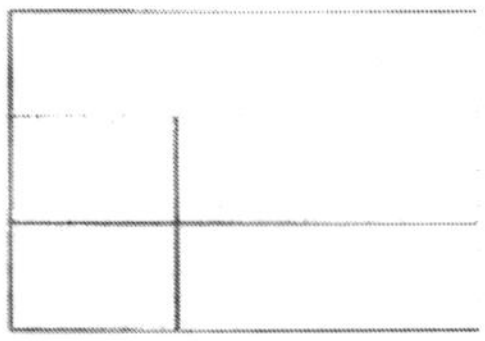

(1) 12 (2) 13 (3) 11 (4) 14

Count No. of parallelograms

11. 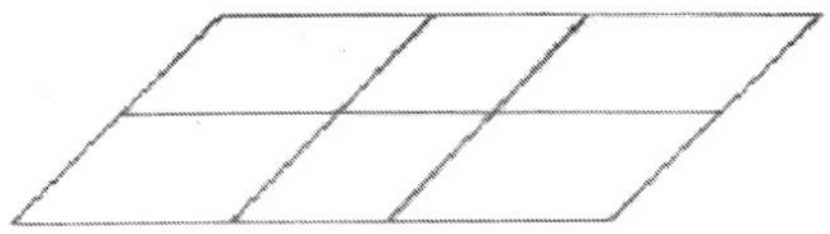

(1) 16 (2) 18 (3) 19 (4) 20

12. 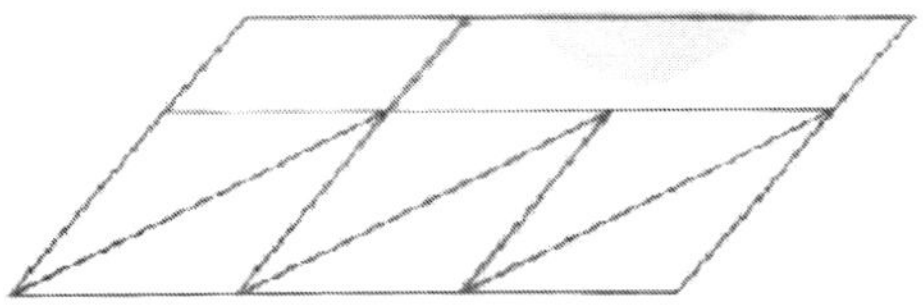

(1) 14 (2) 12 (3) 10 (4) 15

13. 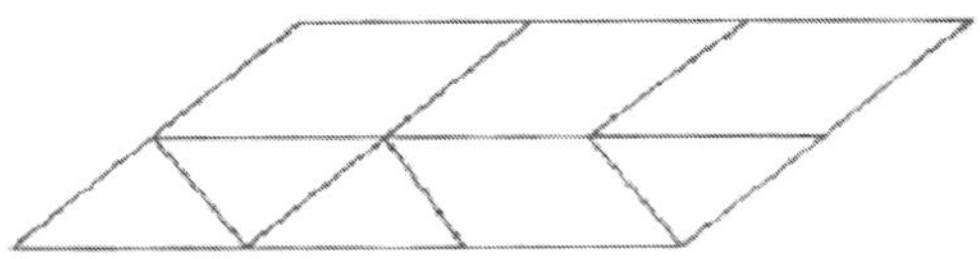

(1) 16 (2) 14 (3) 15 (4) 13

Count No. of straight lines

14.

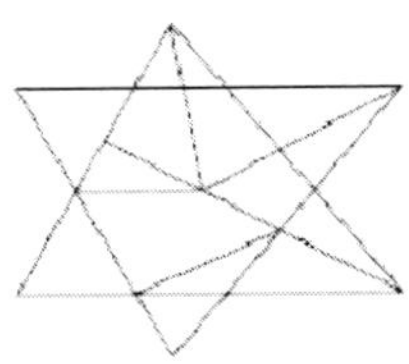

(1) 11 (2) 10 (3) 9 (4) 12

15.

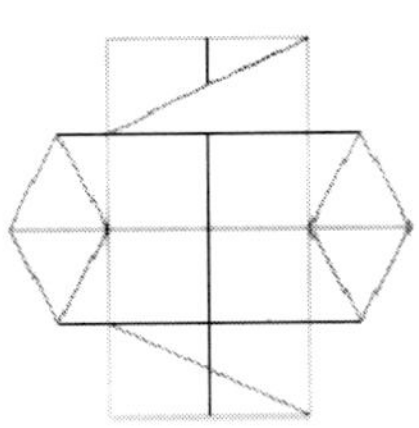

(1) 18 (2) 19 (3) 20 (4) 21

NATA QUESTION BANK

(DRAWING)

Scene Question

1. Imagine you visiting a public garden. In the garden they have a sculpture made of 8 cubes at the centre& you are standing at the corner of a cube Draw a pencil sketch of what you can see from the corner.
2. Imagine yourself to be a bird flying over the ruins of a historical site Make a pencil sketch of what you would see.
3. Imagine that your size has been reduced to 6 cm and you are sitting along with a mouse and a frog in a boat made out of paper in a big bucket inside your bathroom Draw a pencil sketch of what you would see around, sitting alongside your two companions.
4. Imagine that you are standing in the door-way of a bus as it passes by a local street market on a Sunday. Draw a pencil sketch of what you would see from your position in the bus.
5. Imagine that your size has been reduced to 6 cm and you are on the ground with your pet dog in your garden You also see two birds nearby Draw a pencil sketch of what you would see sitting alongside your companions with the view around.
6. Imagine you are reduced to 6 centimeters in height You are standing on a kitchen platform where your mother is preparing some rotis On gas stove, along with griddle there is a pot where sabji is being cooked There are some pots and utensils around on the platform Draw a pencil sketch of the scene as you see from your eyes.
7. Remember your first day to school You were 5 years old and you went to the Kindergarten holding hand of your mother/ father Some children who were already there for the first day were happy while some were crying You were curious to see the play area and number of games there Draw from your memory a pencil sketch of what you saw there.
8. You are standing in a queue at a cinema hall to get the ticket for the feature film that is popular (hit) today You can view others standing in a queue till the booking window, people standing around (not in the Queue) looking at hoardings / banners and those entering the hall beyond Draw a pencil sketch of what you see from your position.
9. You are standing in the Lobby area of a secondary school building located on its 1st floor and overlooking the courtyard surrounded by the classrooms and play area, draw a pencil sketch of what you would see.
10. n the given space draw pencil sketch of the tensed situation inside a HSC (+2) examination hall with you as the supervisor looking at it.

11. In your college cricket team you are a wicket keeper In a match you are kneeling down close to stumps as the spin bowler is approaching to deliver the next ball Draw a pencil sketch of what you see from your position.
12. In the given space draw a pencil sketch of the dilapidated ruins of an old fort.
13. Imagine that you are visiting an art gallery & there is an exhibition of paintings There is nobody in the gallery & you are alone standing in the center of gallery Draw a pencil sketch of what you would see.
14. Imagine yourself to be a Foot ball player representing famous club It's a federation cup final against another top club Stadium is full of spectators At a crucial juncture you are about to execute a Penalty kick Draw a pencil sketch of the scene as seen by you from your position in the ground [50]
15. Imagine that you are inside your house and you are looking out through the peephole of your main door Draw a pencil sketch of what you see in the lobby outside your door through the peephole.
16. Imagine yourself sitting in the last row of an auditorium to see the live dance performance Lights on the stage are on & rest of the auditorium is dark Draw a pencil sketch of whatever you will be able to see sitting there, from your seat.
17. Imagine that your size is reduced to that of a tiny caterpillar and you are moving through a pile of vegetables in a market Draw a pencil sketch of the view of the market as you would see while moving through the pile.
18. Assume Your size is 5cm. it is raining. kids are playing with paper boats in puddles. you are sitting on the board and enjoying the ride. the kids are laughing at you. draw what you see!
19. You are looking out of a window. It's a normal window with a wooden panel & horizontal bars (grills). You can see a playground with play equipment & some children playing. There is a small building & a hospital after that. Draw your view from your imagination.
20. There is a inter school quiz competition going on in an historical school assembly hall. There are two students in each group and there are three groups. The other three sides of the hall is occupied by audience with the quiz master standing in the middle of one side, you are sitting on two top row of a side. Sketch what you see.

2D QUESTIONS

1. Design and draw a logo for a voluntary social organization working to help visually challenged persons. You can use maximum three different shapes and three colors.
2. In the given space, create a geometrical composition by using three primary shapes circle/ triangle and square The composition is to be created by using each shape not more than 4 times. Color the composition using secondary colors.
3. A car manufacturing company wants to design its logo to be used on the front and rear bonnet of the car. The same logo will also be used in advertisements in color You can use primary shapes like square, rectangle, circle, etc and also few letters

(alphabets) to compose the logo Draw the logo in the given space and Color the composition using 2 colors.

4. In the given space, draw a large square and divide the same using 6 straight lines (at any angle) and one curved line. Color the composition using not more than 4 colors. All the lines and rectangle must be drawn freehand.
5. Create and draw a two dimensional composition using profile of a 'Electric Bulb' in the given space and color the same using any three colors of our choice. You may overlap the profiles and use the profiles multiple times.
6. Create and draw a two dimensional composition using profile of a 'Key' in the given space and color the same using any three colors of your choice .You may overlap the profiles and use the profiles multiple times.
7. For lobby of drama theatre in your town design a mural 10 meters long and 2 meters high Draw a proportionate sketch of the mural and color the same using maximum four colors in the given space.
8. Draw a composition using 3 shapes (Circle, Triangle, Rectangle etc) each used twice in the composition that can be used as a logo. Color with appropriate color scheme.
9. Using line profiles of aquatic life (Fish, Tortoise, Octopus, etc) create an interesting composition to serve as a signage for an Aquarium. Color the same using not more than three colors of your choice (Note: Internal details in shapes are not expected. Use not more than 3 basic profiles. Repetition of single profile in different sizes and orientation is allowed Overlapping allowed).
10. Design a logo of 'Hockey game' with the use of rectangle & circle. Draw the logo in the given space and color the logo using not more than 3 colors.
11. Depict, draw and color a household fish tank (Aquarium) as a two dimensional composition with fish of various sizes, shapes and color.
12. Create and draw a two dimensional composition using profile of a 'Leaf' in the given space and color the same using any three colors of your choice .You may overlap the profiles and use the profiles multiple times.
13. Create and draw a two dimensional composition using profile of a 'Shoe' in the given space and color the same using any three colors of your choice .You may overlap the profiles and use the profiles multiple times.
14. A Renowned Indian mobile service company wants to redesign their logo. Draw a logo for them so that it attracts customers of all age groups and color it appropriately.
15. Make an interesting 2d composition with 5 playing cards and using three colors only.
16. Create a logo for motor-cycle Company and color the same by using primary colors only.
17. Design a bed sheet for a children's bedroom using basic geometric shapes. Each shape cannot be used only twice. And maximum 4 colors.
18. Draw a logo 4 kabbadi game using rectangles, circles and triangles. Use only 3 colors.
19. Draw a logo for a TV News channel, First You have to think channel name and then draw a Logo accordingly. Color it with any three colors.
20. Draw the logo of a shoe company using circles and triangles only and color it with not more than three colors.

3D QUESTIONS

1. Make a 3D composition with the 6 glucose biscuits & a ball in the space provided. Also show the effect of Light & shadow on it.
2. In the given space make an interesting three dimensional stable composition using two square boxes, one rectangular box & one pyramid. Also show the effect of light & shadow on the composition.
3. On your grandfathers study desk you find there are 3 thick books, a pair of reading glasses, a magnifying glass, a table clock and glass of drinking water lying there. You place these objects in a manner to make attractive sculpture like composition. Draw in pencil only the composition as seen from one of the angles and also show shades and shadows on it.
4. 3 to 4 Books of sizes 20 cm x 10 cm and 300 to 500 pages each are kept vertically at a distance 8cm from each other on a book rack. The light source on the left at angle of 45 degrees. Draw out the 3D composition showing the shadow pattern.
5. On a dining table where you are seating, in a small plate (18 cm diameter). One Pineapple, Two Mangos, Two Bananas and bunch of grapes are arranged. Draw a pencil sketch of the dish and fruits as seen by you. Imagine light falling on it from left hand side Render the sketch with shades and shadow.
6. A clay pot, A bamboo basket & a brass cooking pot are kept on the dining table You have to keep appropriate materials in all the 3 objects & compose them Draw a pencil sketch of the 3D composition on the table top with the shade and shadow effects showing the materials of the objects.
7. In the given space make an interesting three dimensional stable composition using three cricket balls, one cricket bat, stumps & a cap. Also show the effect of light & shadow on the composition.
8. Draw a three dimensional composition using various size cylinders (Minimum 4) to represent a tall building. Draw using pencil only and show shades and shadows on the composition.
9. Arrange a bucket, a tumbler, an earthen pot, a piece of cloth and rectangular box to make an interesting, stable arrangement like a still life. Draw pencil sketch of the composition showing light and shade in the given space.
10. In the given rectangle make a stable, interesting looking composition using 4 earthen pots of any shape and size placed in a group, show shade & shadow on the composition.
11. Using the objects - 3 notebooks, one orange and two walking sticks create a stable form and draw its view from interesting angle. Then show the effect of light thrown at your form from the left direction and draw the shadow cast by it on the ground.
12. Using 7 cubes of different sizes create a sense of opening and steps. Also show the effect of light and shadow.
13. You have 1 empty bowl,1 glass,2 forks,1 spoon and handkerchief draw a 3d composition giving light and shadow effect like light is coming through your left.

14. Using 4 parts of a luggage draw a composition. Light is falling from the left side. Shade it.
15. Using at least 4 cylinders show a tall building. Show light n shadow.
16. You have six automobile tyres. Arrange them and form a visually attractive sculpture, viewing from one angle and light is coming from the other angle. Show shadow and lightning effect.
17. Compose and sketch a sculpture from 4 cubes. But some cubes are opaque n some transparent give light n shadow.
18. You are provided with 2 prism and 2 pyramid make a stable composition with the effect of light and shade . Assume the light is falling on objects from right hand side . use the space provided.
19. Make a stable 3 D composition with help of 2 bricks , 2 Stone , and 2 wooden logs of same size . Show the effect of light falling from left hand size.
20. With the help of utensils make a stable 3d composition .Show the effect of light.

TEST PAPER-1

Q.1) The length of sides AB and AC in the triangle below are equal. What is the measure of angle ∠ A?

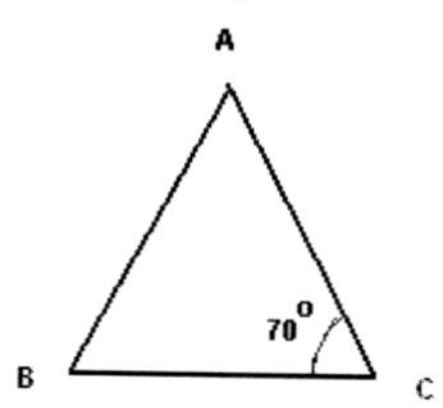

a. 55°
b. 18°
c. 40°
d. 22°

Q.2) Look at this series: 53, 53, 40, 40, 27, 27, ... What number should come next ?

a. 27
b. 13
c. 12
d. 14

Q.3) Out of the five figures given below, four belongs to a group. Identify the figure does not belong to the group.

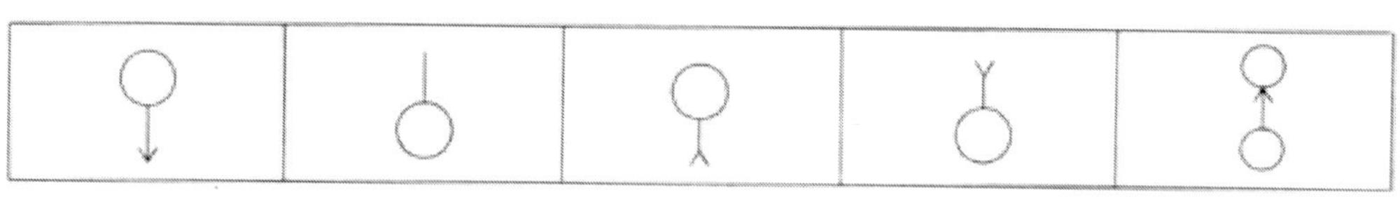

a. "A" does not belong to the group

A B C D E

Q.4) The area of a trapezoid is 0.5h (b1 + b2), where h is the altitude, and b1 and b2 are the lengths of the parallel bases. If a trapezoid has an altitude of 15 inches, an area of 105 square inches, and one of the bases 22 inches, what is the perimeter, in inches, of the trapezoid?

a. 40

b. 30

c. cannot be determined from the given information

d. 50

Q5.) If the patterns shown on left hand side are cut and folded which one of the pattern shown on right hand side with match ?

Problem Figure

Answer Figures

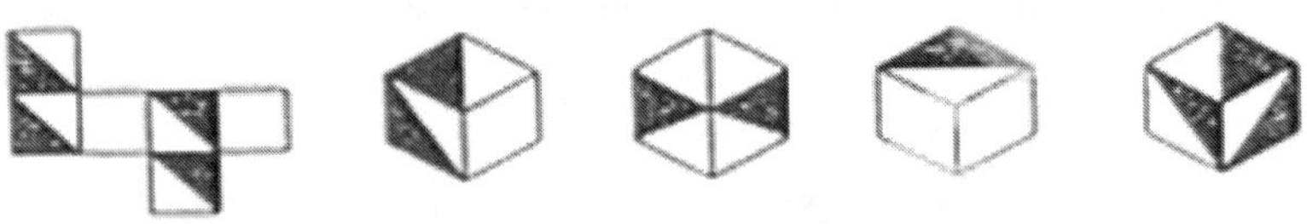

A B C D

a. "B" option is correct

b. "A" option is correct

c. "C" option is correct

d. "D" option is correct

Q6.) If the patterns shown on the left hand side are cut and folded which one of the pattern shown on right hand side will match ?

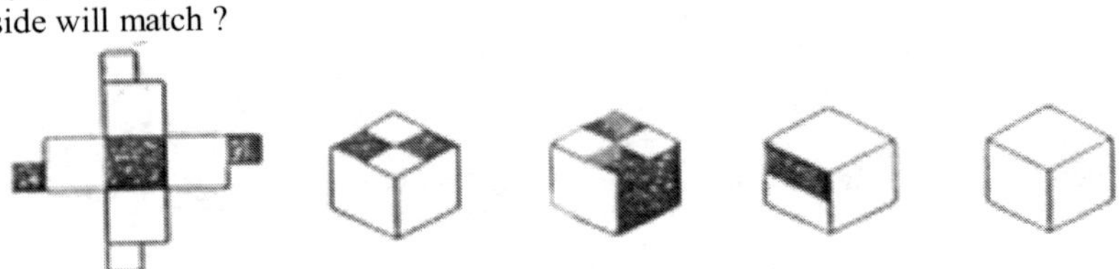

A B C D

a. "A" option is correct

b. "C" option is correct

c. "D" option is correct

d. "B" option is correct

Q7.) If the key word is Quit, fit in the correct synonym in the space in each question.
Which word is the antonym of "sunny", as in "it is sunny outside, today"?

a. Hot
b. Cloudy
c. Wet
d. Windy

Q8.) The Vijaya Nagar empire owes its origin to :

a. Harshvardhana
b. Harihara & Bukla
c. Raja Ram
d. Krishnadev ray

Q.9.) A group of Pieces on the right side when assembled form the figure on the left. Mark the correct set of pieces.

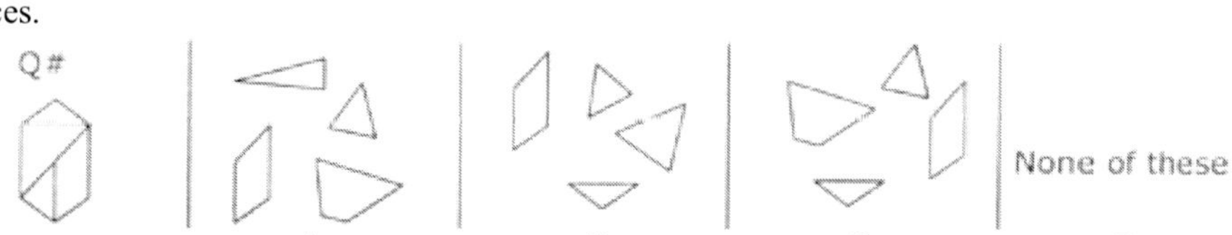

A B C D

a. "D" option is correct
b. "C" option is correct
c. "A" option is correct
d. "B" option is correct

Q.10) One of the 4 alternatives given on the right when folded along the dotted lines will form the figure on the extreme left. Suggest which will exactly form the problem figure.

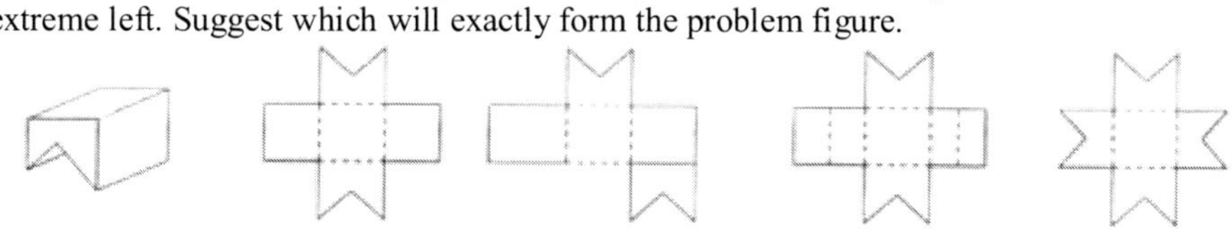

A B C D

a. "B" option is correct
b. "A" option is correct
c. "D" option is correct
d. "C" option is correct

Q.11) Find out the surfaces of solid object shown below

a. 7

b. 8

c. 6

d. 9

Q.12) In the standard (x,y) coordinate plane, the graph of (x + 3)2 + (y + 5)2 = 16 is a circle. What is the circumference of the circle, expressed in coordinate units?

a. 11π

b. 4π

c. 12π

d. 8π

Q.13) Find dy/dx where x and y are related by the parametric equations: x = ln(t) + t and y = t - ln(t)

a. -(t + 1) / (t - 1)

b. (t - 1) / (t + 1)

c. (t + 1) / (t - 1)

d. -(t - 1) / (t + 1)

Q.14) Following the sequence of instruction in question which of the composite figure is obtained

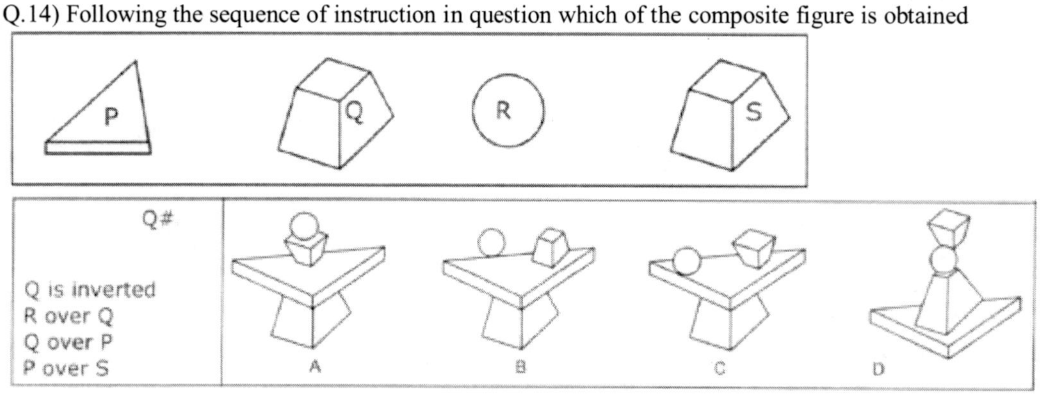

Q.15) 3-Dimension problem figure shows the view of an object; identify correct top view (Plan)

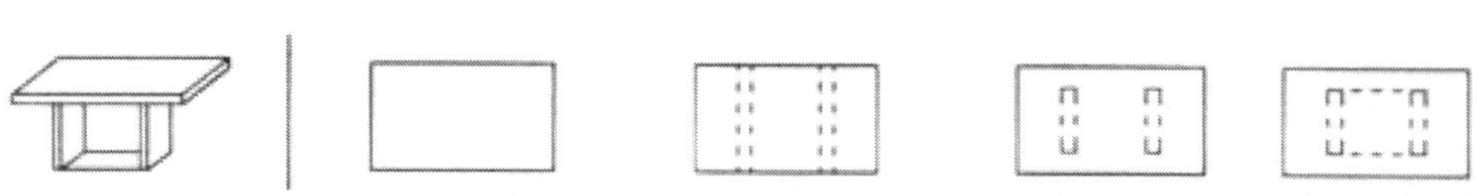

A B C D

a. "C" option is correct

b. "D" option is correct

c. "B" option is correct

d. "A" option is correct

Q.16) One of the 4 alternatives given on the right when folded along the dotted lines will form the figure on the extreme left. Suggest which will exactly form the problem figure.

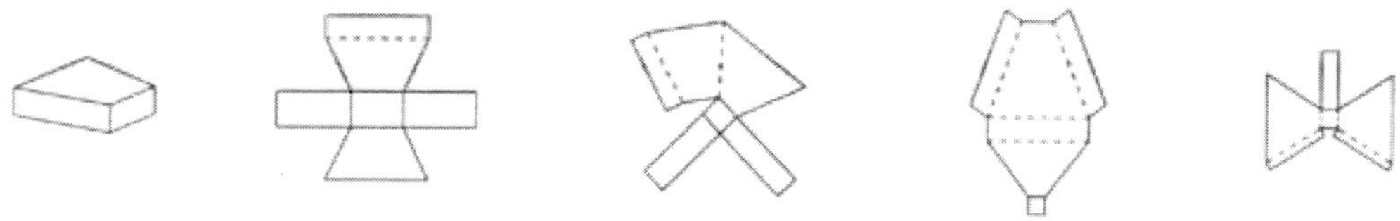

A B C D

a. "B" option is correct
b. "C" option is correct
c. "A" option is correct
d. "D" option is correct

Q.17) Angle A is an acute angle and sin(A) = 11/14. What is the value of cos(A)?

a. none
b. 5/14
c. √(3/14)
d. 5√3 / 14

Q.18) A group of Pieces on the right side when assembled form the figure on the left. Mark the correct set of pieces

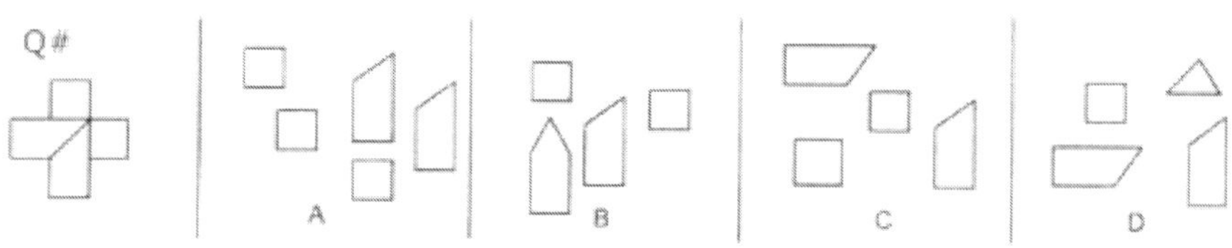

a. "B" option is correct
b. "D" option is correct
c. "C" option is correct
d. "A" option is correct

Q.19) If f(n) = n + √n, where n is a positive integer, which of the following would be a value of f(n)?
I) 5 II) 10 III) 12

a. I and III only
b. I, II and III only
c. III only
d. II and III only

Q.20) A circle with center (4,-5) is tangent to the y-axis in the standard (x,y) coordinate plane. What is the radius of this circle?

a. 4
b. 5
c. √4
d. √5

Q.21) There are n students in a school. If r% among the students are 12 years or younger, which of the following expressions represents the number of students who are older than 12 ?

a. n (100-r) / 100
b. n (1-r) / 100
c. 100(1-r) n
d. n (1-r)

Q.22) Problem shows the Top view of an object. Identify correct 3-D view of the object from the Answer figures

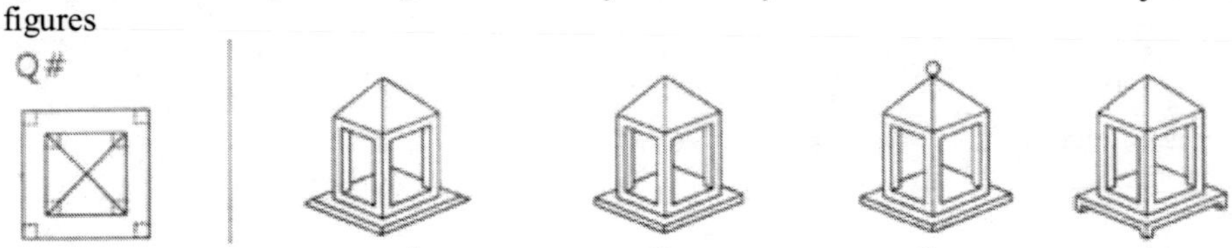

A B C D

a. "A" option is correct
b. "B" option is correct
c. "D" option is correct
d. "C" option is correct

Q.23 ... extre ... ed along the dotted lines will form the figure on the ... gure.

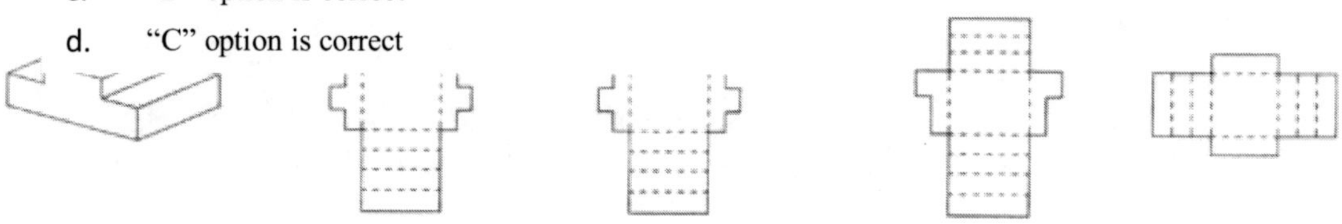

A B C D

a. "C" option is correct
b. "D" option is correct
c. "B" option is correct
d. "A" option is correct

Q.24) Find out the surfaces of solid object shown below.

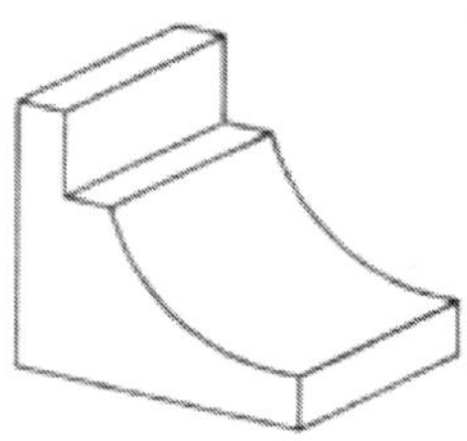

a. 12
b. 10
c. 8
d. 9

Q.25) 3-Dimension problem figure shows the view of an object, identify correct top view (Plan)

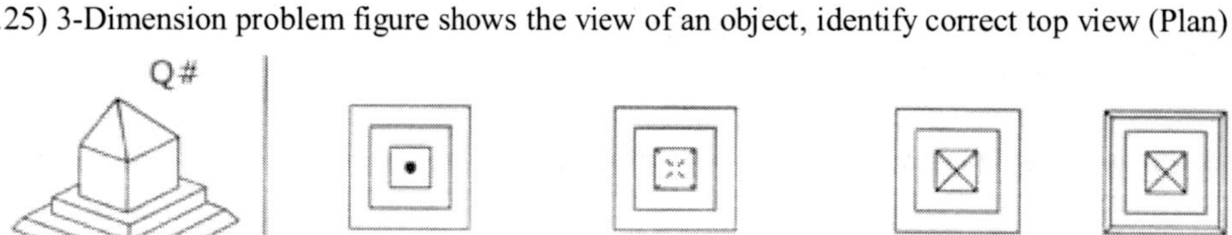

A B C D

a. "B" option is correct
b. "C" option is correct

Q.26) Find out the surfaces of the solid object shown below

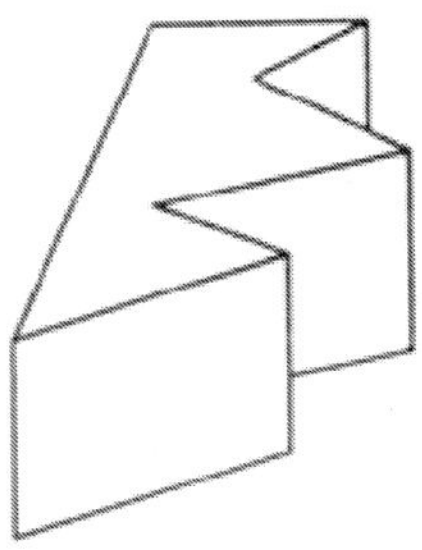

a. 7
b. 8
c. 10
d. 9

Q.27) Following the sequence of instruction in question which of the composite figure is obtained

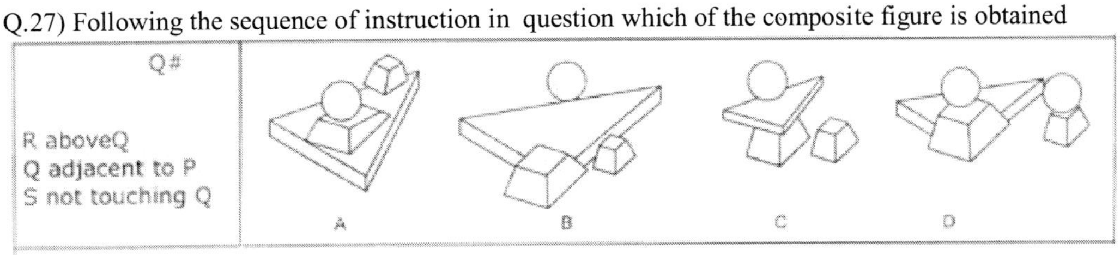

a. "B" option is correct
b. "A" option is correct
c. "D" option is correct
d. "C" option is correct

Q.28) Out of the five figures given below, four belongs to a group. Identify the figure does not belong to the group.

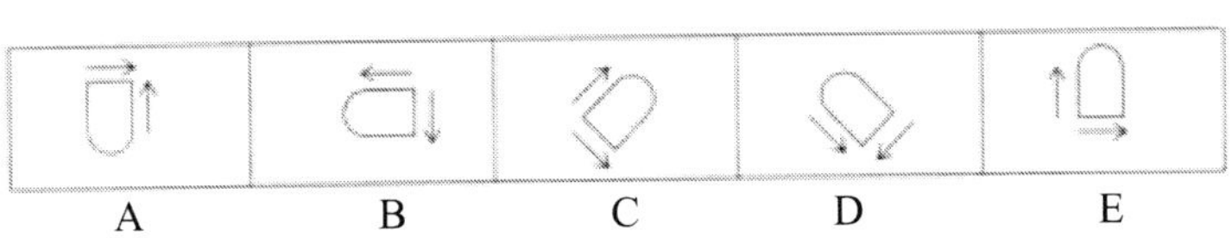

A B C D E

a. "D" does not belong in the group
b. "A" does not belong in the group
c. "C" does not belong in the group
d. "B" does not belong in the group

Q.29) Out of the five figures given below, four belongs to a group. Identify the figure does not belong to the group.

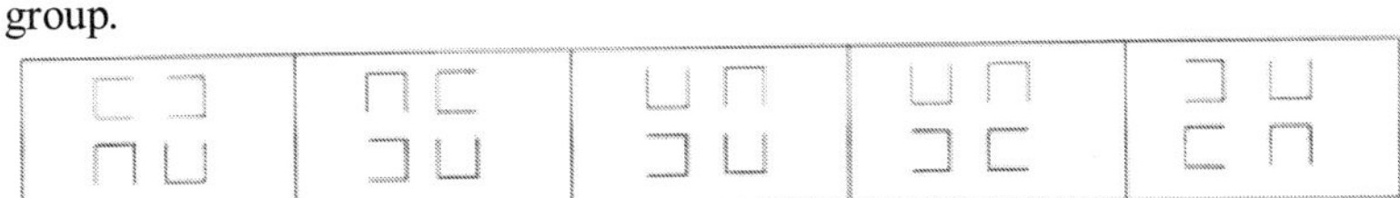

A B C D E

a. "B" does not belong in the group
b. "C" does not belong in the group
c. "D" does not belong in the group
d. "A" does not belong in the group

Q.30) In these series, you will be looking at both the letter pattern and the number pattern. Fill the blank in the middle of the series or end of the series.
B2CD, _____, BCD4, B5CD, BC6D

a. BC3D
b. B3CD
c. BC2D

Q.31) Look at this series: 22, 21, 23, 22, 24, 23, ... What number should come next ?

a. 23

b. 24

c. 22

d. 25

Q.32) One of the 4 alternatives given on the right when folded along the dotted lines will form the figure on the extreme left. suggest, which will exactly form the problem figure.

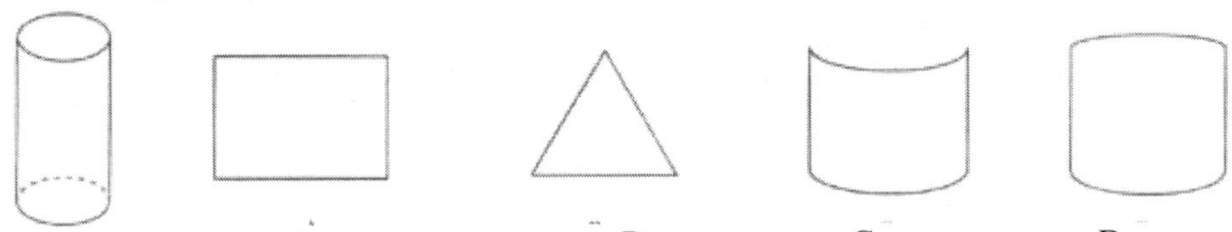

A B C D

a. "C" option is correct

b. "A" option is correct

c. "D" option is correct

d. "B" option is correct

Q.33) For all x >2, (2x2 + 2x - 12) / (x - 2) simplifies to

a. 2(x+3)(x-2)
b. 2(x+3)
c. 2(x-2)
d. none

Q.34) 3-Dimension problem figure shows the view of an object, identify correct top view (Plan)

Q#

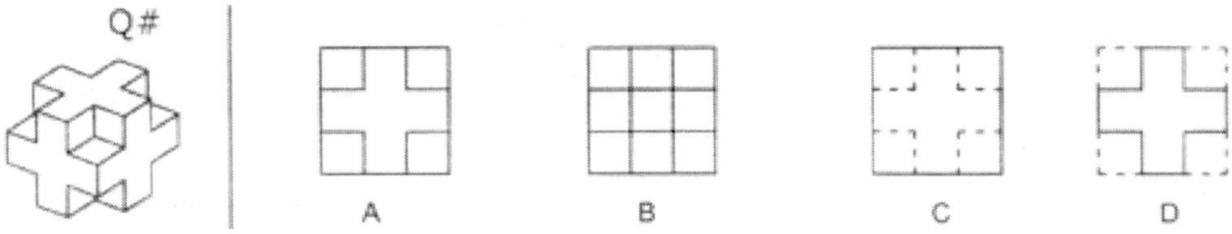

A B C D

a. "D" option is correct

b. "B" option is correct

c. "A" option is correct

d. "C" option is correct

Q.35) If a and b are both even numbers, which of the following COULD be and odd integer?

a. (a+b)2

b. (a-b)2

c. (a+1)2+(b+1)2

d. (a+1)/ (b+1)

Q.36) The total surface area of all six sides of the rectangular box below is equal to 128 square inches. What is x in inches?

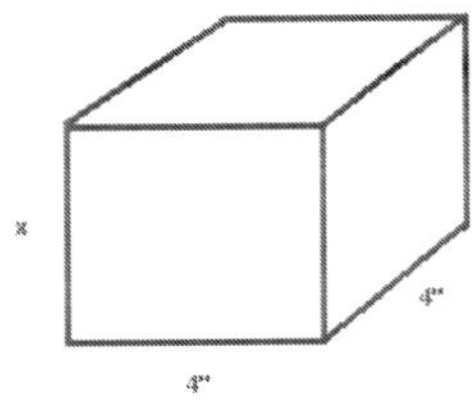

a. 5

b. 4

c. 6

d. 8

Q.37) One of the 4 alternatives given on the right when folded along the dotted lines will form the figure on the extreme left.Suggest, which will exactly form the problem figure.

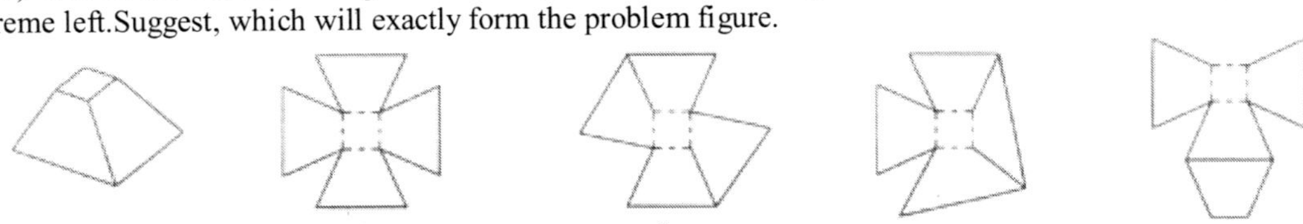

a. "D" option is correct

b. "C" option is correct

c. "B" option is correct

d. "A" option is correct

Q.38) The set of all values of K so that the graph of f(x) = x4 - 14x2 + 24x + K has two distinct x intercepts is given by
Response:

a. (-infinity , -11) U (-8 , 117)

b. (-100, -11) U (-11 , 130)

c. (-infinity , +infinity)

d. (0 , +infinity)

Q.39) In the figure below, half a period of sin(x) from 0 to Pi is split into two regions (yellow and green) of equal area by a line through the origin. The line and the sine function intersect at a point whose x coordinate is K. What equation does K satisfy ?

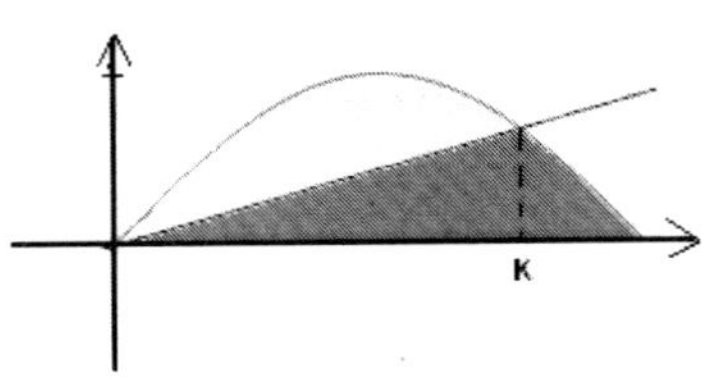

a. K cos(K) = sin(K)

b. sin(K) = K

c. K sin(K) + 2 cos(K) = 0

d. (2 + K) sin(K) + 2 cos(K) = 0

Q.40) Problem shows the Top view of an object. Identify correct 3-D view of the object from the Answer figures

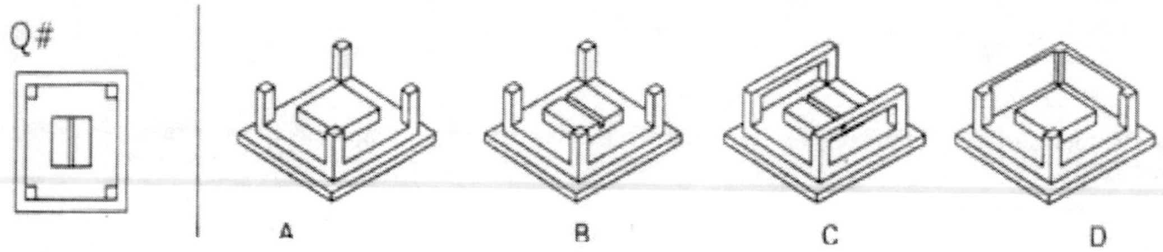

a. "C" option is correct
b. "A" option is correct
c. "D" option is correct
d. "B" option is correct

Q.41) Who is The Architect of Sydney Opera House "a multi-venue performing arts centre" in the Australia.

a. Alvar Aalto
b. JørnUtzon
c. Alvaro siza
d. Antonio Gaudi

Q.42) One of the 4 alternatives given on the right when folded along the dotted lines will form the figure on the extreme left. suggest, which will exactly form the problem figure.

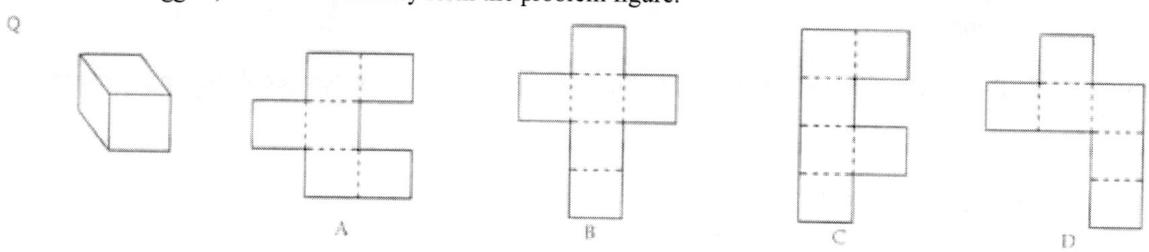

a. "C" option is correct
b. "D" option is correct
c. "B" option is correct
d. "A" option is correct

Q.43) The two legs of a right triangle measure 6 and 8 inches respectively. What is the area of the circle that contains all 3 vertices of the triangle?

a. 36Pi
b. 25Pi
c. 64Pi
d. 48Pi

Q.44) One of the 4 alternatives given on the right when folded along the dotted lines will form the figure on the extreme left. suggest, which will exactly form the problem figure.

A B C D

a. "B" option is correct
b. "D" option is correct
c. "A" option is correct
d. "C" option is correct

Q45.) The 'Stupas' at sanchi portray, the art and sculpture of :

a. Early Aaryans
b. Buddhists
c. Muslims
d. Jains

Q46.)I the letter pattern and the number pattern. Fill the blank in the middle of the series or end of the series.
FAG, GAF, HAI, IAH, ____

a. HAK
b. JAI
c. JAK
d. HAL

Q47.) Find the number of rectangle in the given object:

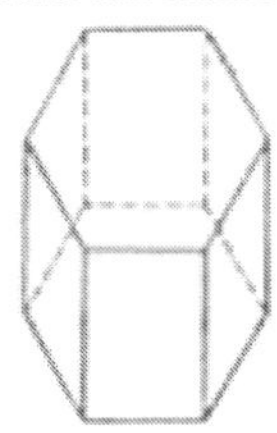

a. 7
b. 6
c. 15
d. 10

Q48.) Central Building Research Institute is located at :

a. Mumbai
b. Roorkee
c. Chennai
d. New Delhi

Q49.) Ayodhya is situated on the bank of river :

a. Saryu
b. Yamuna
c. Ganga
d. Gomati

Q50.) If the key word is Quit, fit in the correct synonym in the space in each question. Which word is the antonym of "happy", as in "you make me very happy"?

a. Content
b. Sad
c. Joyful
d. Laughing

Q51.) A mixture of water and alcohol can be separated by

a. Evaporation
b. Decantation
c. Distillation
d. Filtration

Q52.) 'Buland Darwaza' was built by :

a. Akbar
b. Aurangzeb
c. Ashoka
d. Shahjahan

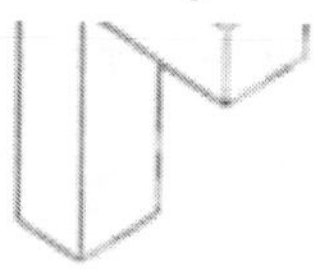

a. 2
b. 4
c. 6
d. 8

Q54.) If the patterns shown on the left hand side are cut and folded which one of the pattern shown on right hand
side with match ?

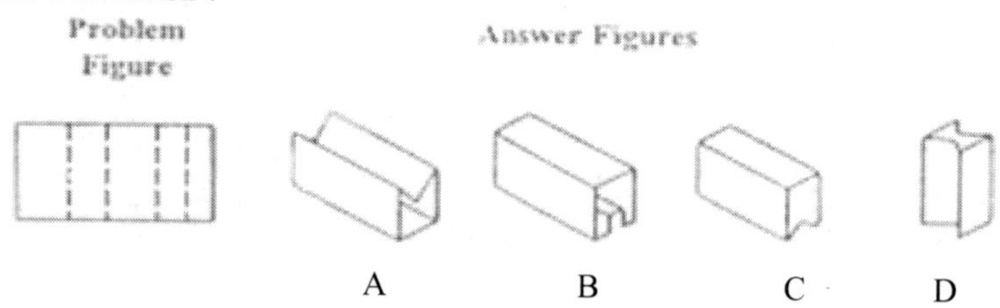

a. "A" option is correct
b. "D" option is correct
c. "C" option is correct
d. "B" option is correct

Q55.) The question shows a photograph of an architecturally important building. Choose the correct name of building from answer choices

a. Hagia Sophia, Constantinople
b. None of these
c. Sufi Sophia, Constantinople
d. St. Sophia, Constantinople

Q56.) A good way to figure out the relationship in a given question is to make up a sentence that describes the relationship between the first two words. Then, try to use the same sentence to find out which of the answer choices completes the same relationship with the third word.
Marathon is to race as hibernation is to

a. sleep
b. bear
c. dream
d. winter

Q57.) If the patterns shown on the left hand side are cut and folded which one of the pattern shown on right hand side with match ?

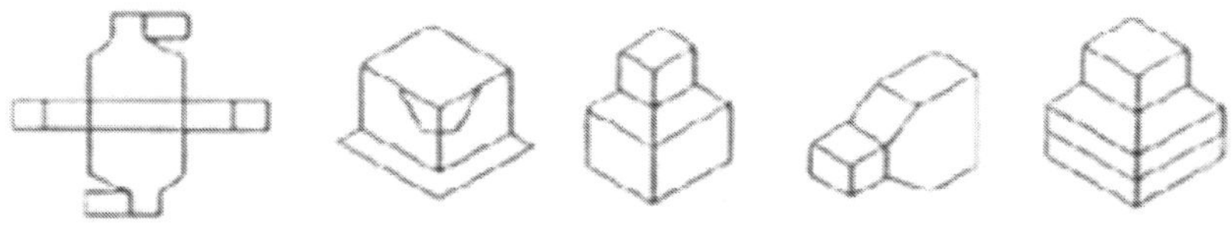

A B C D

a. "B" option is correct
b. "A" option is correct
c. "D" option is correct
d. "C" option is correct

Q58.) Escalators help in :

a. horizontal movement only
b. none of these
c. Vertical & horizontal movements
d. Vertical movement only

Q59.) If the patterns shown on the left hand side are cut and folded which one of the pattern shown on right hand side with match?

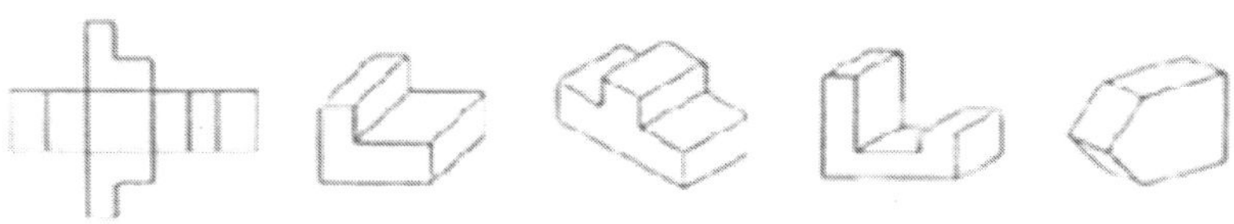

A B C D

a. "A" option is correct
b. "C" option is correct
c. "B" option is correct
d. "D" option is correct

Q60.) A good way to figure out the relationship in a given question is to make up a sentence that describes the relationship between the first two words. Then, try to use the same sentence to find out which of the answer choices completes the same relationship with the third word.
Window is to pane as book is to

a. Cover
b. Novel
c. Page
d. Glass

TEST PAPER-2

Q1.) When did state of Meghalaya came into being ?

a. 1975

b. 1972

c. 1974

d. 1970

Q2.) one of the 4 alternative given on the right when folded along the dotted lines will form the figure on the extreme left. suggest, which will exactly form the problem figure ?

A B C D

a. "B" is correct

b. "C" is correct

c. "A" is correct

d. "D" is correct

Q3.) one of the 4 alternative given on the right when folded along the dotted lines will form the figure on the extreme left. suggest, which will exactly form the problem figure ?

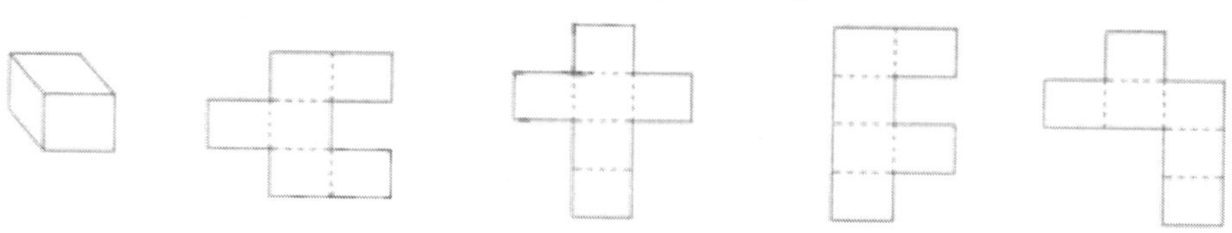

A B C D

a. "B" is correct

b. "A" is correct

c. "D" is correct

d. "C" is correct

Q4.) The maximum strength of a state legislative Assembly in india can be :

a. 500

b. 600

c. 400

d. 550

Q.5.) Given to the question has an underlined word followed by four answer choices. You will choose the word that is a necessary part of the underlined word.
<u>lightning</u>

a. Electricity
b. Rain
c. Thunder
d. Brightness

Q6.) The manufacturer of a certain item can sell all he can produce at the selling price of Rs. 60 each. It costs him Rs. 40 in materials and labour to produce each item and he has additional costs (overhead) of Rs. 3000 per week in order to operate the plant. The number of units he should produce and sell in order to make a profit of at least Rs. 1000 per week, is :

a. 250
b. 400
c. 200
d. 300

Q7.) One of the 4 alternative given on the right when folded along the dotted lines will form the figure on the extreme left. suggest, which will exactly form the problem figure ?

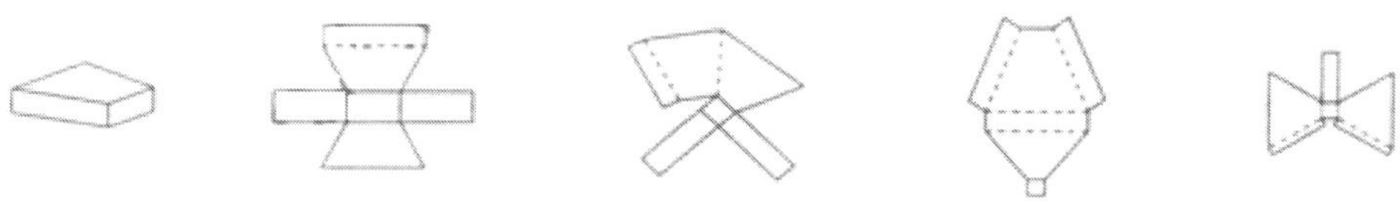

A B C D

a. "D" is correct
b. "C" is correct
c. "A" is correct
d. "B" is correct

Q8.) Which one of the following statements regarding alternate and corresponding angles formed by the intersection of a line with two parallel lines is not correct?

a. Internal angles on the same side are supplementary
b. Alternate angles are equal
c. Corresponding angles are equal
d. The bisectors of alternate angles are non- parallel

Q9.) If the key word is Quit, fit in the correct synonym in the space in each question.
He easily .... his career.

a. Left
b. Abandoned
c. departed
d. Stopped

Q10.) Vijayawada is situated on the bank of river :

a. Cauveri
b. Krishna
c. Tungabhadra
d. Godavari

Q11.) The question shows a photograph of an architecturally important building.Choose the correct name of building from answer choices.

a. Aachen Cathedral
b. Abteiburg Museum
c. Allewelt House
d. Academic Bookshop

Q12.) One of the 4 alternative given on the right when folded along the dotted lines will form the figure on the extreme left. suggest, which will exactly form the problem figure ?

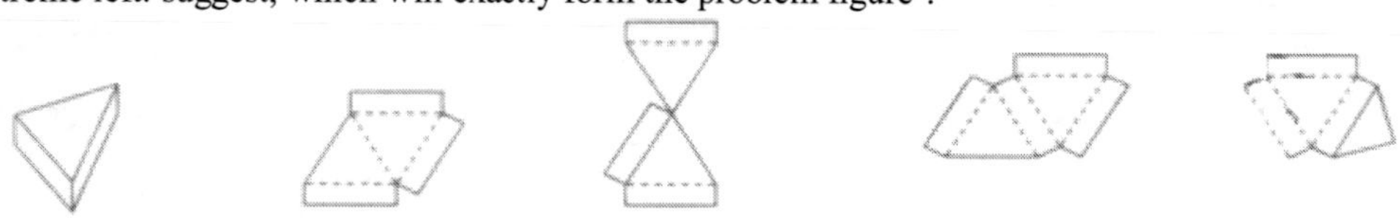

A B C D

a. "D" is correct
b. "C" is correct
c. "B" is correct
d. "A" is correct

Q13.)A regular rectilinear figure has each of its internal angles as 60°. The figure has :
Response:

a. 5 sides
b. 3 sides
c. 4 sides
d. 6 sides

Q14.) The architect of 'Parliament House'in New Delhi is :
Response:

a. Warren Hastings
b. Le Corbusier
c. Christopher Renn
d. Herbert Baker

Q15.) A plane figure is bounded by straight lines only. If 'n' is the number of these lines, then the least value of 'n' is :

a. 3
b. 2
c. 1
d. 4

Q16.) Who designed the Eiffel Tower ?

a. I.M. Pei
b. J. Roche
c. Gustav Eiffel
d. E. Jeanneret

Q17.) Which one is a cold blooded animal ?

a. Penguin
b. Peacock

c. Tortoise

d. Whale

Q18.) If the key word is Quit, fit in the correct synonym in the space in each question
You have to .... smoking because it's not good for you !
Response:

a. abandon

b. Quit

c. Resign

d. Leave

Q19.) One of the 4 alternative given on the right when folded along the dotted lines will form the figure on the extreme left. suggest, which will exactly form the problem figure ?

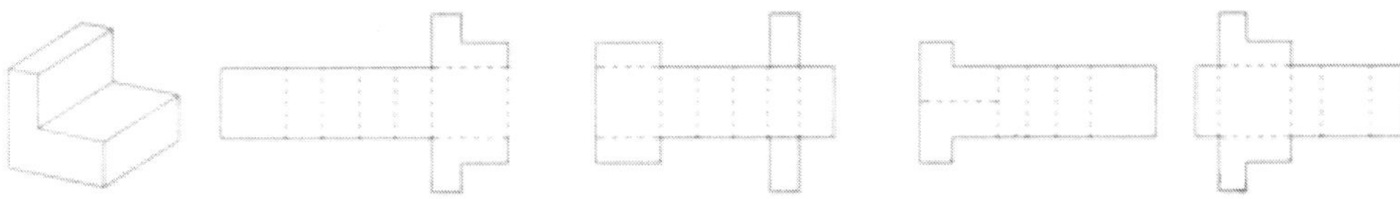

A B C D

a. "D" is correct

b. "C" is correct

c. "A" is correct

d. "B" is correct

Q20.) Given to the series, look for the degree and direction of change between the numbers. In other words, do the
numbers increase or decrease, and by how much
Look at this series: 2, 1, (1/2), (1/4), ... What number should come next?

a. 1/8

b. 1/16

c. 1/3

d. 2/8

Q21.) One of the 4 alternative given on the right when folded along the dotted lines will form the figure on the extreme left. suggest, which will exactly form the problem figure ?

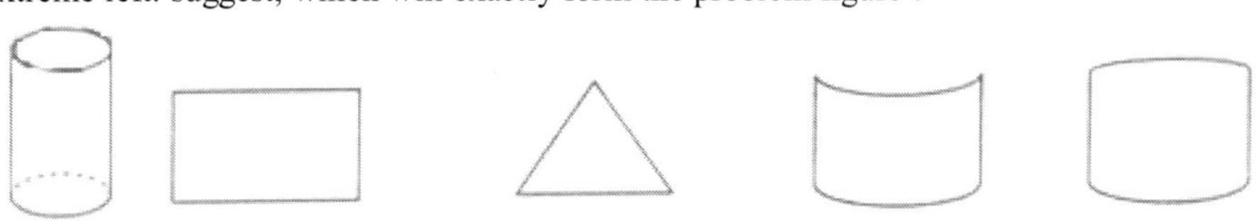

A B C D

a. "B" is correct

b. "D" is correct

c. "A" is correct

d. "C" is correct

Q22.) One of the 4 alternative given on the right when folded along the dotted lines will form the figure on the extreme left. suggest, which will exactly form the problem figure ?

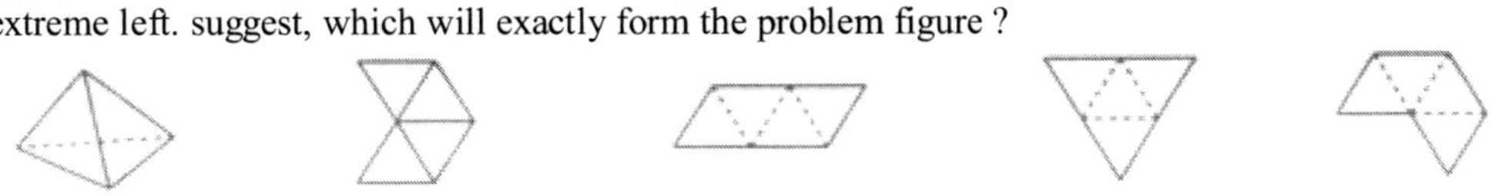

A B C D

a. "C" is correct
b. "D" is correct
c. "B" is correct
d. "A" is correct

Q23.) Given to the question has an underlined word followed by four answer choices. You will choose the word that is a necessary part of the underlined word.
election
a. November
b. president
c. nation
d. voter

Q24.) 'The Fountainhead' - a story about an architect is written by :
a. Jamesjoyce
b. Wilbur smith
c. Henry james
d. Ayn Rand

Q25.) The biggest lake in indiais :
a. Wular Lake
b. Sambhar Lake
c. Chilka Lake
d. Dal Lake

Q26.) If the key word is Quit, fit in the correct synonym in the space in each question
The teacher asked the noisy students to .... talking
a. abandon
b. give up
c. leave
d. quit

Q27.) The literacy rate in India, according to census 2001, is
a. 66.29%
b. 51.2%
c. 65.38%
d. 55.38%

Q28.) Each question has an underlined word followed by four answer choices. You will choose the word that is a necessary part of the underlined word.
Book
a. pages
b. pictures
c. fiction
d. learning

Q29.) Given to the series, look for the degree and direction of change between the numbers. In other words, do the numbers increase or decrease, and by how much
Look at this series: 7, 10, 8, 11, 9, 12, ... What number should come next ?

a. 13
b. 12
c. 10
d. 7

Q30.) The question shows a photograph of an architecturally important building.Choose the correct name of building from answer choice

a. Alexandra Road Housing
b. Abteiburg Museum
c. Academic Bookshop
d. Air Force Academy Chapel

Q31.) Which country is known as " the Land of Rising sun " ?

a. Japan
b. Australia
c. korea
d. china

Q32.) Each question has an underlined word followed by four answer choices. You will choose the word that is a necessary part of the underlined word.
harvest

a. crop
b. stockpile
c. autumn
d. tractor

Q33.) One of the 4 alternative given on the right when folded along the dotted lines will form the figure on the extreme left. suggest, which will exactly form the problem figure ?

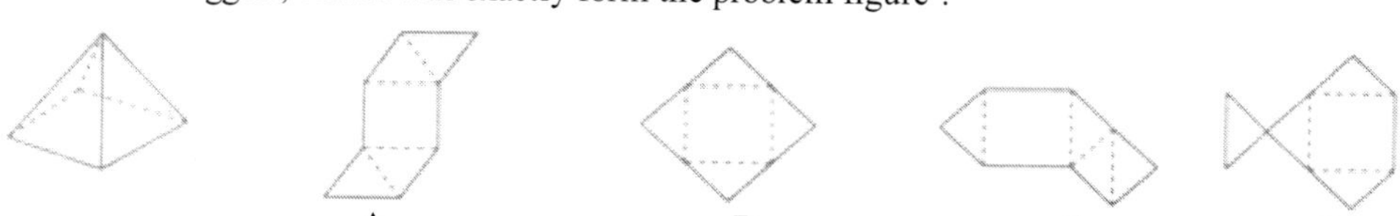

A B C D

a. "A" is correct
b. "C" is correct
c. "D" is correct
d. "B" is correct

Q34.) One of the 4 alternative given on the right when folded along the dotted lines will form the figure on the extreme left. suggest, which will exactly form the problem figure ?

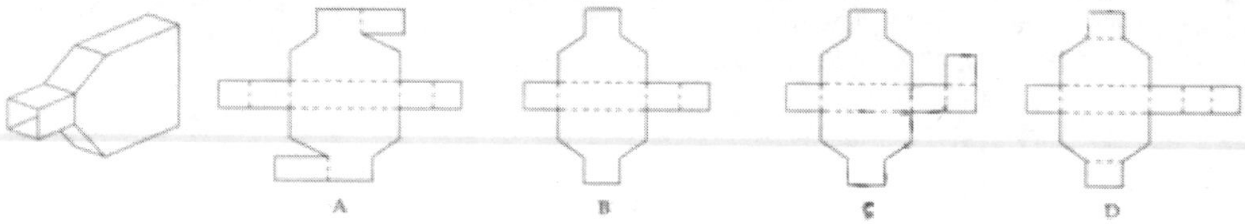

a. "D" is correct

b. "A" is correct

c. "C" is corrcet

d. "B" is correct

Q35.) Given to the question has an underlined word followed by four answer choices. You will choose the word that is a necessary part of the underlined word.
monopoly

a. Exception

b. Exclusive

c. Rich

d. Corrupt

Q36.) One of the 4 alternative given on the right when folded along the dotted lines will form the figure on the extreme left. suggest, which will exactly form the problem figure ?

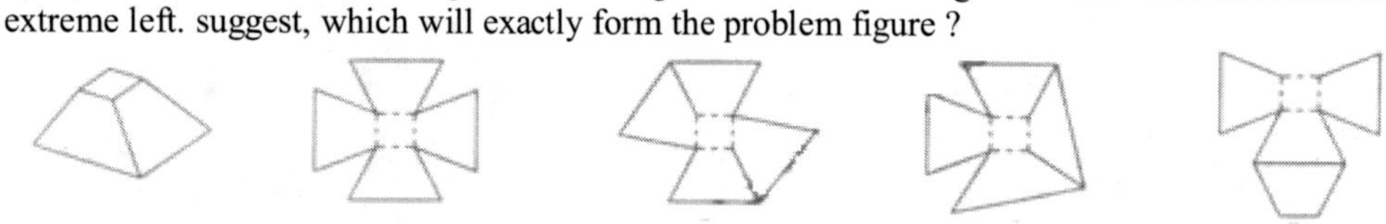

A B C D

a. "D" is correct

b. "A" is correct

c. "C" is correct

d. "B" is correct

Q37.) Each question has an underlined word followed by four answer choices. You will choose the word that is a necessary part of the underlined word.
desert

a. Flat

b. Oasis

c. Cactus

d. Arid

Q38.) The question shows a photograph of an architecturally important building.Choose the correct name of building from answer choices.

a. Academic Bookshop

b. Adziogol Lighthouse

c. Abteiburg Museum

d. Angkor Wat

Q39.) India's first underground nuclear test took place at :

a. Karnataka

b. Gujarat

c. Kerala

d. Rajasthan

Q40.) River Damodar originates from :

a. Chota Nagpur Plateau

b. Christopher Renn

c. Aravali Hills

d. Tibet

Q41.) If in the triangles ABC and DEF, angle A is equal to angle E, both are equal to 40o , AB : ED = AC : EF and angle F is 65°, then angle B is :

a. 75°

b. 65°

c. 85°

d. 35°

Q42.) The energy from the sun comes to us due to

a. Chain reactions

b. Nuclear fusion

c. Chemical reactions

d. Nuclear fusion

Q43.) Everywhere at the equator, the :

a. Latitude is 90°

b. Longitude is 0°

c. Latitude is 0°

d. Longitude is 90°

Q44.) If the patterns shown on the left hand side are cut and folded which one of the pattern shown on right hand side with match ?

A B C D

a. "D" option is correct

b. "C" option is correct

c. "B" option is correct

d. "A" option is correct

Q45.) If the patterns shown on the left hand side are cut and folded which one of the pattern shown on right hand side with match ?

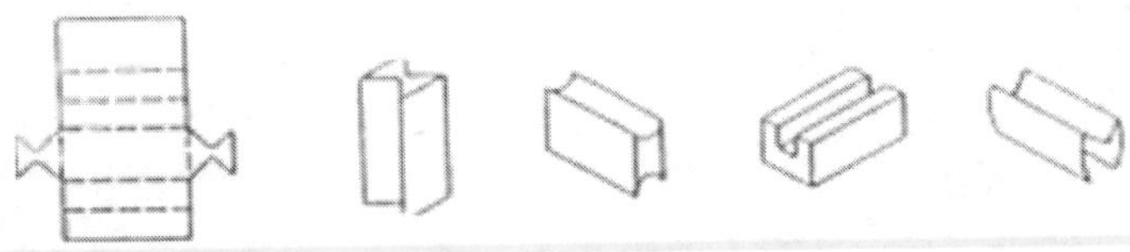

A B C D

a. "D" option is correct
b. "B" option is correct
c. "A" option is correct
d. "C" option is correct

Q46.) If one cubic cm of silver weighs 10 grams and 8 grams of silver costs Rs. 30, then the cost of silver cube of edge 4 cm will be :

a. Rs. 1200
b. Rs. 800
c. Rs. 2400
d. RS. 1920

Q47.) The question shows a photograph of an architecturally important building. Choose the correct name of building from answer choices

a. Peters Dame Cathedral
b. Notre Dame Cathedral
c. Notre Dame Bapistry
d. San Fransico Cathedral

Q48.) If the key word is Quit, fit in the correct synonym in the space in each question.
Which word is the antonym of "bad", as in "he was bad today"?

a. Unlucky
b. Terrible
c. Good
d. Ugly

Q49.) In these series, you will be looking at both the letter pattern and the number pattern. Fill the blank in the middle of the series or end of the series.
ELFA, GLHA, ILJA, _____, MLNA

a. OLPA
b. KLLA
c. KLMA
d. LLMA

Q50.) The gas used in fire extinguishers is :

a. Carbon dioxide
b. SO2
c. Carbon monoxide
d. Chlorine

Q51.) Which one of the following metals was not known to the people of the indus valley civilization ?

a. Copper
b. Iron
c. Bronze
d. Silver

Q52.) If the patterns shown on the left hand side are cut and folded which one of the the pattern shown on right hand side with match ?

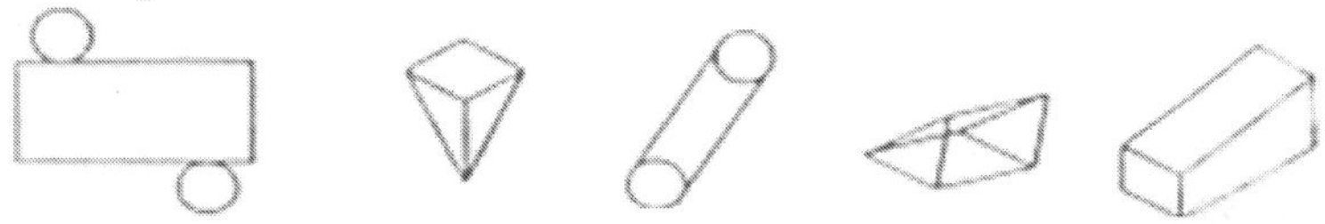

A B C D

a. "C" option is correct

b. "B" option is correct

c. "A" option is correct

d. "D" option is correct

Q53.) A rectangular sand box is 5 metres wide and 2 metreslong.How many cubic metres of sand are needed to fill the box to a depth of 10 cm ?

a. 1 cu m

b. 100 cu m

c. 10 cu m

d. 1000 cu m

Q54.) Nights are cooler in the deserts because :

a. The sky is generally cloudy

b. sand radiates heat less quickly as compared to the earth

c. sand radiates heat more quickly as compared to the earth

d. The sky is generally clear

Q55.) In these series, you will be looking at both the letter pattern and the number pattern. Fill the blank in the middle of the series or end of the series.

SCD, TEF, UGH , ____, WKL

a. IJT

b. UJI

c. VIJ

d. CMN

Q56.) In these series, you will be looking at both the letter pattern and the number pattern. Fill the blank in the middle of the series or end of the series.

CMM, EOO, GQQ, _____, KUU

a. ISS

b. GRR

c. ITT

d. GSS

Q57.) Typhoid is a disease connected with the :

a. Intestine

b. Liver

c. Teeth

d. Skin

Q58.) A good way to figure out the relationship in a given question is to make up a sentence that describes the relationship between the first two words. Then, try to use the same sentence to find out which of the answer choices completes the same relationship with the third word.

Odometer is to mileage as compass is to

a. Needle

b. Speed

c. Direction

d. Hiking

Q59.) The question shows a photograph of an architecturally important building. Choose the correct name of building from answer choices

None of these
Hexagon
Parliament, USA
Pentagon

Q60.) In these series, you will be looking at both the letter pattern and the number pattern. Fill the blank in the middle of the series or end of the series.
B2CD, ..., BCD4, B5CD, BC6D

a. B2CD
b. BCD7
c. BC3D
d. B3CD

ANSWERS:

TEST : 01

Q1. c	Q2. d	Q3. d	Q4. c	Q5. b	Q6. a	Q7. b	Q8. b
Q9. d	Q10. d	Q11. b	Q12. d	Q13. d	Q14. d	Q15. c	Q.16 c
Q17. d	Q18. c	Q19. c	Q20. a	Q21. a	Q22. c	Q23. d	Q24. d
Q25. d	Q26. d	Q27. c	Q28. d	Q29. b	Q30. a	Q31. d	Q32. b
Q33. b	Q34. c	Q35. d	Q36. c	Q37. d	Q38. a	Q39. c	Q40. d
Q41. b	Q42. c	Q43. b	Q44. b	Q45. b	Q46. c	Q47. b	Q48. b
Q49. a	Q50. b	Q51. a	Q52. a	Q53. c	Q54. a	Q55. a	Q56. a
Q57. d	Q58. c	Q59. a	Q60. c				

TEST : 02

Q1. b	Q2. a	Q3. b	Q4. b	Q5. b	Q6. c	Q7. b	Q8. b
Q9. a	Q10. b	Q11. a	Q12. a	Q13. c	Q14. a	Q15. a	Q.16 a
Q17. d	Q18. c	Q19. a	Q20. c	Q21. c	Q22. a	Q23. c	Q24. c
Q25. a	Q26. c	Q27. c	Q28. d	Q29. c	Q30. b	Q31. a	Q32. b
Q33. b	Q34. a	Q35. c	Q36. c	Q37. a	Q38. a	Q39. c	Q40. d
Q41. a	Q42. c	Q43. c	Q44. a	Q45. c	Q46. c	Q47. d	Q48. c
Q49. b	Q50. a	Q51. b	Q52. b	Q53. a	Q54. c	Q55. c	Q56. a
Q57. a	Q58. c	Q59. d	Q60. c				